The Independent Guide to the Mac

Everything you need to know about the world's coolest range of computers

Hello...

WELCOME TO THE INDEPENDENT GUIDE TO THE MAC, the one-stop shop for every new or aspiring Mac user. Whether you've just bought your first Mac, or you're on the cusp of taking the plunge, this book will tell you everything you need to know about the operating system and software on these remarkable machines. We cover all the major suites and applications, like iLife, iWork and Microsoft Office, and our extensive collection of masterclasses and workshops will guide you through performing essential everyday Mac tasks, to get you up and running quicker than you ever imagined.

We'll also cover the iPod and iPhone, Apple's revolutionary media players and mobile phone. These have quickly dominated their particular sectors, and they're perfectly matched to the Mac, making Apple's computers among the best you can get for entertainment and connectivity.

We'll assume no prior knowledge of the Mac, and start by introducing you to the basic concepts and elements of the operating system, before moving on to the platform's best software, and how you can make it work for you. We've also included a comprehensive glossary at the back, which will define any technical terms you may come across.

The Mac is a remarkable machine. It's stable and attractive, and great for less experienced computer users thanks to its friendly operating system, Mac OS X. This has been through several variations over the years, and while much of what we talk about in this volume applies equally to all of them, we'll concentrate primarily on the two latest releases: 10.4 Tiger, and 10.5 Leopard. Any new Mac you buy today will ship with Leopard, and it offers so many advances on previous releases that if the machine you're using (or you've just bought second-hand) is running anything earlier than Mac OS X 10.4 Tiger, we'd recommend you seriously consider upgrading. Check out the minimum system requirements on Apple's site at *apple.com/macosx/techspecs*.

The Mac has long been considered a computer solely for creative users, who spend their day designing, composing or laying out pages, but that's no longer true. A wide range of attractive machines, intuitive software and a vibrant community of developers and users means the Mac is enjoying something of a renaissance right now. This is your chance to be a part of it.

Nik Rawlinson

The Independent Guide to the Mac

EDITORIAL
FAX 020 7907 6369
EMAIL *mailbox@macuser.co.uk*

EDITOR Nik Rawlinson
ART EDITOR Camille Neilson
PRODUCTION EDITOR Jon Lysons
DEPUTY EDITOR Kenny Hemphill
CONTRIBUTORS Ian Betteridge, Christopher Brennan, Tom Gorham, Rod Lawton, Keith Martin, Howard Oakley, Christopher Phin, Misha Sakellaropoulo, Alan Stonebridge
IMAGES Danny Bird, Pio Blanco, Linda Duong, Peter Mac, Faissal Otmani, Chris Robson and some images courtesy of Apple

ADVERTISING
020 7907 6000, Fax 020 7907 6600
ads.macuser@dennis.co.uk
ADVERTISING DIRECTOR Paul Rayner 020 7907 6663
ACCOUNT MANAGER Alexandra Skinner 020 7907 6623
AD PRODUCTION EXEC Lawrence Brookes 020 7907 6062

INTERNET
ONLINE EDITOR Nik Rawlinson 020 7907 6361
SENIOR SALES EXEC Gary Rayneau 020 7907 6661
MANAGING DIRECTOR Pete Wootton 020 7907 6299

PUBLISHING & MARKETING
020 7907 6000, fax 020 7636 6122
MANAGING DIRECTOR Ian Westwood 020 7907 6355
RESEARCH DIRECTOR Lesley Downey 020 7907 6110
LIST RENTAL MANAGER Nerys Church 020 7907 6140
CIRCULATION MANAGER Kate Du Cros

DENNIS PUBLISHING LTD
DIRECTOR OF ADVERTISING Julian Lloyd-Evans
NEWSTRADE DIRECTOR Martin Belson
FINANCE DIRECTOR Brett Reynolds
GROUP FINANCE DIRECTOR Ian Leggett
CHIEF EXECUTIVE James Tye
CHAIRMAN Felix Dennis

Typography Neue Helvetica © Heidelberger Druckmaschinen AG, licensed by Linotype *linotype.com* Collis © 1993 The Enschedé Font Foundry *teff.nl/fonts/collis*
Printed in England by Southern Print, 17-21 Factory Road, Upton Industrial Estate, Poole, Dorset BH16 5SN
Distribution Seymour Distribution 020 7396 8000

MacUser, incorporating *Apple User, DTP, MacShopper* and *MacBuyer*, is published fortnightly by Dennis Publishing Ltd, 30 Cleveland Street, London W1T 4JD, a company registered in England number 1138891. Entire contents © 2008 Dennis Publishing Ltd licensed by Felden. *MacUser* is an independent journal, not affiliated with Apple Computer Inc. 'Apple' and the Apple logo, 'Macintosh', 'Mac', the Mac logo and 'MacUser' are the trademarks of Apple Inc.
PERMISSIONS AND REPRINTS
Material in *MacUser* and the *Independent Guide to the Mac* may not be reproduced in any form without the publisher's written permission. *MacUser* is available for licensing overseas. For details contact Richard Bean, international licensing director *licensedir@dennis.co.uk*.

HOW TO CONTACT US
MAIL MACUSER, 30 Cleveland Street, London, W1T 4JD
EMAIL *mailbox@macuser.co.uk* **WEB** *www.macuser.co.uk*
PHONE 020 7907 6000 Fax 020 7907 6369
EMAIL AND WEB
To contact the editorial team *mailbox@macuser.co.uk*

260 PAGES OF MAC KNOW-HOW ☞

WELCOME

Welcome to the Mac

Welcome to the Mac, the most extraordinary and groundbreaking computer ever conceived.

It's more than 30 years since Steves Wozniak and Jobs got together to found Apple, and while the company enjoyed early success, it really only came to the public's attention with the launch of the revolutionary semi-transparent iMac. This squat, by today's standards, conventional device was to revive the company's fortunes, and inspire a whole range of follow-ups, including the MacBook, Mac mini, iPod and iPhone.

Whether you've just bought home your first Mac or you're a beginner just finding your feet, you'll find plenty here to help you get the most out of your new machine. Before that, though, we'll take a look at Apple's current line-up to help you understand where your computer sits or, if you've not yet taken the plunge, decide which is the right Mac for you.

Why should you buy a Mac?

If you're still considering making the leap from a PC or if you're about to buy your first Mac then fear not because it is one of the easiest computers to use. It also comes pre-loaded with a great software bundle so you can be up and running in no time at all, and once you've taken the plunge you'll never look back.

If you've not yet bought your first Mac, you're probably wondering why you should. Maybe you've never had a computer before, or perhaps you're on the cusp of making the switch from a PC, and you have a few concerns about compatibility, ease of use and value for money. Either way, there are good reasons to invest in a Mac rather than a computer running Windows and we're sure that once you've taken the plunge you'll never look back.

Macs, as you'll already have noticed, look great on the outside, and if you've ever opened one up you'll know that they look just as good on the inside, too. Apple's own operating system, Mac OS X, is the most beautiful and intuitive operating environment money can buy. It is also stable and secure, being built on top of the industry-standard Unix environment, which greatly reduces its vulnerability to virus, spyware and other harmful infections.

The Mac is the ultimate start-and-go machine. With a single company controlling both the hardware and the operating system, you can be sure that the two will work together without any glitches. If you want a computer you can use from the off and that is reliable, buy a Mac. If you want a computer you can fix and diagnose on a regular basis, buy a PC. How do we know? Because the team that put together this book uses both Macs and PCs, and while we often have to tweak our PCs to keep

them happily chugging along, the last time we did any serious Mac maintenance is lost in the mists of time. The last time any of us had a system crash can be counted in terms of months, not days and weeks.

There is less confusion over what you should be buying when you invest in or upgrade a Mac. Unlike Microsoft, Apple doesn't make myriad different versions of its operating system. It has only two: one for servers, which will be of no interest to most consumers, and one for desktop and portable machines, which we can all use.

This means that you have to pay only one price to get every available feature offered by Mac OS X, not look at your budget and decide what you can afford. Compare that to Microsoft's Windows Vista range, where there are no less than five different editions: Ultimate, Business, Home Premium, Home Basic, Business and Enterprise. Which one is right system for you? Who knows. Be warned, though, that

if you opt for the cheapest, Home Basic, you'll be missing a lot of key features.

But it's not just the operating system that you get when you buy a Mac. PC users will already be familiar with getting a load of applications pre-installed on their machines when they arrive, but these are usually trials, which either expire after a certain period, or have had many of their most impressive features trimmed to encourage you to upgrade to the full edition.

Macs are different: they come pre-loaded with a fantastic software bundle. The included iPhoto (see page 50) makes photo editing, organising and printing simple, with professional features for making books and web sites from your galleries. iMovie (see page 64) grabs video footage from the best camcorders and lets you transform it from a series of shaky shots into a coherent film of which you can be proud. Don't believe us? American Mac user Jonathan Caouette made a movie called *Tarnation* using iMovie,

Images Courtesy of Apple

which was shown at the Sundance Film Festival and invited to both the New York Film Festival and the Directors' Fortnight at Cannes. Once you've edited your movie, you can burn it to disc using iDVD (see page 68).

iTunes (see page 54) does for music what iPhoto does for your pictures. It keeps everything organised, lets you build playlists to suit any mood, and download music and podcasts from its integrated online store. It also connects seamlessly to the iPod, the world's best-selling portable music player. GarageBand lets you create your own tunes the easy way – by dragging and dropping pre-recorded snippets in the order in which you want them to play – and iWeb (see page 60) does much the same for websites, greatly simplifying the process of getting your pages up online.

Beyond these, you'll find a first-class media player in the shape of Front Row, messaging tools, a web browser, email and calendar applications, and a range of third-party software tailored to whichever Mac you've bought.

Macs last, too. Apple's advertising team could also be forgiven if it took a leaf out of Volkswagen's book and highlighting how many of its machines go on and on and on,

and how many get re-sold online, or passed on to friends. Take a look at the Macs for sale on eBay (*ebay.co.uk*) and you'll see that for many, there's very little difference in the prices between buying new and picking one up second-hand. This may be bad news if you were hoping to save a bit of money by nabbing some slightly older technology, but it's good news should you later decide to sell up and switch back to the PC, not that we think you will. Invest in a Mac today and you could still be enjoying its benefits in 10 years' time.

This is a great environmental benefit, as it means less of them will end up in landfill sites, leaching their dangerous components alongside all the dead PCs. In the US, Apple runs an extensive recycling scheme, taking back old machines you have bought through its stores and handling its safe disposal for you, leaving you feeling better about moving on to your next great machine.

At the start of their lives, new Macs are built with the environment in mind, too. The aluminium casings of the MacBook Pro, MacBook Air and Mac Pro are easily recycled and, following encouragement from environmental groups, Apple no longer uses many harmful chemicals in the production of

its products and, by the end of 2008, should have eliminated PVC, brominated flame retardants and arsenic from all of its products, despite the fact that these harmful chemicals, which some other manufacturers continue to employ, make the production process easier and cheaper.

It has slimmed down the size of the boxes in which it ships its computers, saving on packaging and the fuel consumed in shipping them, and its portable products, ranging from notebooks to iPods and iPhones, have excellent power management, allowing their batteries to run for longer than most PC equivalents on a regular charge, saving on energy consumption.

All-in-all, there are many good reasons to choose a Mac instead of a PC, and with excellent compatibility between the two you shouldn't be scared of making the switch. Mac applications are great at reading Windows files, and the same is true in reverse, making it easy for you to continue working on the documents, such as spreadsheets, that you've already produced on your PC, and share work with your PC-using colleagues and friends. ✪

Mac myths exposed

Time and time again you come across a range of arguments against buying a Mac, whether they're from family, friends or work colleagues who all use Windows-based computers. We take you through some of the most common myths to debunk them, so you can make a more balanced judgement about buying a Mac.

MACS ARE EXPENSIVE

No they're not. They may have a higher up-front price than some equivalent PCs, but in the long run Macs often work out cheaper. When Windows Vista launched it required up-to-date hardware – so up-to-date, in fact, that many users found they couldn't run it at all without a major upgrade. It was the same story for Windows XP, and 2000 and Me before it.

With Apple producing both the hardware and the software, it can ensure that this doesn't happen. The two are so finely crafted to work hand-in-hand that when Mac OS X 10.4 Tiger shipped, it was compatible with machines up to seven years old.

There are countless tales of people still using Macs 10 or more years old, either because they've been handed down through the years or because they bought them new and have never stopped using them. When you average the up-front cost of such a machine over such an extended working life, it usually ends up much cheaper than an equivalent PC, which would have become cluttered, fragmented and ground to a halt.

MACS HAVE A LIMITED RANGE OF SOFTWARE

What exactly do you want to do with a Mac that you think might not be possible? Every Mac sold ships with a browser (Safari), email client (Mail) and basic word processor (TextEdit). iLife provides video and photo editing tools (iMovie and iPhoto), a web design application (iWeb), DVD burning software (iDVD) and iTunes for downloading, buying and playing back music and podcasts.

There are dozens of office suites, including Microsoft Office, which is compatible with its Windows equivalent, and high-end design tools like Photoshop, InDesign and Dreamweaver, all from Adobe, are arguably better on the Mac than they are on PC.

We'd defy you to find a mainstream task that a Mac can't perform just as well as a PC, if not better. Plus, the Mac is far easier to program than a PC thanks to the great development software Apple and other publishers have put together. This has encouraged an army of third-party coders to knock out some great applications – at very low prices – that you simply can't get for Windows.

MACS ARE INCOMPATIBLE WITH MOST PERIPHERALS

While it's true that some devices still don't work with the Mac, it's unfair to say that most peripherals are incompatible with the Mac. Pretty much every printer, scanner and multi-function device will work with a Mac straight out of the box, and although other gadgets like webcams have had difficulty working on the Mac, shareware and open source projects are plugging the gap for drivers. And when it comes to printers, the Mac's Unix-based printing system has been tried and tested for many years on a wide range of non-Mac operating systems, allowing you to use a range of generic drivers if the one for your printer has never been ported to the Mac.

A wide range of ostensibly Windows-only products, like Microsoft keyboards with a Windows key beside the space bar, and of course two-button mice (Apple used to only make mice with a single button) work just fine without any drivers.

As the Mac gets more popular, more and more hardware developers will write Mac drivers for their peripherals, giving Mac users everywhere a bigger choice of add-ons than ever before.

MACS DON'T RUN WINDOWS

Oh yes they do. Since Apple started using Intel processors in its computers they've been more like regular Windows PCs than ever before. As such, you can actually install Windows on your Mac. There are two ways to do this, namely dual-booting and virtualisation. It's not as difficult as it sounds, and it means you can effectively have two computers in one. We cover this in more detail on pages 98-105, Windows on the Mac.

▲ Both the same MacBook, but one is running Windows and the other Apple's native operating system Mac OS X.

MACS ARE INCOMPATIBLE WITH A LOT OF WEBSITES

No they're not. A good, efficient, compatible website should be coded in such a way that it complies with guidelines set down by the World Wide Web

▲ Most online banking websites work just as easily in Safari as they do in Firefox or Internet Explorer.

Consortium – the so-called W3C. The Mac's default web browser, Safari, is written to interpret these pages, and should have no problems with any website that is properly written. Even if it does have problems with some sites, there are

▲ The BBC website is a perfect example of a website that complies with the guidelines from W3C.

alternatives like Firefox and Opera, both of which also available for Windows PCs.

Unfortunately, however, lazy developers sometimes block Mac browsers from viewing their sites because they think there's a remote possibility they could be a security risk. This is untrue, of course, but the online banks can sometimes be the worst culprits here, and it's usually because they don't have the time, resources or simply inclination to even bother checking.

How do we know? Because simply telling the browser to fib about what it is, and pretend to be something more widely-used, such as Internet Explorer running under Windows, will often let you access the site. And guess what? No problems.

So websites aren't incompatible with Macs, but perhaps some Windows-based web designers are.

MACS ARE ONLY FOR DESIGNERS

That would be true if designers were the only people who ever wanted to create spreadsheets, word process documents or write PHP code. But they're not, so it isn't.

The Mac is just a computer, like any other – technically a PC – and the fact that it appeals to designers dates back to the days when it was the first consumer PC to ship with a graphical user interface driven by a pointer and a mouse. All of the rival PCs at the time had text-based interfaces, which were great for writing and doing your sums, but no good for design.

So if you wanted to be a designer you bought a Mac, then recommended Macs to the next generation of designers who the did the same, all the way down the line to the present day.

While it's true that many designers buy Macs, it's not true that they're the only ones who buy them. Or indeed that they're the only people for whom they're built.

MACS DON'T CRASH

Well, much as we'd like to hold this one up we have to admit that there is a whisper of a lie in it. Macs do crash, but not nearly so often as Windows PCs. You can safely expect to go many weeks, or even months, without a crash on a properly maintained Mac and, as a bonus, should one of your applications throw a fit and break down, it is unlikely to bring down the whole of the operating system, so the data in your other applications should remain safe.

▲ Commonly called the spinning beachball of death, fortunately you don't see it that often.

MACS AREN'T PCS

PC stands for Personal Computer. The Mac is a computer, used by one person at a time; that is personally. Thus it's a PC. ✕

iMac

With its all-in-one design, the latest incarnation of the iMac, a descendant of the computer that revitalised Apple's fortunes, looks fantastic. However, it isn't just the looks that are impressive, the specs are also very formidable, making the iMac a very powerful machine to have on your desktop whether you choose the 20in or 24in model.

DESKTOP MAC
iMac

Price £799 (£680 ex VAT) for 2GHz 20in; £949 (£808 ex VAT) for 2.4GHz 20in; £1149 (£978 ex VAT) for 2.4GHz 24in; £1429 (£1216 ex VAT) for 2.8GHz 24in
Pros Looks gorgeous + Superb 1080p HD-compatible screen + Excellent performance + 2.8GHz Core 2 Extreme option
Cons None

In August 2007 two things happened: the sun started shining again and a new iMac was unveiled. We're fairly sure the two events aren't connected, but what is certain is that Apple's design team has done it again; it's balanced form and function even better than before. Sure, in the most basic sense the new iMacs are just a revamp of an old all-in-one, flat-panel product design. But in every other sense these are things of rare beauty that make the previous flat-panel models look plump and even a touch garish. We're no stranger to Apple's design unveilings, but we weren't expecting to feel this much desire for the new iMacs.

The iMac's body is now a sleek matte aluminium shell with a matte black rear. The 20in or 24in LCD flat screen is set inside a black frame and protected with flush-fit, high-impact, scratch-resistant glass. Unlike Apple's laptop ranges, gloss is the only option. But before you get on your high-horse about this, it is worth noting that Apple's glossy screens give a noticeably better contrast ratio than the non-glossy designs. The result is richer, deeper blacks that improve the appearance of all kinds of content.

The 20in iMacs have a display resolution of 1680 x 1050 pixels, while the 24in models

have 1920 x 1200 pixels. The larger size is perfect for playing high-end 1080p HD video; the 20in screens can handle 720p HD videos with ease.

All the models include the same embedded iSight camera, which, set into the black frame that runs around the display, is even more discreet than before. About the only thing we missed from previous models was the side magnet that held the remote control. It was a nice touch that kept the tiny device from getting lost and it's a shame it's gone, but that's a minor quibble. In terms of overall physical design, these are effectively flawless. There are LCD displays more bulky on their own than this iMac is with the complete computer packed inside.

So has anything been compromised in the effort to squeeze everything inside the slim-line chassis? According to our tests, the answer is an emphatic 'no'. It isn't a match for a beefy Mac Pro, of course, but the 2GHz and 2.4GHz Intel Core 2 Duo processors perform very well. There's even an option to fit a 2.8GHz Intel Core 2 Extreme processor, although you have to start with the 24in 2.4GHz iMac to get this ability in the build-to-order list of options.

The graphics hardware for the entry-level model is now a 128MB ATI Radeon HD 2400 XT, a very good step up from the previous entry model's Intel GMA 950 'integrated graphics' support. The 2.4GHz models have a 256MB-equipped ATI Radeon HD 2600 Pro graphics card. Every model comes with an

8-speed SuperDrive that supports 4-speed double-layer DVD burning, so the optical drive is no longer a decision point.

The entry-level iMac now comes with a 250GB Serial ATA hard drive, while the two 2.4GHz models are graced with 320GB drives, all spinning at a decent 7200rpm. The high-end 2.8GHz iMac comes with a 500GB drive as standard but, of course, build-to-order drive options for up to 1TB can be selected for most models.

The bundled mouse is a variety of the normal Mighty Mouse scrollerball, but the keyboard is a new and slightly strange slimline design. It is exceptionally low, which is a good thing, ergonomically speaking. Opinions around the our office and elsewhere are divided. Those who use desktop keyboards, particularly with Windows PCs, tend not to be that happy with it, preferring a bigger, more noticeable distance of travel for the key caps. Those who have used MacBooks, however, will feel right at home as this keyboard looks and feels exactly the same as the portable model. Except, of course, for the extended sets of keys off to the right; no messing with virtual numeric keypads if you use one of these. We think that most people who aren't keen on it now will come to like it after a little while;

► The latest iMacs come in just two screen sizes – 20in and 24in. Both have a glossy screen to give deeper blacks.

◄ You can't help but be impressed by the iMac's looks – even the keyboard is super slim.

when we used it for regular work we found it to be comfortable and responsive.

The USB ports on the keyboard are now USB 2 ports; previous keyboards all used USB 1.1-speed ports, which made them not much use for anything more demanding than a mouse. The controller keys along the top of the keyboard are arranged slightly differently from previous designs. The brightness controls (F1 and F2) are standard but the F3 key is the 'All Windows' Exposé trigger and F4 kicks Dashboard into life and back again. F5 and F6 are unadorned with extra functions, but keys F7 through F9 are generic reverse, play/pause and forward controls, and F10 to F12 are now the volume control keys.

Curiously, there are F keys right up to F19. All this feels pretty logically organised, although it may take current users a little while to get used to things being in different places. If you use these F keys for anything else you'll need to hold down the Fn modifier key to get the traditional F key trigger behaviour. Notebook users will automatically look to the lower left of the keyboard for this, but in fact it has taken the place of the Help key in the home/end block of keys.

Finally, the one small, but clearly potential problem with the keyboard design is the recessed USB ports tucked below the keyboard's edge on either side. If you plan to use USB memory sticks you'd better make sure these have slim profiles or be ready to plug them into the iMac's back instead.

The ports on the back of the new models are arranged horizontally rather than vertically. The analog audio out and in ports are near the right-hand edge, followed by three USB 2 ports, a FireWire 400 port and, new on iMacs, a FireWire 800 port, gigabit Ethernet and Apple's now-standard (for consumer Macs anyway) mini-DVI port for connecting a second display or projector.

Down at the bottom of the iMac, positioned centrally between the two downward-firing speakers, is a grille that is held in place by a single screw. This provides access to the memory slots – still just two, but thanks to the newer Intel CPU design these allow a maximum of 4GB of Ram to be installed and used. Pleasingly, Apple fits all models with a single 1GB SO-Dimm, so you still have one slot free for adding more Ram without having to remove anything first.

The stereo speakers are driven by a 24-watt amplifier and their downward orientation spreads the audio quite effectively without requiring physically separate units. While no computer speakers are going to out-perform a proper hi-fi setup, or even a good set of powered speakers, these are rich, responsive and clear, and have enough power to fill a room with music without straining. They may not keep a party going, but they're more than enough for casual music enjoyment while you and your colleagues get on with your work or play.

One consequence of Apple's use of aluminium for the body is the loss of the

material as a differentiator between the consumer and pro Macintosh lines. Previously, all consumer designs were encased in a sleek white plastic (or metal and white plastic for the Mac minis), with the all-metal bodies reserved for the professionals. That's no longer the case but, in truth, with product designs this iconic the sharing of material finishes isn't going to make any difference. It will be interesting, though, to see whether aluminium is used in future consumer laptop designs. Given that Apple is pointing out the recyclability of the glass and metal it uses in the new iMacs, this is starting to seem quite likely.

If you have the space for it, the 24in screen is simply amazing and well worth the extra cost. Although both main processor options are good, we'd recommend the 2.4GHz processor over the 2GHz, so that puts the £1149 24in 2.4GHz iMac squarely in the frame. And don't forget the option of a 2.8GHz Intel Core 2 Extreme CPU; this built-to-order option is only available for this model, and we'd seriously consider coughing up the extra £160. Or has the sun gone to our heads? ✪

Mac Pro

The configure-to-order Mac Pro is Apple's heavyweight desktop computer aimed at creative professionals who need power to handle large files, such as video and high-resolution photographs, as well as have open several high-end applications. As such the Mac Pro forms that backbone of Apple's range of Macs.

DESKTOP MAC
Mac Pro

Price £1749 (£1488 ex VAT)
Pros Fast + Easy to upgrade + Lots of expansion options
Cons Not enough Ram or hard drive capacity in base specification + No Blu-ray option + Wifi not included as standard

It may have been released without the fanfare of a keynote speech or special event in its honour, but Apple's latest Mac Pro is an important step forward for the company's professional desktop line-up.

It's the first Mac range to feature Intel's Harpertown quad-core processor, and in its basic configuration ships with two of them running at 2.8GHz. Dual processor options with 3GHz and 3.2GHz processors are also available, as is a single processor, quad-core 2.8GHz model.

Harpertown is a 45nm, low-voltage processor, which dissipates significantly less heat and therefore requires less cooling, and thus consumes less power, than previous Xeon processors shipped in the Mac Pro. The processors have 12MB of Level 2 cache, split as 6MB per pair of cores, allowing each core to grab all 6MB when necessary. The dual 1600MHz frontside buses shuttle data between processor and system controller at up to 2.5GB/sec, a 20% improvement on the previous Mac Pro according to Apple. Memory throughput has also been improved, by 160%, according to the company's figures.

The basic memory configuration is 2GB in a pair of 1GB 800MHz DDR2 fully-buffered Dimms. Given that the Pro has a

maximum capacity of 32GB in eight slots, and that even the MacBook now ships with 2GB Ram, the Mac Pro's base specification seems miserable. And the usual warnings about buying memory from Apple in order to upgrade apply: don't. Third-party dealers will charge you a fraction of the price and fitting it in the Mac Pro is child's play.

If the standard Ram provision is miserable, it's at least matched by the capacity of the hard drive. To include a 320GB drive, and charge an additional £60 to upgrade it to 500GB, at a time when a 500GB 7200rpm Sata drive can be bought and installed alongside the existing 320GB drive for the same price shows an astonishing lack of awareness of current market pricing. To ship a £1749 professional computer with a hard drive below 500GB is, frankly, astonishing, particularly when the Pro's consumer sibling, the iMac, has a 500GB drive. The Mac Pro does score highly in its ability to house up to 4TB of storage in its four drive bays and in its support for hardware Raid using the optional Mac Pro Raid card and for 15,000rpm serial attached storage drives.

The standard graphics controller is an ATI Radeon HD 2600 XT with 256MB Ram, a decent mid-range card with two dual-link DVI ports, and a step up from the Nvidia GeForce 7300GT shipped with earlier Mac Pro models. There are also other graphics controller options available, including the ability to add a further three Radeon HD 2600s in order to drive eight, 30in displays. If you earn a living from 3D graphics however, you might want to go for Nvidia's GeForce 8800GT or Quadro FX 5600 instead.

It's worth noting that the Mac Pro has a total of four PCI Express slots, and so if you plan on installing say, a Raid card and a fibre channel controller, you'll be

limited to two graphics cards. Bear in mind too, that two of the Mac Pro's four slots are PCI Express 2 slots with twice the bandwidth of the slower interfaces.

Other options include the ability to add to the Mac Pro's 16x Superdrive with another 16x Superdrive. However, there is no option to add a Blu-ray drive, which will no doubt infuriate anyone who was hoping that now that the format war is settled Apple would add a high-capacity optical drive at the very least as an option. You can also add 802.11n wifi support – something which, interestingly, is included as standard with every other Mac – but not Bluetooth, despite the presence of a Bluetooth logo on the build-to-order page on the Apple Store.

In our tests, the Mac Pro didn't live up to Apple's claims of being twice as fast as the quad-core 2.66GHz model. It showed a 35% improvement in processor performance in our benchmarks and a 50% increase using the Cinebench graphics benchmarking suite. That's still a very decent return and we have no qualms over its performance.

It's the base specification that lets the Mac Pro down. Only 2GB Ram and 320GB hard drive is just not good enough for a professional workstation. Also, the lack of a Blu-ray drive is disappointing. We just feel there is something better from Apple is just around the corner. This update seems to have been rushed out so that Apple could ship a Harpertown Mac rather than because it had spent several months working on a machine that would do justice to its professional customers.

It may be understandable that at a time when it's focusing on the iPhone, Apple has concentrated less on the Mac Pro. That has to change if the company wants to build on the excellent platform it's made for itself in the creative professional market.

▲ The innards of the Mac Pro are easily accessible, making the upgrading of hard disks incredibly easy.

▲ To get the most out of the Mac Pro's capabilities, a large monitor, such as Apple's 30in display, is essential.

▲ Smart design makes installing massive amounts of memory, adding expansion cards and increasing storage easy.

▲ There are plenty of ports to connect external devices.

Images Courtesy of Apple

MacBook

The entry-level MacBook is Apple's budget range of notebooks and is the cheapest Mac you can buy with everything included to get you up and running. But don't think that just because these are budget machines Apple has skimped on the parts; each one compares favourably with the professional line of MacBook Pros.

NOTEBOOK
MacBook

Price £699 (£595 ex VAT) for 2.1GHz; £829 (£706 ex VAT) for 2.4GHz white; £949 (£808 ex VAT) for 2.4GHz black
Pros Good value + Good performance + Plenty of Ram on top two models
Cons Black model is expensive + Shared graphics Ram + Only one screen size option

The MacBook isn't just the cheapest portable Mac on the market. It also has the virtue of being the least expensive Mac with everything provided in the box – only the barebones Mac mini undercuts it and, despite being several hundred pounds less than the MacBook Pro, many of the specifications are the same. Apple has avoided the temptation to use older, slower parts to keep the price low, and for many this latest revision is powerful enough to see them through a hard day's work.

The price differential with the Pro models is a reflection of the MacBook's good value for money. The low price pitches it at budget-conscious users and it is indeed a fine machine for running common desktop applications such as Mail, Safari, Microsoft Office and even Photoshop.

All of Apple's current notebooks use Core 2 Duo processors on an 800MHz system bus, and the 2.4GHz MacBooks use the same processor specification as the cheapest MacBook Pro, which runs at the same clock speed and has 3MB of shared L2 cache. The other Pro models have 6MB of cache, while the MacBook Air has 4MB. In addition, every Mac notebook uses 667MHz DDR2 SD Ram, though the cheapest MacBook has less than 2GB.

Favourable comparisons extend to the 5400rpm hard disks that are standard on both the MacBook and MacBook Pro, though only the Pro is upgradable to 7200rpm disks as a build-to-order option. The MacBook can't be ordered with a faster drive.

The bone of contention for some will be the integrated Intel graphics processor (GPU), which is also used on the MacBook Air. A dedicated processor from Nvidia is reserved for the Pro models. This precludes some high-end applications from running, such as Motion and Premiere Pro, as well as some of the latest games to be released for the Mac.

The GPU isn't all bad news though. Unlike the old iBooks, the MacBook can extend the desktop to a second display of up to 1920 x 1200 pixels. This is lower than the resolution sported by the MacBook Pro, which is intended to be used for HD video authoring. In contrast the MacBook caters only for playback.

The GPU has no dedicated memory of its own. Instead it shares 144MB of Ram and grabs another 16MB from the system resources when running a second display.

Other features that previously were paid-for upgrades are now included as standard on even the budget range. All three MacBooks come with wifi, Bluetooth and even an iSight camera built-in above the screen. Glass-half-empty types might wish to remove these features and grab a discount (impossible) but the inclusion of these at £699 serves only to highlight just how strongly the MacBooks stand against their sibling ranges.

The three MacBooks offer little variety in their specifications. Each has a 13.3in screen and a 5400rpm hard disk that can be upgraded to 250GB if required. The only upgrade options that you really need to consider when buying a MacBook are the hard disk capacity and Ram.

The base system comes only with a Combo drive and in a move that seems designed to create an artificial barrier between this and the other models, it can't be upgraded to a SuperDrive. If you plan to use iDVD or back up huge amounts of data, the mid-range model is your starting point. Otherwise the cheapest model still plays DVDs and is perfectly capable of running essential applications like a web browser, email and office software.

Budget permitting, it would still be wise to upgrade the low-end MacBook's Ram to 2GB to keep it running smoothly, especially if you need to run several large applications at the same time. Casual users who spend minimal time at the computer will find the standard 1GB sufficient though. All models can be upgraded to 4GB but spare yourself the expense unless you'll be working with high-resolution photos and running many other applications in the background.

The 2GB included in the other two models is ample for most tasks. But if you do decide to upgrade the Ram, it's much cheaper to buy it from a third-party supplier and fit it yourself than it is to buy from Apple as an upgrade option.

Rather than upgrading the internal hard disk, it's better to splash out on an external disk for use with Time Machine. Just £30 upgrades the internal hard disk from 120GB to 160GB but £50 will net a 250GB external USB disk. It gives a space for backups that's more convenient than burning optical media.

By upgrading the hard disk of the mid-range model, its specification matches the black MacBook. The priciest model carries a premium for its stylish black casing – a princely £60.01. Our benchmarks showed little difference in the two models, so it's only worth going for the top model if you insist on standing out from the crowd.

IS THIS ONE RIGHT FOR YOU?

A MacBook is kitted out well in terms of hardware and extra features – it has all of the essential networking options and plenty of ports for connecting peripherals over USB and FireWire.

Aside from the Air, the MacBook is the most portable of all Mac notebooks with its small but functional screen and full-size keyboard. It's suitable for desktop use when space is limited.

The MacBook is a real winner for Apple. With the notebook market increasing and Apple's market share on the up, it's an ideal way for newcomers to jump platforms. Without specific application needs to warrant extra expense, the MacBook should have wide appeal. And it's a solid workhorse to keep track of photos, music and email.

ALL MODELS

2.27kg + 13.3in glossy widescreen + 1280 x 800 pixel display + Intel GMA X3100 graphics processor
Quoted battery life 4.5 hours of wireless productivity

Price £699
Specifications 2.1GHz Intel Core 2 Duo + 1GB + 120GB hard disk + 24x Combo drive

Price £829
Specifications 2.4GHz Intel Core 2 Duo + 2GB + 160GB hard disk + 8x double-layer SuperDrive

Price £949
Specifications 2.4GHz Intel Core 2 Duo + 2GB + 250GB hard disk + 8x double-layer SuperDrive

3 REASONS TO BUY

Expansion ports: Of the entire portable range only the 17in MacBook Pro has more USB ports. The MacBook's single FireWire port is sufficient for most home users, especially with so many consumer-orientated video cameras that record to hard disk or DVD via USB connections.
Generous features: The only things that separate the base model from the others are a Combo drive and a slower processor. Just make sure that it has enough disk space and Ram to cope with the tasks you'll throw at it. Remember that the whole range benefits from wifi, Bluetooth and a built-in iSight camera.
Price: The two cheapest models are ideal for those after a solid Mac that can handle everyday tasks without needing to be at the cutting edge of performance and style.

3 REASONS TO THINK AGAIN

Restrictive screen: The 13.3in screen crams in 1280 x 860 pixels and Spaces makes it easy to manage. A 15in MacBook Pro is comfier for prolonged use at a desk though, and its higher resolution leaves plenty of space for iChat and other small windows at the screen's edge.
Integrated Intel graphics processor: This rules out running some applications. If only ATI and Nvidia graphics processors are listed in system requirements, the software won't run on a MacBook at all – the only portable solution is the Pro range.
Portability: The MacBook weighs 2.27kg.

► The MacBook's ports are on its left-hand side. From top to bottom, they are the Kensington cable lock slot, audio line out, audio line in, two USB ports, FireWire 400, Mini-DVI, Gigabit Ethernet and the MagSafe power port.

MacBook Pro

While MacBooks are the budget notebooks in Apple's line-up, the MacBook Pros are at the pinnacle of the range and geared towards creative professionals. These notebooks are at the limit of comfort where portability is concerned and, as such, the MacBook Pros are more akin to a desktop replacement than a computer for the road.

NOTEBOOK
MacBook Pro

Price £1299 (£1106 ex VAT) for 15in 2.4GHz; £1599 (£1361 ex VAT) for 15in 2.5GHz; £1799 (£1531 ex VAT) for 17in 2.5GHz
Pros Dual-link graphics chip + LED on all models + Hi-res display option on 17in models
Cons Less portable than MacBook + Only 2GB Ram + Processor is only moderately more powerful than MacBook

At the very peak of the range is the MacBook Pro. There are three models, all every bit the powerhouses that the name suggests, which means that they're ideally suited for applications that require extreme number-crunching power. The hard disk can also be upgraded to a faster rotational speed to keep things running more nippily.

Fittingly they're equipped with better processors and larger, higher-resolution screens. This latest refresh also marks the first time that an LED screen has been available on the 17in model. In addition, the Pro models can run graphics-intensive applications thanks to their dedicated processors. These have their own supply of memory which leaves more of the Mac's Ram for memory-hungry applications.

The MacBook Pro's price falls between that of the two MacBook Air models. But where the top-range Air has a more cutting-edge, power-efficient system, the Pro edges towards a full desktop replacement.

The cheapest MacBook Pro uses the same 2.4GHz processor found in some MacBooks, even matching the amount of L2 cache. The other models take the Core 2 Duo only a tad higher – up to 2.6GHz if built to order, which in addition gives double the amount of L2 cache. As expected these

factors have contributed to slightly higher speed results on the Pro range.

Like the MacBook, all three offerings come equipped with 5400rpm hard disks. But they're upgradable to 7200rpm, though that means a reduction in capacity of 50GB on the top two models. Curiously the 17in model can also be upgraded to a 300GB disk but the rotational speed drops to 4200rpm – the same as the MacBook Air's hard disk, although at a considerably higher capacity.

Upgrading to a 7200rpm drive makes sense but we can't see the logic in paying for the privilege of a slower drive. It's likely to have detrimental results when put to use in a video-editing environment and we recommend that only home users with a thirst for portability and an HD display should even consider it. If you need extra capacity, it's better to invest in an external drive for use with Time Machine, as with the MacBook's hard disk upgrades.

Also exclusive to the 17in model is an optional 1920 x 1200 pixel display. This is the only notebook from Apple to offer full 1080p display, and it will really come into its own when used in conjunction with a second display.

The entire Pro range is fitted with Nvidia graphics processors with dual-link DVI support. This allows connection to a 30in Apple Cinema Display that offers enough space to edit 1080p video while viewing toolbars and other screen furniture around the edge. The use of such large displays is a reason for two models being equipped with 512MB of memory on the graphics processor.

The 17in model is the closest you'll come to a true replacement for a desktop, though the type of screen should be considered very carefully to ensure that it's suitable for your preferred tasks.

Anyone who works extensively with video or photographs should avoid the glossy screens in favour of the anti-glare option; both are available at all screen sizes, including the optional high resolution (1920 x 1200 pixel) display on the 17in model. The screens with a glossy finish are great for watching DVDs but, in our experience, the effect proves to be a hindrance in colour correction work.

The 15in models have two USB ports, while the 17in Pro raises this to three, affording the opportunity to simultaneously attach a range of devices such as an external mouse, a flash drive and a TV tuner. In addition there are two FireWire ports – one 400 and one 800 – which means that video professionals can hook up a fast FireWire 800 drive to take advantage of its performance benefits, leaving the other port free for a DV or HDV camera.

The ExpressCard/34 slot should not be overlooked either, as it offers even more expansion opportunities that also are exclusive to this group of MacBooks. Commonly it has been used to add more FireWire and USB ports to connect external hard disks – and even eSata disks get ultra-fast performance.

While the MacBook Pro isn't as portable as the MacBook Air, the port can also be used to add a memory card reader so that you can forget about packing a USB cable to connect a digital camera at a photoshoot.

Provided that they're being put to demanding, professional tasks, these models require the most careful thought about Ram – 2GB should again be sufficient for casual purposes.

Video professionals working with HD footage and rendering and compositing applications will benefit from adding more Ram, though the MacBook Pro still allows only a maximum of 4GB to be fitted.

IS THIS ONE RIGHT FOR YOU?

Though we've already mentioned it, it's worth emphasising that the MacBook Pro occupies a privileged position: it's the only portable Mac that's able to run certain applications. It's also a good choice if you're reluctant to install an iMac or Mac Pro and don't want to be tied to a desk. Even the bulkier 17in model is still good for anyone who likes to move around the home – it's just too uncomfortable for regular carriage.

In a professional capacity, the 17in model is best for those working with HD video, high-resolution photos and graphic design that demands a lot of screen space. These apart, the 15in model is fine for most tasks, while remaining comfortably portable – it weighs only a little more than the MacBook.

ALL MODELS

2GB Ram + 8x double-layer SuperDrive
Quoted battery life 5 hours of wireless productivity; except for the £1799 model, which is 4.5 hours

Price £1299
Specifications 2.45kg + 2.4GHz Intel Core 2 Duo with 3MB shared L2 cache + 15.4in wide-screen LED + 1440 x 900 pixel display + 200GB hard disk + Nvidia GeForce 8600M GT with 256MB GDDR3 SDRam

Price £1599
Specifications 2.45kg + 2.5GHz Intel Core 2 Duo with 6MB shared L2 cache + screen and pixel display as per £1299 model + 250GB hard disk + Nvidia GeForce 8600M GT with 512MB GDDR3 SDRam

Price £1799
Specifications 3.08kg + processor as per £1599 model + 17in wide-screen + 1680 x 1050 pixel display + 250GB hard disk + Nvidia GeForce 8600M GT with 512MB GDDR3 SDRam

3 REASONS TO BUY

Raw power: The dedicated graphics processor makes the Pro models the only contenders for running certain applications such as Premiere Pro CS3 and Motion 3. These notebooks – especially the 17in one – are closest to a portable Mac Pro.
Better dual-monitor support: All Pro models are sensibly outfitted with a dual-link DVI port that can power the 30in Apple Cinema Display. It provides enough space to edit 1080p content without having to constantly hide and reveal tool palettes.
Expansion ports: Having two FireWire ports is a great bonus for video pros and those demanding the best performance from external disks. FireWire 400 devices can be attached to the FireWire 800 port with a suitable cable. The ExpressCard/34 slot allows even more to be added.

3 REASONS TO THINK AGAIN

Cost: A 250GB hard disk upgraded, mid-range MacBook still costs £440 less than the cheapest MacBook Pro. Specific applications should be the prime motivator for spending nearly half a grand on the latter. Unless you absolutely need the Nvidia graphics processor, it's better to gravitate towards the regular MacBook.
Portability: The 15in model approaches the comfort limits of portability. The 17in is heavy to carry at more than 3kg.
Photo editing: Photoshop isn't hardware accelerated and won't make best use of the dedicated graphics processor.

▲ From top to bottom, the left side of the MacBook Pro features the ExpressCard port, audio out, audio in, a USB port (two on the 17in model) and the MagSafe power port. On the right side are a full-size DVI port, Gigabit Ethernet, FireWire 800 and FireWire 400 ports, another USB port and a Kensington cable lock slot. ✪

MacBook Air

Apple claimed that the MacBook Air was the world's thinnest notebook on its launch in early 2008 and, when experienced in the flesh, it doesn't fail to impress any friends or colleagues. It's also unbelievably light, making it the ideal machine for those who spend a lot of working life on the road and have to lug around their computer.

NOTEBOOK
MacBook Air

Price £1199 (£1020 ex VAT) for 1.6GHz 80GB hard disk; £2028 (£1726 ex VAT) for 1.8GHz 64GB solid state drive
Pros Beautifully engineered + Very light + 2GB Ram
Cons Expensive for specification + No optical drive + Few expansion ports

The star attraction at Steve Jobs' January keynote in 2008 was undoubtedly the MacBook Air. Greeted with huge interest by the industry and the public alike, its light weight and lean looks impressed many.

The sleek lines are achieved by dispensing with unnecessary bloat. Gone are most of the expansion ports and the optical drive, which has allowed Apple to reduce the height of the machine to 0.4cm at its thinnest point. Yet the Air is comfortable to use as it retains the screen and keyboard size of the MacBook, making it feel like a regular MacBook rather than the cramped and cumbersome sensation of some ultraportables.

The MacBook Air uses Core 2 Duo processors like the rest of the line-up, though the available clock speeds are the slowest of all. It's even further removed from the MacBook Pro's performance than the cheapest MacBook which, once upgraded to 2GB, is a better-suited machine to handling a barrage of tasks throughout the day. The hard disk and Ram are quite easy to replace in the MacBook and MacBook Pro but with the Air, all components are sealed inside the case, which is screwed shut. Anyone brave enough to open it would find that only the hard disk and battery can

be replaced. By necessity of the design everything else is part of the logic board.

This impacts on the Ram, which is limited to the 2GB fitted as standard, whereas other MacBooks can be upgraded to 4GB. The 1.6GHz model's 4200rpm Parallel ATA hard disk will have more impact on general performance though; it's the slowest in any Mac. The optional solid state drive's price pushes the Air well beyond even the price of the 17in MacBook Pro – though they're polar opposites when it comes to power and portability, that's a heavy price to pay.

The Air's battery is also fixed inside the case. Apple can replace it at the end of its life but it can't be swapped on the move. Replacements cost £99 and you will be without the unit for up to five days. If you need power for longer consider any other Mac notebook and buy a second battery.

A slimline USB SuperDrive is available for ripping CDs to iTunes, watching DVDs and installing software that comes only on a disc. With the slim pickings currently available on the UK's iTunes Store, you'll have to carry this if you want to watch DVDs on the move. You'll also need a USB hub to plug in more than one device at a time. Note that there's neither a FireWire port for connecting a DV camera nor an Ethernet port for locations that offer only a cabled network connection unless you buy an optional dongle.

The MacBook Air makes many compromises to achieve its slim stature but it stands head and shoulders above the rest of the range on portability and Apple's famed design aesthetics. Even its nearest competitor, the regular MacBook appears bulky and heavy by comparison.

However, there's no overlooking the MacBook Air's limitations. The build-to-order options are even fewer than those of the MacBook, so it's even more important to choose the right spec in the first place

because it's a closed box and upgrading it later is not an option you can take. Unless you can afford the 64GB solid state drive at an additional £639, the only other option is the 80GB drive that is standard on the cheaper Air model.

That model comes with the slowest Core 2 Duo processor of all Mac notebooks, clocked at 1.6GHz. Thankfully, this can be upgraded to the same 1.8GHz processor of the solid state drive-equipped model, while retaining the slow but inexpensive hard disk. Until solid state drive prices fall, this is the most economical way to benefit from the Air's physical characteristics while theoretically extending its battery life slightly.

There are no real upgrades for the 1.8GHz model – only extra peripherals like the USB SuperDrive. It includes everything in the box, which is just as well since it costs £2028. It's a shame that price doesn't include the external SuperDrive, though the extra £65 that the drive costs will mean little to anyone who is seriously considering the solid state drive option.

The Air isn't an ideal notebook if you're reliant on external devices. First there's the expense of extra cables such as the USB to Ethernet adapter – and the situation is made worse if you need to copy files to a flash drive or if you dislike trackpads when working at a desk and want to use an external mouse. There's only one USB port, so you're left to carry a USB hub too, which works a little against the Air's portability. If you need to use more than one USB device and portability isn't such a big issue, a MacBook is a far better option.

The MacBook Air uses the same integrated Intel graphics processor as the plain MacBook, again limiting applications and the resolution of a second display. As ever, serious video professionals should skip over this and look at the Pro range.

▼ MacBook Air's three ports from top to bottom are the Micro-DVI port, USB and a headphone jack.

IS THIS ONE RIGHT FOR YOU?

The MacBook Air's hardware features are lean. When it was introduced, much attention was lavished on its multi-touch trackpad but this has already filtered across to the pro range; if it is to garner support and flourish, expect to see it on the regular MacBook at some point. It certainly shouldn't sway a buying decision until that happens.

The lack of expansion opportunities means it's unsuitable as a main computer except for infrequent users, who would be better off with the cheaper MacBook. The Air is capable enough to run Photoshop but is best suited to those who already own a capable Mac and who crave a lightweight Mac notebook on the road – provided that there's a mains power source to charge it every few hours.

ALL MODELS

Width 32.5cm
Depth 22.7cm
Height 0.4 to 1.94cm
Weight 1.36kg

Specifications 2GB Ram + 13.3in glossy widescreen LED + 1280 x 800 pixel display+ Intel GMA X3100 graphics processor
Quoted battery life 5 hours of wireless productivity

Price £1199
Specifications
1.6GHz Core 2 Duo with 4MB shared L2 cache + 80GB hard disk

Price £2028
Specifications 1.8GHz Core 2 Duo with 4MB shared L2 cache + 64GB solid state drive

3 REASONS TO BUY

Weight: The Air is almost a kilo lighter than the plain MacBook yet the case feels reassuringly durable – just as well since you could forget that you're carrying it.
Full-size screen and keyboard: Despite its portable aspirations, the Air features the same screen size and resolution as the MacBook – and doesn't lose anything when it comes to the physical interface.
Abandon physical media: Music, video and software downloads take up a lot less space than discs and printed manuals. The lack of a built-in optical drive will mean little if you've adopted the download culture. If the Air will play second fiddle to a desktop Mac, it can share the optical drive for those increasingly rare instances when software ships only on a disc – these days, even Adobe CS is available as a download.

3 REASONS TO THINK AGAIN

Cables: Many of the missing features can be added to the Air but it means carrying cables. A hub is also needed to play music from your iPod – and there are no adaptors as standard for using an external mouse and hooking up to an Ethernet port.
Slower parts: The hard disk uses older Parallel ATA disk technology. You can upgrade to a smaller 64GB solid state drive but it's a massive £639.
Integrated battery: Without mains power in easy reach, the Air isn't suitable for prolonged use. The battery is replaceable (by Apple) only when its life has expired.

Mac mini

If you have a Windows PC, complete with a monitor, keyboard and mouse then Apple's lowest priced desktop machine, the Mac mini, provides a cheap way of sampling the Mac environment. However, its hardware specs, packed into its small biscuit tin sized casing, does have its limitations, but then its price is unbeatable.

DESKTOP MAC
Mac mini

Price £399 (£340 ex VAT) for 1.83GHz;
£499 (£425 ex VAT) for 2GHz
Pros Inexpensive + Compact
Cons Poor graphics performance + Not a significant upgrade

◄ **Same look – all the changes to the new Mac mini take place on the inside.**

Apple's Mac mini really grabbed people's attention when it launched back in January 2005. But when the cheapest model rose to about £400 its relevance was questioned, and it has been regarded as a product line on the way out, which is why the launch of the new Mac minis came as such a surprise to industry observers.

Although the cheapest Mac mini still costs £399, a figure beaten by several budget PCs, Apple still believes it has a market and has kept it up to date with the recent advances. The new line uses the same Intel Core 2 Duo processors found in other Macs, the cheaper model running at 1.83GHz and the better at 2GHz. The faster model also has 4MB of Level 2 processor cache memory, shared between the two cores, while the slower model has the same 2MB used in the previous line.

Sadly, both still have the same Intel GMA 950 graphics processing used in the previous minis. This is okay for undemanding work but unlikely to satisfy the needs of wannabe gamers. Without dedicated graphics processing designed to handle 3D game requirements at least fairly well, the new Mac minis will always disappoint.

At least the standard Ram allocation is better than before. Both models come with 1GB of Ram, half of its 2GB maximum. Unfortunately, this is split across two 512MB memory cards, so you have to remove at

least one if you ever want to upgrade. Hard disk space is a little better, with 80GB or 120GB rather than 60GB or 80GB capacities. These are still the slower 5400rpm models, but most Mac mini users won't be bothered by the difference between these and the more expensive 7200rpm drives. The optical drive choice remains the combo model at the cheap end and basic SuperDrive for the top model, although the SuperDrive now supports double-layer (DVD+R Dual Layer) disks.

And that's it. You'd be right to think the difference between the new and previous generations of Mac minis is not exactly staggering. It's a welcome upgrade but a small one, more an exercise in keeping the minis in their place in the Mac pack than grabbing customers' attention.

Performance was in line with what we would expect from a Core 2 Duo-based Mac running at these speeds with no extra hardware support. Graphics performance was roughly equivalent to the MacBook range: more or less identical for Cinebench 3D rendering times and fractionally faster with the OpenGL lighting routines. We got similar results from Xbench, although the CPU-specific tasks inched ahead, allowing for differences in processor speed, and the graphics-based tests just about kept up.

With these comparisons in mind, it should be obvious that the Mac minis are

the desktop equivalent of MacBooks. If you've considered getting one of those portables but would rather spend less on the hardware, perhaps a Mac mini is the answer. But don't forget to factor in the cost of buying a screen, keyboard and mouse if you don't have one already. Sure, these are pretty cheap these days, but it all adds up.

What about using a Mac mini as a media centre? That's one logical use, but now that the Apple TV is available, and works so well, this alternative use for Mac minis is no longer such an attractive idea.

There is one yardstick where it wins out over other desktop Macs and probably virtually any desktop PC as well. Although you'll need to factor in the screen, the Mac mini itself remains a very low-power device, peaking at about 110W (similar to a regular lightbulb) compared with up to 280W for the iMac and a staggering 1440W (at peak power usage) for the Mac Pros. This means that a Mac mini has a much smaller impact on your carbon footprint, which is handy if you just need Internet access and basic office tools.

The Mac minis are cheap (although not quite as cheap as they first were), they use impressively little power, and they're still attention-grabbingly small. But they're not particularly well suited to those with even moderately demanding needs. Don't dismiss them by any means, but do think carefully before handing over your cash. ⊗

Apple TV

When the iPod was released it marked a significant departure for Apple as it branched out from making computers. And now Apple TV marks another departure as it takes its hardware and software into the living room by giving you the ability to watch film and TV shows, play music, view photos on Flickr and video on YouTube.

MULTIMEDIA HARDWARE
Apple TV

Price £199 (£169 ex VAT) for 40GB;
£269 (£228 ex VAT) for 160GB
Needs High-definition TV capable of 1080p 60/50Hz, 1080i 60/50Hz, 720p 60/50Hz, 576p 50Hz or 480p 60Hz; HDMI or Component input
Pros Buy music and TV shows from your living room + Works seamlessly with or without iTunes
Cons Limited connectivity options + No movie downloads or rentals + Lacks PVR functionality + Expensive

◄ The major disappointment with Apple TV is that, as yet, there are no movie rentals for the UK.

When Steve Jobs announced that the Apple TV had failed, it was an unusual admission that sometimes Apple doesn't get it right. The first version failed for several reasons, so Apple has re-focused its living-room offering with take two of Apple TV. If you had invested in a first generation Apple TV, you'll be glad to know that this improved Apple TV is simply a software upgrade, which can be downloaded for free.

A 40GB and 160GB model are available for £199 and £269 respectively. However, the Apple TV software has been radically remodelled and now it can be used without the aid of a Mac. Setup is a breeze and if you want to tie your Apple TV to your Mac the process is as simple as it was with the original software.

The main menu has lost the Front Row styling and is simply a table with content types on the left and the options within these are displayed on the right. The movies option is there but it only allows you to watch trailers or view movies that you've copied to an iTunes library. The difficulties of negotiating international movie licences mean that film downloads or rentals aren't available in the UK at present.

We do get TV shows from a selection of networks in the UK. Navigating the download options is simple and elegant. When you choose a show to download, you're asked for your password and then the transfer begins. We chose an episode of *The West Wing* and it was ready to watch within a few seconds of the download beginning. That's quite impressive if you bear in mind that this is a 50-minute programme. Image quality is very good, though it's not exceptional; we'd say it's on a par with DVD content – no better no worse.

Buying music on your Apple TV is a simple process. You can navigate through with a selection of hand-picked albums that Apple thinks you'll enjoy. If Morrissey and the soundtrack to *Juno* aren't to your liking though, you can search for alternatives. This requires that you use the Apple remote to select individual characters but the predictive search does a good job of narrowing down the choices. We only had to type 'eme' to get to Emerson, Lake and Palmer for instance.

Podcasts, Photos and YouTube navigation are all much the same. The Flickr integration is a nice touch and being able to add multiple contacts increases the appeal of the photo aspect of the Apple TV. Watching video of teenagers dancing to the latest chart topper doesn't yet hold a mass appeal but the Apple TV does offer a good method of transferring this online technology to the living room. When the quality of the video and the production values improve, however, the YouTube content will be really worthwhile.

We're still a little hesitant to recommend the Apple TV even in this much improved second coming, although the changes to the interface and the ability to purchase music and TV shows is really excellent. However, there are still a few insurmountable failings. The lack of PVR functionality, or ability to add one is disappointing and, though we can understand why we don't have movie downloads or rental yet, it's still frustrating.

If this had been the Apple TV take one, there's no doubt we'd have been raving over it but this is the second swing of the bat for Apple and though it's not the miss of Apple TV 1 it's not the home run we wanted either. ⊗

iPod line-up

The iPod, arguably, kick-started the resurgent Apple as it has attracted millions of devotees with its stylish looks, while its halo effect has pulled in many more computer users who bought their first Mac after buying an iPod. The current line-up of iPods means that there's one that will match every budget and pocket.

MEDIA PLAYERS
iPod range

Price shuffle 1GB: £32 (£27 ex VAT), 2GB: £49 (£42 ex VAT); nano 4GB: £99 (£84 ex VAT), 8GB: £129 (£110 ex VAT); classic 80GB: £159 (£135 ex VAT), 160GB: £229 (£195 ex VAT); touch 8GB: £199 (£169 ex VAT), 16GB: £269 (£229 ex VAT), 32GB: £329 (£280 ex VAT)

By the time Steve Jobs left the stage at the Moscone Center on 5 September 2007, he had announced the most radical shake-up of the iPod line-up and iTunes Store since the launch of Apple's first portable music player in 2001.

The iconic white iPod, which has existed in one form or another since its launch in 2001, has gone. In its place is the iPod classic, now only available in silver and black. The iPod has been replaced at the pinnacle of the line-up by the iPod touch, a widescreen, touch-sensitive, wireless iPod. The touch takes its cues from the iPhone but completely redefines what constitutes a portable music player by allowing you to download music directly from the iTunes Store.

As well as announcing the iPod touch, and a modest upgrade to the iPod classic, Jobs took the wraps off a shorter, fatter version of the nano. The look of the new nano is a shock. We've become used to the long, thin shape, and its new proportions somehow looked wrong at first. But in the flesh, rather than in photographs, the new look works very well.

Only the shuffle is unchanged, except for its range of new colours.

It isn't just the hardware that has been refreshed, though. Jobs announced ringtone downloads, which cost 99 cents each in addition to the price of the song from which they're created. A ringtone editor allows you to choose which part of the song you use as a ringtone.

In the most surprising move of the day, Jobs also announced a tie-in with Starbucks that will allow iPhone and iPod touch owners to connect to the iTunes Store over the wifi network in a branch of Starbucks. Users can download the song that is currently playing in that café, as well as the nine songs that preceded it.

iPod touch

The announcement of the iPod touch wasn't exactly a surprise: rumours of a widescreen, touch-sensitive iPod with built-in wifi have been circulating for more than a year. And given that Apple already had the bones of the device in the iPhone, the touch seems a natural and logical move. Despite the lack of surprise, though, the confirmation of the new iPod was greeted enthusiastically, particularly as it can be used as a mobile web browser and web email device wherever there's a wifi network.

The iPod touch features the same multi-touch interface as the iPhone, and includes Cover Flow — Apple's visual metaphor for flipping through record sleeves in a stack. In addition to playing music, it has built-in applications for viewing photos, watching movies, connecting to YouTube, and a version of Safari for web browsing. PDA-type applications include a calendar, contacts book, clock and calculator.

With one push of a button on the touch's screen, users can connect

directly to the iTunes Store whenever they're connected to a wireless network. This means that for the first time, iPod users don't need a Mac or PC to download music. Another, perhaps more controversial, application is symbolised by a Starbucks logo; iPod touch and iPhone users will be able to walk into a Starbucks, connect to iTunes over its wifi network and download the currently playing song, as well as the nine songs that played immediately before it. Initially the service will be available only in major cities in the US, but Starbucks is expected to roll it out to its stores around the world over

▲ The iPod touch uses the same touch-screen display as the iPhone as well as having wifi capability.

Images Courtesy of Apple

◄ Apple's current line-up of iPods comes in four flavours, which means there's one for every different-sized pocket.

the next few years.

The iPod touch's screen is the same 3.5in widescreen, 480 x 320-pixel display seen on the iPhone. But the device itself is shorter and thinner than the iPhone, presumably due the absence of a phone and camera inside.

The built-in wifi adaptor supports 802.11b and 802.11g standards but not the draft n specification supported by Apple's Macs. This shouldn't be too much of a problem in a handheld device though.

Battery life has been a thorn in Apple's flesh since it shipped the very first iPod. So its reassuring to note that even with such a large screen, Apple quotes 22 hours of playback for music and five hours for video.

The touch, like the iPhone and the nano, uses flash memory. That's why it's so thin and is able to run for a reasonably long time on one charge. But it also seriously limits its capacity. The three available capacities, 8GB, 16GB and 32GB, fall far short of the capacities of the hard disk-based iPod classic.

For those of us with large music libraries, who've become accustomed to copying everything from iTunes to the iPod, this presents a problem: either choose a classic, or start to be very strict about what music you copy to your iPod and how often you sync it with your Mac.

This dilemma was unavoidable – it wouldn't have made sense for Apple to swap the flash memory for a hard drive: doing so would have meant a fatter case and shorter battery life. Yet there must be thousands of potential touch users who will be put off by the low storage capacity. Storage is even more limited when you consider that one of the touch's main attractions is the ability to play video on a reasonable (for a handheld) sized screen.

VIDEO FORMATS

The touch supports the same audio and video formats as other iPods. That means there's still no support for Windows Media Audio or Video. While this is unlikely to be an issue for most Mac users, it remains a bone of contention among consumer groups who believe that the cost to Apple of licensing Windows Media would amount to a few pence per iPod, and that the reason for its exclusion is to lock iPod owners out of the stores that sell music in Windows Media-protected formats.

Supported video formats are H.264 and Mpeg-4, with a maximum resolution of 640 x 480 pixels (which is scaled down to the touch's display resolution of 480 x 320 pixels).

Despite being a small device, and dwarfed by rivals like the PSP, the touch remains a good option for viewing video on the move, and that screen – once you get used to using it for moving pictures – isn't as small as you might first think.

The touch is a fully-featured, great fun device. If you can live with the low storage capacity, then the only decision you have to make is whether to buy the 8GB, 16GB or 32GB model.

► The touch is skinnier than the iPhone, but then it lacks most of its innards.

iPOD TOUCH VS iPHONE

The 16GB touch costs the same as the 8GB iPhone. Of course, there are contract costs to pay for the iPhone, but that's true of any mobile phone bought on a contract. So assuming an iPod touch owner would also have a separate mobile phone and pay a similar monthly fee for the contract, it's a straight comparison between the iPhone and 16GB touch.

The advantage of buying the touch is that it has more storage, it's smaller and allows you greater flexibility in choosing a contract for your mobile. There is also a benefit in keeping devices separate – if you lose one or it gets broken, you haven't lost everything.

The benefits of the iPhone are that you get a camera and phone included in the price, but then you lose storage capacity. Advocates of a single device would say that carrying only one device around is a definite plus. There are other, less obvious benefits to the iPhone, though. It has a volume control on its side, which is missing on the touch. While this may have been included on the iPhone specifically to allow you to change volume without moving the phone from your ear, it would have benefited the touch too. As it stands, the only way to change the volume on the touch is to unlock the screen and use the multi-touch interface.

There's no Bluetooth on the touch, although this is barely an issue given that syncing and file transfer through the Dock is fast and straightforward. The iPhone buys you quite a lot. If you find a contract you're happy with, it's probably well worth it. ⊕

Images Courtesy of Apple

◄ The current nano is now smaller than its predecessors and sports the ability to play back video, but whether you would want to on its small screen is another matter.

iPod nano

The new iPod nano's wide form factor is a shock – and in photographs it looks like a backward step. Thankfully, when you see one close-up, all the misgivings fade. It may lack the svelteness of its predecessor, but this nano is no fatty. It is still incredibly thin, and its anodised aluminium shell looks every bit as good as it did on the last generation of nano. Think of an After Eight mint, slightly elongated, a little bit thicker and coated in coloured aluminium, and you get the picture.

From the front, the nano looks like a shorter, fatter version of the iPod classic, but it's much thinner, thanks to its use of flash memory, rather than the classic's 1.8in hard disk. Also, the nano's headphone socket and hold switch are on the bottom, next to the Dock connector, rather than on the top. When you look at it up close, it's the most appealing nano yet.

The reason Apple has changed the shape is, of course, because the nano can now play video. Whether anyone wants to watch video, or even look at photographs, on a screen that's only two inches across its diagonal remains to be seen. We have our doubts.

The 320 x 240-pixel screen is 65% brighter than its predecessor, which should help, but for those of us with less-than-perfect eyesight, there's little fun to be had watching movies, TV shows or music videos on a screen that size.

The nano now comes in capacities of 4GB and 8GB, and six colours: silver, blue, green, black, pink and the Product Red Special Edition. The 4GB nano is available only in silver.

Battery life is a reasonable 24 hours for music and five hours for video, according to Apple. Charging the nano fully over USB takes about three hours, while charging to 80% of the battery capacity takes an hour and a half, according to Apple.

As with the classic, the nano features a new user interface that makes the most of its colour screen and display abilities. It supports the Cover Flow interface, which enables you to browse albums by cover art. On the nano and classic, scrolling through albums is done using the Click Wheel. The nano's screen may be bigger and brighter than before, but text is still quite difficult to read. And our fears about watching videos were confirmed when we tested it. You can see what's going on, but watching for any more than a few minutes at a time is uncomfortable.

Additionally, using Cover Flow seems to place significant demands on the processor, and the operating system becomes sluggish and unresponsive. This isn't a deal breaker by any means, and you can always switch Cover Flow off, but it's worth noting.

Despite our initial fears on seeing pictures of it, the new nano is every bit as attractive as its predecessor. The video features may be superfluous for most. But it remains an excellent music player for anyone who wants something more portable than the classic but with more storage than the shuffle.

iPod classic

The iPod is dead. Long live the classic. Ditching the white iPod makes sense for Apple now that it seems to be moving away from white as its favoured colour scheme for consumer products (the MacBook is now the only white Mac in Apple's range of computers).

Apple hasn't just changed the colour scheme though; the classic has ditched its ancestor's plastic and stainless steel

► The iPod shuffle now comes in a range of colours, that include silver, blue, green, purple and the Product Red Special Edition.

casing for a metal shell, and is now slimmer than ever.

The classic is the only iPod in the range to use a hard drive rather than flash memory for storage. For many users this will be enough to sway the decision of which iPod to buy in its favour. Using a hard drive means that its storage capacity is significantly higher than the flash-based nano and touch. The two classics currently available have storage capacities of 80GB and 160GB.

The 80GB version is remarkably thin for a hard disk-based device, and while the 160GB version is noticeably thicker, it still feels slim compared with, say, a fourth-generation iPod. These two capacities are much more realistic for users with large music libraries, and for downloading video content.

Sadly, the classic's screen is nowhere near as good as the touch's for watching video. At 2.5in across its diagonal, it's bigger than the nano's, but well short of the touch. And its 320 x 240-pixel resolution is the same as the nano's. The interface makes full use of the colour display for Cover Flow, while the menu items such as the graphic equaliser have been spruced up.

Our only complaint with the classic is that, as with the nano, there is a definite lag between making selections and something happening when Cover Flow is enabled. It was enough of an irritation for us to decide not to use Cover Flow.

That inconvenience aside, the classic is a worthy update to the hard disk iPod line. It will have to compete with the touch for attention, and there's no doubt that with the iPhone, both it and the touch will get nearly all the publicity, but the classic has plenty of life left in it and could yet prove itself to be the iPod for grown-ups.

iPod shuffle

If the iPod classic is the iPod for grown-ups, the shuffle is the iPod you can give your kids without worrying too much about them losing it. Its price of £32 or £45 is hardly pocket money, but it's as close as you'll get in the portable music player market.

The shuffle hasn't changed at all, except in the range of colours available. It now comes in silver, blue, green, purple and the Product Red Special Edition.

As with all previous shuffles, it doesn't have a dock connector. It connects to its supplied dock through the 3.5mm headphone jack, which also carries data.

The shuffle may be the smallest, and least exciting of the iPods, but that doesn't mean Apple has paid any less attention to the details of its design. The headphone socket, which bulges from the rear of the case, has been used as a hinge for the clip. The Click Wheel is specially designed – as it has been since the first shuffle – to take account for the fact that it's too small to operate in the same way as the Click Wheel on the classic. And the hold and shuffle switches look like tiny chrome rivets.

The suffle comes in two sizes: 1GB and 2GB. Apple's quoted battery life is 12 hours on a full charge, which takes four hours.

The shuffle isn't for everyone, but if you don't mind syncing regularly and want an inexpensive iPod, it's perfect. ❷

◄ The iPod classic is now the media player of choice for those users with a large music library.

► The headphone socket is on one side of the shuffle, while the on/off switch and shuffle switch are on the other.

iPhone

Unveiled to the world in January 2007, the iPhone quickly became one of the most talked about electronic product announcements. Yet it was almost six months later before the first iPhones went on sale in the US, with the UK following four months after that. The iPhone certainly looks amazing, but does it manage to live up to the hype?

SMARTPHONE
iPhone

Price £269 (£229 ex VAT) for 8GB;
£329 (£280 ex VAT) for 16GB
Pros Great design + Innovative touch-screen + Best Internet experience on a phone
Cons Separate adaptor required for third-party headphones + Edge standard is relatively slow + Sealed battery

Long after the initial frenzy has calmed and the iPhone finds its ubiquitous place among the masses, Apple's first foray into the telecom business will certainly be remembered as one of its most anticipated and ambitious product launches in history.

Rumored to be in development for more than five years – and some accounts suggest it actually was – the iPhone's long-awaited arrival marks a significant milestone not only for Apple aficionados, but for anyone who relies on that most common piece of digital kit.

With six months of hype between its first announcement and delivery, did it live up to expectations? The simple answer is yes, the iPhone really is as cool as the ballyhoo that preceded its launch suggested it would be.

At the first glance, it's apparent that Apple has delivered a level of elegance and class never before seen in the mobile market. Even ignoring the iPhone's two most impressive accomplishments, its innovative touch-screen display and Mac OS X-based operating system, the iPhone trumps the design of every other handset we have held. It simply looks and feels terrific in hand.

The iPhone's dimensions resemble that of the 80GB iPod classic but it appears more svelte on account of its longer design and completely curved and chrome-accented edges. It is less than half an inch thick, making it stunningly thin for a smartphone. The iPhone also feels remarkably solid due to its metal and glass construction.

Apple has learned from its experience with the iPod – that while consumers may love a sleek finish, they abhor the scratches that accompany them. Accordingly, the rear is finished in brushed aluminum and the glass front is exceptionally durable, like the face of a good watch that can take a beating and still emerge unscathed.

Without being activated, the iPhone passes only for an elegant paperweight: out of the box, not even the non-mobile features will work without signing up for service through iTunes. Those who envisioned tapping their wifi network for Internet access on the iPhone and taking advantage of its iPod capability without marrying themselves to a monthly plan are out of luck.

On the bright side, Apple has taken an ingenious route in delegating activation to iTunes, as owners can have their phone up and running in under a minute by completing just a few screens of required information. It is so simple, it's easy to forget that in addition to the price of admission to the iPhone party, you have also committed yourself to a two-year contract whose charges will at least triple the price of the iPhone itself.

The iPhone's touch-screen feels immediately natural to use, although it can take some practice to discover what part

▲ This is what comes in the box, but it's all you need to hook the iPhone up to iTunes and get it running.

of your finger actually makes contact with the screen first. Perfecting your pointing instrument is made easy on account of the instantaneous response that the iPhone delivers, and the animated interface elements Apple has sprinkled throughout the iPhone only make the experience better (delete an email and watch it get sucked down into the trash can).

Like a laptop's trackpad, the touch-screen magic works by sensing the change in capacitance created by your finger, meaning it needs only to contact the screen, not actually 'press' it. This makes operating the iPhone an extremely light-weight task that won't tire your fingers and hopefully will

► The touch-screen is the iPhone's most prominent feature. All the iPhone's features are accessed through touching it.

mitigate some of the stress injuries that repetitive thumb typing can create among smartphone users. It also makes the iPhone useless in the hands of a gloved operator, a potential point of inconvenience when using the device in the winter.

Typing on the iPhone's virtual keyboard is easy, despite the fact that your digit will dwarf the miniature key caps. When a key is pressed, the iPhone responds with the audible click of a typewriter and the pressed key momentarily expands above your finger, allowing you to easily verify that it was the one you wanted.

It takes little time to familiarize yourself with typing on the iPhone, although typos will always be an inevitable fixture. Fortunately, Apple has that mostly covered with its clever error-correction algorithm, which monitors what you're typing and automatically corrects misspelled words, eliminating the need to make corrections. If you see a mistake in your typing, carry on and the iPhone will likely fix it for you.

The iPhone ships with most of the functionality expected in a smartphone, including a calendar, address book, and email client that can be synchronised across multiple systems via iTunes. Of those three, the iPhone's capabilities best shine through with Mail, which like Safari on the iPhone looks and acts much like Mail on Mac OS X.

Rich HTML email is fully supported and attached photos can be viewed directly in Mail. A selection of other documents, including PDF, Word and Excel can also be viewed when sent as attachments or downloaded from Safari.

While both Mail and Safari are miles ahead of most competitors' mobile apps, they aren't quite fully featured desktop replacements. Flash and Java are not supported and any files not compatible with the iPhone's document viewer can't even be saved for

viewing later on your computer. Another significant shortcoming likely to be solved in a future software update is the inability to select, copy, or paste text on the iPhone.

The iPhone makes it a breeze to take photos with its modest 2-megapixel camera and email them, but oddly multimedia messaging support (MMS) is missing.

Similarly, SMS text messaging is elegantly deployed in the form of iChat-like conversations with each contact you have, but iChat itself is missing, an inexcusable omission in the age of instant messaging.

The iPhone's iPod functionality exhibits more of this give-and-take. Apple has packed the best iPod ever into the iPhone, with features like wide-screen video viewing and Cover Flow, but in the process has crippled the iPhone's versatility by mandating that its media library be tied to a single computer.

Content can only be managed through playlists on that computer, so forget about popping that new tune on your iPhone that you bought at work through iTunes if your iPhone is linked to your computer at home. Songs also can't be used as ringtones.

Also, unlike iPods, the iPhone can't be used a portable hard drive, although that too could theoretically be added through software.

One aspect of the iPhone that owners of the first-generation will never be able to improve is the Edge wireless data support, which is considerably slower than the more modern 3G standard. Edge is roughly two-to-three times faster than a 56K dial-up connection and is perfectly suited for email and casual Web browsing, but it wasn't uncommon to wait at least 30 seconds or more for a page to load. The iPhone's Maps functionality also takes a hit in convenience when you're on the road and need directions quickly.

Edge also makes the iPhone less fit to function as a wireless modem tethered to

your computer, perhaps that's the reason why Apple opted to not include such support despite the iPhone's obvious appeal among road warriors.

The iPhone compensates for Edge by including wifi capability, something that only a minority of smartphones on the market currently feature. If you have a wifi access point at work, school, or home like many people now do, chances are the iPhone will spend more time connected to the Internet that way than over Edge.

The iPhone does a commendable job of managing its wireless connectivity to conserve battery life, ever important in any portable device, but even more so in the iPhone, whose battery can't be removed and replaced with a fresh one. Apple claims the iPhone offers up to 8 hours of continuous talk time or 24 hours of music playback on a single charge and our own testing came very close to those numbers.

Most owners will regularly use their iPhone for a mix of voice, data and media functions, and they'll want to make it a habit to charge the iPhone at least every night to ensure ample juice for the day ahead.

Apple does make charging more convenient by including a dock with the iPhone, which features the same 30-pin connector as iPods. This means the car charger you bought for your iPod nano will also work with the iPhone, as will most other iPod accessories.

Despite its array of mostly minor annoyances, the bulk of which Apple should be able to address through promised software updates, the iPhone exemplifies the marvels of modern technology.

Like the iPod before it, Apple opted not to pioneer the market that the iPhone now finds itself in but, to the benefit of consumers, has blazed a trail that is simply miles ahead of competitors. ⊗

MAC OS X

Mac OS X

Apple doesn't only build computers: it also makes the software that runs them. Mac OS X, Apple's equivalent to Windows, is stuffed full of useful features that make your life easier and Macs more fun to use.

With an industrial strength email application, a speedy web browser, organisational tools like iCal and Address Book, there is plenty built in to get you up and running from day one.

Over the next 14 pages we'll run you through all of the key features of Mac OS X, explain its smart, clean interface and show you how to make changes through System Preferences to have it running just the way you need it.

Interface

The Mac OS X interface is composed of windows, icons, menus and pointers, making it a classic Wimp environment. That's why it's so easy to use.

INTERFACE

1 The **Menubar** runs across the top of the screen. At the moment it is showing the options associated with managing your files. However, it will always tailor itself to your current application, with the bold word on the very left indicating which application that is.

2 The **Dock** is where you'll store your most common applications. You can drag applications icons on and off it to add or remove them. When an application needs attention, its icon will bounce.

3 **Stacks** are special Dock icons found in Mac OS X 10.5 Leopard, which fan out to reveal the contents of a folder on your hard drive. By default it will show your Documents and Downloads folders, but you can create new Stacks by dragging folders onto the Dock to the right of the vertical dividing bar.

4 The **Trash Can** holds all of your deleted documents so that you can rescue them if you didn't mean to erase them. Files, applications and folders can be sent to the Trash by dragging them to it from the Desktop or any Window. To empty the trash, right-click (or click while pressing Ctrl on the keyboard) on the Trash icon and select Empty Trash from the menu.

5 This icon shows your currently active **Space**. Spaces are virtual screens (see page 44) that allow you to run several applications at once. Switch between spaces using Ctrl and 1, 2, 3 or 4 as appropriate.

6 The **Desktop** is your main working area. It is the backdrop to all of the open windows on your Mac, and is also a place where you can temporarily drop files you are working with. However, you should never use it for permanent file storage.

7 The **red button** on a window closes it, the **amber button** minimises it to the Dock, and the **green button** switches between a full-size and shrunken view of the document. Note that this is different to the maximise button in Windows, as while that fills the whole screen with your application, the Mac's green button simply makes the application the largest appropriate size for your work.

8 The **lozenge** on the top right of a window shows and hides an application's toolbar, allowing you to hide distracting buttons that you may no longer need once you have learnt each application's keyboard shortcuts.

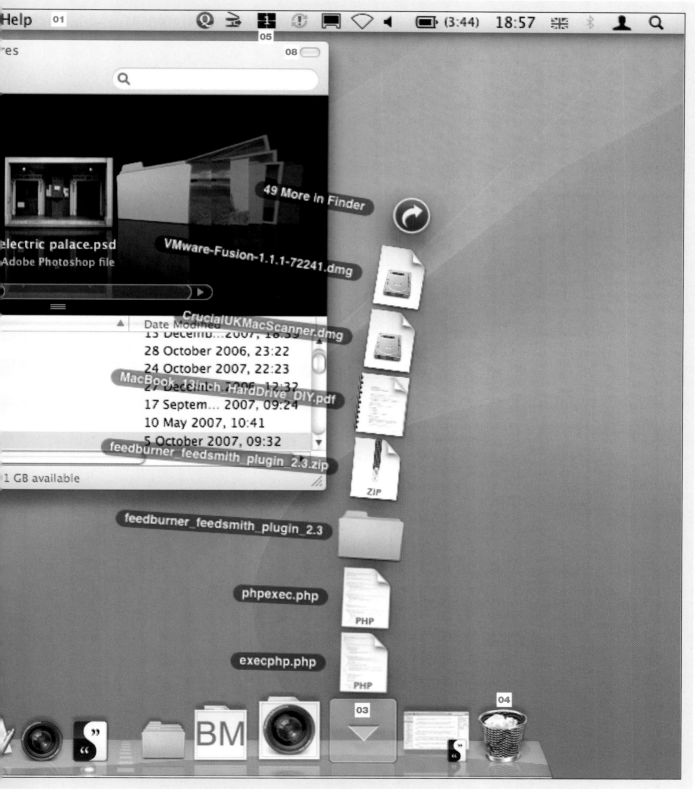

System Preferences

When you need to tweak your settings in Mac OS X, turn to System Preferences, found in the Apple menu. It's the fastest way to tailor your Mac to your needs.

INTERFACE

System Preferences is the part of Mac OS X that lets you control how it works. The closest equivalent on a PC is Windows Control Panel. In Mac OS X 10.5 Leopard, System Preferences is represented by a set of grey cogs. In Mac OS X 10.4 Tiger and earlier it is a white light switch with an Apple logo. It can also be accessed through the Apple menu in the top-left corner of the screen.

System Preferences is split into logical sections, with each feature represented by an icon. You can also search for features using the box at the top of the panel, and it is intelligent enough to understand Windows terms, so while the picture on your Desktop is called the Desktop Background and accessed through the Desktop & Screen Saver option, typing Wallpaper (the Windows equivalent) into the search box will highlight that option in System Preferences.

1 Accounts is used to add new users to your computer, allowing several members of one household to share a single computer while keeping their documents, email and bookmarks separate.

2 International controls the languages and formats used by your Mac. This is where you could add new language options for the spell checker, or change the date and currency symbols.

3 You add new printers through **Print & Fax**, which will search the ports on your Mac or a network to which you are connected and lets you specify an appropriate driver file. The driver file tells the Mac how to communicate with the printer.

4 You can change the resolution of your screen through **Displays**, and control how your Mac spans the Desktop and its applications across multiple screens attached simultaneously.

5 .Mac is Apple's Internet service for synchronising contacts and calendars across multiple Macs, backing up your files, publishing websites and accessing email online. You control what it synchronises and how it manages your allocated space here.

6 Mac OS X's **Parental Controls** were expanded in version 10.5 Leopard to allow you to specify how long your child can use the computer, who they can chat to and email, and what websites they can visit, all the while logging what they do.

7 The bottom row of **System Preferences** will gather together all of the extra settings tools for any third-party applications you install.

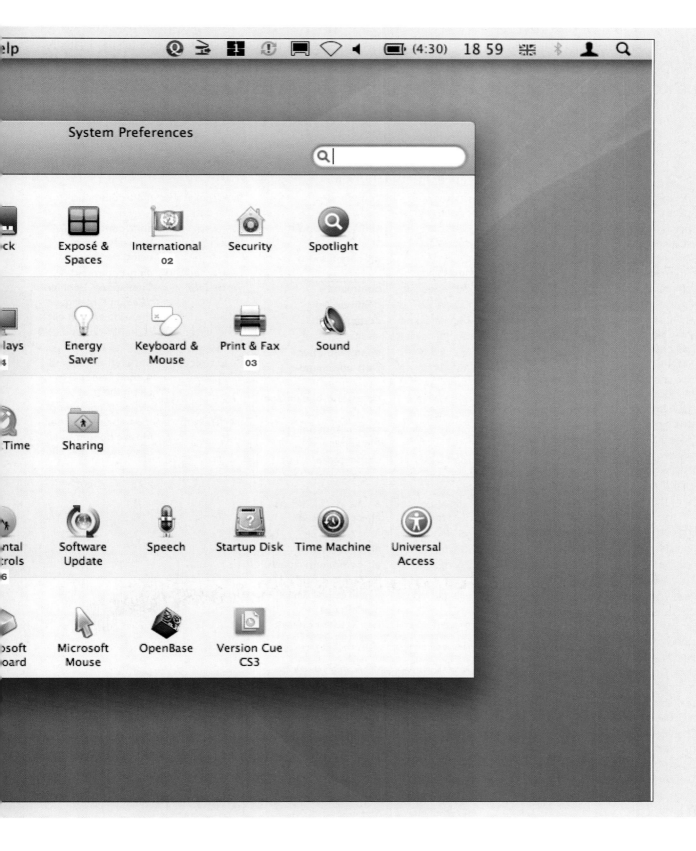

Keyboard shortcuts

You'll get a lot further in a lot less time by learning a few handy keyboard shortcuts. These let you perform common tasks without having to hunt through your menus using the mouse or trackpad. The longer you use your Mac, the more you'll learn, but it's worth keeping this list of the most common – and most useful – shortcuts handy as you get to know your Mac better. Remember that the more shortcuts you know the less time you'll spend mousing, and the more time you'll save.

MAC OS X

Show all active Spaces	**F8**
Show all windows in Exposé	**F9**
Show all windows in the current application	**F10**
Move all windows off the desktop	**F11**
Show the Dashboard Widgets	**F12**
Hide or show the Dock	**alt-command-d**
Show Spotlight search box	**command-space**
Close current window	**command-w**
Quit current application	**command-q**
Force quit	**alt-command-escape**
Log out	**shift-command-q**
Undo last action	**command-z**
Select all	**command-a**
Copy selection	**command-c**
Paste selection	**command-v**
Cut selection (remove to clipboard for later pasting)	**command-x**
Open Computer in Finder	**shift-command-c**
Open Home folder in Finder	**shift-command-h**
Open Desktop in Finder	**alt-command-d**
Open Applications folder in Finder	**alt-command-a**
Open Utilities folder in Finder	**alt-command-u**

FILE MANAGEMENT

Open a new Finder window	**command-n**
Create a new folder	**shift-command-n**
Create a new smart folder	**alt-command-n**
Get a file's info	**command-i**
Open a file	**command-o**
Duplicate a file	**command-d**
Quick Look a file	**space**
Find a file	**command-space**
Add file to favourites	**shift-command-t**
Send file to the trash	**command-backspace**
Empty the trash	**shift-command-backspace**
Eject a disc	**command-e**

ZOOMING

Turn zoom on and off	**alt-command-8**
Zoom in	**alt-command-=**
Zoom out	**alt-command-- (dash)**
Zoom in and out with the mouse	**by scrolling the wheel or ball while holding ctrl**

(Note that universal access must be enabled before you can zoom the screen, adjust the contrast or reverse out the screen display. Do this by opening System Preferences and navigating to Universal Access where you'll find the necessary checkboxes to enable it.)

APPLICATIONS

Open Preferences	**command-,**
Hide this application	**command-h**
Hide all other applications	**alt-command-h**

DISPLAY

Save screen shot to the desktop	**shift-command-3**
Save selection to desktop	**shift-command-4, then select area using the mouse**
Save window to the desktop	**shift-command-4, then space. Position mouse pointer over the window and click.**
Send screen to the clipboard	**ctrl-shift-command-3**
Send selection to clipboard	**ctrl-shift-command-4, then select area using the mouse**
Send window to the clipboard	**ctrl-shift-command-4, then space. Position mouse pointer over the window and click.**

SAFARI

New window	**command-n**
New tab	**command-t**
Switch to next tab	**command-}**
Switch to previous tab	**command-{**
Open location (web or network address)	**command-l**
Send page contents by email	**command-i**
Automatically fill out form	**command-a**
Re-load page	**command-r**
Enlarge text	**command-+**
Reduce text size	**command-- (dash)**
Bookmark current page	**shift-command-d**
Show bookmarks	**alt-command-b**

(Note that use of tabs requires tab features to be switched on through Safari's preferences pane.)

TEXTEDIT

Show document properties	**alt-command-p**
Print	**command-p**
Check spelling	**command-;**
Paste text but match current style	**shift-alt-command-V**
Bold	**command-b**
Italic	**command-i**
Underline	**command-u**
Show fonts	**command-t**
Enlarge font	**command-+**
Reduce font	**command-- (dash)**
Left align	**command-{**
Right align	**command-}**

MAIL

New message	**command-n**
Reply to message	**command-r**
Reply to all recipients	**shift-command-r**
New note	**ctrl-command-n**
Delete message	**command-backspace**
Bounce message	**shift-command-b**
Forward message	**shift-command-f**
Mark message as spam	**shift-command-j**
Erase spam	**alt-command-j**
Paste as quotation	**shift-command-v**
Show or hide BCC field	**alt-command-b**
Get new mail	**shift-command-n**

Mail

One of the best email applications on any computer is Mail, which found only on the Mac. It is bundled as part of the operating system, and as such it integrates well with the other key components, including Address Book, iCal, iChat and the downloads folder found in Mac OS X 10.5 Leopard. An extensive set of built-in tools lets you define rules that help cut down on unwanted commercial email (spam) and route incoming emails to specific folders based on their content.

Apple couldn't have chosen a better name for its email application than Mail. Its closest equivalent on Windows PCs is Outlook Express. Microsoft makes an equivalent of the full-blown Outlook for the Mac called Entourage, which is available as part of Microsoft Office for Mac (see page 114). However, we think you're better off sticking with Mail rather than switching to Microsoft's rival for two reasons: many people feel it works in a far more logical and smooth way than Entourage, and it integrates better with other applications in the operating system. Plus, of course, it's free.

The first time you start it up, you'll be walked step-by-step through the process of adding your first account, using the details supplied by your Internet Service Provider (ISP). Mail will run through a series of checks to make sure that it can connect to their servers and download your messages and, all being well, you'll be sent to the inbox from which you can start messaging your friends and colleagues.

Mail connects with Address Book, so even if you don't remember your contacts' email addresses, you can still send them messages by just typing their name. Mail will immediately start to sort through your address lists, and as soon as it finds a match, will fill it in. If it's the wrong one keep typing and it will try again.

JUNK MAIL
The Internet is now plagued with junk emails – so-called Spam. Mail is good at recognising these and filtering them out, so if you find that your inbox is creaking under the weight of irrelevant incoming messages, go to Mail > Preferences > Junk Mail and check the box beside Enable junk mail filtering.

You have several options here, and we would recommend choosing to move junk mail to the junk mail box, which will keep your inbox nice and tidy while still allowing you to pop into the junk mail folder now and

then to check that it's not filtering out anything you really ought to read.

Mail doesn't always get it right the other way, too; it sometimes drops junk mail in your inbox. Every time it does this you should correct it, as the more times you put it right, the less often it will make the same mistake in the future. Click on the erroneous message and then tap Command-Shift-j, or the Junk button on the main Mail toolbar.

CREATING MAILBOXES AND SMART MAILBOXES
Maintaining an efficient mailbox means sorting through your messages as they arrive. The temptation, of course, is just to leave them in the inbox where the list of communiques will grow to almost unmanageable proportions in no time at all. You should therefore set up separate mailboxes in which you can file your messages according to subject or sender and, once they're in place, rules to do this for you.

Mailboxes are added by clicking on the '+' button at the bottom left-hand corner of the Mail interface and selecting New Mailbox… Give it a name and click on OK and you'll see that it appears in a new section of the sidebar called On My Mac. If you can see this section, but not your new mailbox, click on the disclosure triangle to the left and it should drop down.

You will also have seen the option to create a Smart Mailbox when pressing the '+' button. This lets you define rules that will automatically sort matching messages. Try creating one now. Again, give it a name, then use the input boxes and drop-down menus to define the criteria that, when matched, will redirect a message to your new folder.

You can combine multiple criteria by adding new lines to the box by pressing the '+' button to the right of each line to add a

▲ Use the Rules setting (Mail > Preferences... > Rules) to filter your email and direct messages matching certain conditions to specific mailboxes.

▲ A simple but very effective way of handling your Mail inbox is to set up a Rule. Here, we added a rule that colour codes all the emails from a particular sender, in this case Apple.

new one below it. You can also, usefully, define criteria that should not be matched. For example, if you worked for Dennis Publishing, had set up Mail to pick out both your home and work emails, and wanted to route all non-internal messages to another mailbox, you would select From in the first drop-down and Does not contain in the second, then enter dennis.co.uk in the third box.

Click on OK to create the new smart mailbox and you'll be given the opportunity to run the filter on all messages in the presently open mailbox.

Note that no message sent to a Smart Mailbox is actually taken out of your inbox. You should therefore think of a Smart Mailbox as a lens through which you can see just a selection of all of the emails in your main inbox. If you have set up a mailbox to display only unread messages, therefore, they will not be counted as part of that mailbox when read, but remain within your main inbox for future reference.

Note that Smart Mailboxes don't always automatically update. For example, when reading messages in a folder that only contains unread messages, you may notice

that the now read message remain in place despite the message count decreasing. To get around this quirk, click out of the mailbox – say onto your Inbox – and then back into the Smart Mailbox.

CREATING RULES

Rules work in a similar way to Smart Mailboxes, but offer greater flexibility and don't always have the ultimate goal of moving your messages from one place to another. Although you can divert messages to various locations within or outside the Mail application (you can automatically delete, redirect or bounce unwanted messages, for example), they are most powerful when used to mark up incoming emails for easy identification.

For such a powerful tool, it is surprising that Apple has hidden away the Rules function in Mail's preferences pane. Click on Mail > Preferences > Rules and then Add Rule to define one of your own.

As with the mailboxes, you'll need to give each new rule a name. It doesn't matter what you call it, as it will never appear in the

Mail interface, but you should choose one that you will understand next time you come back to edit it. We're going to call our example rule Dennis Markup, as we're going to use it to re-colour all messages received from Dennis Publishing, but leave them in the inbox rather than putting them into a Smart Mailbox.

Now skip down to the line below 'If any of the following conditions are met' and ensure that the drop-down boxes and input lines match the ones we set up for our Smart Mailbox above, so that reading across the line we get 'From' 'Contains' 'dennis. co.uk'. Now move to the box below 'Perform the following actions', and select 'Set Color of Message' in the first drop-down, 'of background' in the second, and then a colour in the third. We'd select yellow as it's sufficiently different from the standard white background, but not so pronounced that it clashes.

Click on OK and then select the option to apply the rule to all messages in the open mailbox. All messages from the domain dennis.co.uk will now be clearly visible because they have a yellow background. ✖

iCal

What's the point of hanging a kitten-adorned calendar on your wall when you have a Mac? iCal, Mac OS X's integrated calendaring application, can track all of your appointments and tasks, flashing up alarms when things become due so you never miss a meeting or deadline. It integrates perfectly with Mail to capture incoming meeting requests and, if you have a .Mac account, it will let you publish your calendar online so that colleagues can keep tabs on where you might be.

When you want to track your appointments and jobs in Mac OS X, the first place to turn is iCal. It's a sophisticated calendaring application that ties in with Mail to automatically add appointments and invite attendees to meetings.

When you first fire it up, you'll have two calendars: work and home. Clicking on each one in the left-hand column switches between them, while checking and unchecking the boxes beside each name will show and hide each one, so you can have just the most relevant calendar at any one time visible on the screen, or everything at once if you so wish.

You'll notice that each calendar is colour coded, and these colours are replicated on any entries you create so that you can see at a glance whether they relate to your personal or professional life.

In Mac OS X 10.5 Leopard, there is a third calendar: Birthdays. This draws its data from contact cards in Address Book, assuming you have entered your contacts' birthday details.

Of course, there are times when two (or three) calendars simply isn't enough. You might want a separate calendar to track fixtures in your local football league, remind you when your recycling is due to be collected and when to put the bins out. In that case you would click on the '+' button at the bottom of the screen, give your new calendar a name and start adding entries.

There are three display modes in iCal – day, week, and month view – and you switch between using the buttons at the top of the window. The arrows to either side of them will step you one increment forwards and one backwards from wherever you are,

so if you're displaying whole months, the right-hand arrow will take you to the next month. If you're showing days, the left-hand arrow will take you one day back.

You can move more quickly between different days using the small calendar view that appears in the lower left-hand corner of the iCal window. Clicking on any day here will take you to the appropriate place in the main window, while clicking on the Today button will take you back to the current date.

Once you enter an item in your calendar, by double-clicking in the appropriate day in the main part of the screen, it will be displayed as a coloured box (matching the colour of the calendar on which it is entered) taking up as much of the day as is relevant. If it is an all-day event, it will be displayed as a more discrete bar at the top of that day's entry. If you got the date or time wrong then don't go to the hassle of re-entering them manually – just click and hold on the entry and drag it to a new point in the calendar.

For more substantial edits, such as changing meeting venues or adding alarms so that you'll be reminded of an event before it begins, click once on an event and press Command-i to open up the editing dialog.

TO-DO LISTS

iCal is also the best bundled application for managing your to-do lists, as it will track due dates and display them beside your appointments. Press Command-k to create a new to-do job and, once entered, Command-i to create a due date and priority, which will allow you to sort your jobs in order of importance of impending deadline.

To-dos created using Mail will also appear in iCal, and when checked off as being completed in Mail they will also be marked as done in iCal. If your to-dos don't show, click on the thumbtack, bottom right. ✪

▲ In iCal, each of the calendars are colour coded. Home and Work are there as standard but you can add your own.

Address Book

Ever since the earliest days of computers, they have been used to store and manage contact details. Indeed some of the earliest applications were little more than digital versions of the old Rolodex address books found in offices nationwide in the days of rotary telephones and manual typewriters. It's only natural, then, that the Mac should sport a first-class, attractive address book that works flawlessly with its email application and even helps you track your contacts' birthdays.

The address book built into Mac OS X is more important than you might imagine. No mere store of names and email addresses, it integrates with other key applications, such as iCal, though which it maintains a calendar of your contacts' birthdays, and iTunes, which will send its contents to an iPod or iPhone. It works with iChat, Mac OS X's IM tool (see page 42) to automatically populate your contacts list, and tell you who is online.

The main window is divided into three panes handling groups, names and full contact details. The first of these – Group – lets you organise your contacts logically by dragging them from the Name section into sections that you define by clicking on the '+' button at the foot of the window.

No actual change is made to any contact card when it's placed in a Group, and all contacts remain both searchable and corralled in the All group. The benefit of organising them in this way, though, is that you can then restrict which contacts are synced to different devices rather than taking all of your contacts with you.

In this way, you can set up lists of purely personal or business contacts, and sync the business contacts to your mobile phone using iSync, and the personal contacts to your iPod or iPhone using iTunes.

In its default state, Address Book is a perfectly usable and flexible piece of software. However, by giving it a few simple tweaks you can tailor it to your precise requirements. Click on Address Book > Preferences > Templates and you can specify the exact fields that are displayed on each card, allowing you to add such business essentials as a phonetic pronunciation of the first and family names of each contact, job titles, departments and even maiden names and nicknames.

You can have it automatically format phone numbers to comply with specific

▲ Address Book is more than a store for contact details as it integrates with a host of other applications to share data.

country customs through the Phone tab, and specify which country that should be using the General tab.

YOUR OWN PERSONAL CARD

Business cards and email signatures may still rule the day when it comes to passing on your own details, but electronic cards, or vCards, are an increasingly important tool for keeping contacts updated with your various moves and developments.

These are standard data files that conform to an internationally-agreed standard and can thus be passed from one computer to another with relative confidence. Your first job when setting up Address Book should therefore be to input your own card. Do this by creating a new record, filling in all of the details you want to

pass on. Bear in mind that it is not necessary to complete every field, and that leaving out your mobile number or personal email address won't throw up any errors.

When complete, click on the Edit button at the bottom of the window to close off the record (you can go back and change things later by clicking that button again) and then click on Card > Make this my card.

Now, every time you want to send your details to a contact click on Card > Go to my card, and drag your name from the Name column into an email, which you then send.

Even if you don't plan on emailing your details to family and friends, it's worth setting up a card for yourself, as various applications, such as email, business card creation and financial tools use it as a fast and efficient way to automatically populate various fields about yourself.

iChat

Sometimes even lightning-fast email is just too slow. On those occasions when you need an answer right now you have to revert to either the phone or an instant messaging application. While the Mac can't help greatly with the first of those options, it is well tooled for the latter with a first-class messaging client called iChat. This can handle regular written notes, alongside audio and video conferencing using the Mac's integrated iSight camera, speakers and mic.

iChat is Mac OS X's integrated messaging application. The closest equivalent on the PC is AOL Messenger with which it is totally compatible. The most popular PC equivalent, however, is MSN Messenger or Windows Live Messenger, thanks to a bundling deal with Windows.

Microsoft's messaging applications also work on the Mac, so if all of your contacts use them they may suit you better, as you'll not be able to talk to them using iChat. However, iChat is very closely integrated with the operating system as well as being very attractive.

The first time you run iChat, you'll be taken through the set-up process, during which you'll need to enter an existing AOL or .Mac username. If you don't already have one, you can get a free AOL address from *aol.co.uk*, and a .Mac username from *mac.com*.

You will also be taken through setting up any built-in or attached webcam, microphone and speakers, which will allow you to use iChat as a simple video conferencing system with other users on the same system.

Assuming you are using Mac OS X 10.4 Tiger or later, you can video conference with up to two other people. If you are using Mac OS X 10.3 Panther, you can video conference with just one person, but nothing earlier than that can use video conference features at all.

BONJOUR

You will be asked if you want to use Bonjour messaging. This lets you connect to other users on the same network as yourself. If you are using your Mac at home, or you're the only Mac user in your office then you can safely decline, but if you work with other

Mac users then enabling this will allow you to send messages to each other without them passing over the Internet.

Contacts with messenger details in Mac OS X's Address Book will automatically be added to your iChat contacts list – assuming they are AOL or .Mac Buddy details. To add your own, click on the '+' button at the bottom of the window and enter the necessary details, remembering to select Aim or .Mac as appropriate from the account-type drop-down.

To chat with any of your contacts, simply double-click their name and start typing. The two sides of your conversation will appear as speech bubbles within the iChat window. To video conference, click on the green video icon to the right of their name. If it looks like there are more than one of these icons for any one person stacked up on top of each other, then they are capable of taking part in multi-party conferencing. Anyone showing a telephone symbol can chat using audio, but will be unable to take part in video chats because they do not have a compatible camera connected.

Between your name at the top of the window and the contacts list that takes up the major part of the interface you'll see a status line, which most likely says Available. Clicking on it drops down a list of alternatives, with whichever one you select being reflected in your contacts' own contact lists. A wide range of default options have already been entered, including one to post the name of the current song playing in iTunes as your status, but by selecting either 'Custom Available' or 'Custom Away' you can write your own, such as 'Here, but busy, so only chat if it's urgent'.

You can also monitor your contacts' statuses and change your own online, offline and do not disturb settings through the menubar if you have activated this option through iChat's Preferences.

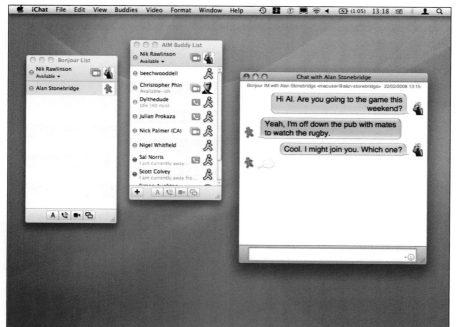

▲ iChat is the IM application that comes with Mac OS X and is a great way of getting in contact with your friends.

Seeing too many beach balls lately?

Speed up your Mac with **Drive Genius 2!**

Spaces

Spaces is a radical feature of the latest edition of Mac OS X that lets you have several 'virtual' screens running at the same time. It has been common in Linux and Unix operating systems for several editions now, and it allows you to either group similar applications together in discrete working environments, or run several applications in full-screen mode. It saves both the cost and environmental impact of buying multiple monitors, which may not work with older machines anyhow.

Spaces is new to Mac OS X 10.5

Leopard. It allows you to have as many as 16 different working areas, each able to run several applications at once, or display a single application in full screen. It is activated through Exposé & Spaces in System Preferences.

You can display all active Spaces, including those with no applications running inside them by pressing F8, or switch between spaces using Ctrl and the number of the Space (Ctrl-2 for Space 2, for example). Of course, this means you can only access up to nine Spaces using the keyboard. If you have between 10 and 16 Spaces active, you'll have to use the cursor keys or the Spaces drop-down on the menubar. This is a four-paned icon with the number of the current Space in the middle. Clicking it drops down a list of all available

Spaces from which you can pick the one you want. If this menu is not visible on your menubar, it must be activated through System Preferences. Click on Exposé & Spaces, then the Spaces tab, and check the option for Show Spaces in menu bar.

If you have a good visual mind, you can skip straight to the Space you need using the cursor keys – the four arrow buttons at the bottom of the keyboard to the right of the space bar. Combine these with Ctrl to move through the Spaces in turn. This allows you to quickly navigate to screens beyond the first nine. In a 16-Space configuration, for example, you could step from Space 1 to space 10 by pressing Ctrl and down twice, then Ctrl and right once.

There are times when the Spaces shortcuts can interfere with key combinations in other applications. Version 1 of Apple's

own Aperture, for example, uses control and the number keys for rating photos, and this will take precedence over Spaces' controls. You may therefore need to change the default key combinations by using the drop-down menus in System Preferences.

But Spaces is more than just a clever way of expanding your Desktop without paying for extra monitors and graphics cards: it is a neat way to organise your working environment by having your most commonly-used applications open on different screens.

SPACES AND APPLICATIONS

Once an application is up and running you can drag it to different Spaces by holding down on its title bar and pulling it to the edge of the screen in the direction of the Space you want. So, to move Word from Space 1 to Space 2, you would take it to the right-hand edge of your screen and hold it there for a second until the new Space slides into view.

However, the Application Assignments section of Spaces' preferences pane lets you specify where applications should open by default. If you therefore always open Mail, Safari and Address Book each morning, you may want to assign each one to a different space, rather than having to drag them there once they've already been opened.

Click the '+' button below the Application Assignments panel and select the first application from Finder window that pops up. Click on Add to return to the pane and then assign it to a Space using the drop-down menu to the right of the panel. Repeat this for every other application you want to assign and then try launching them, either from the Dock or from your Applications folder to see how each one is immediately sent to its allocated Space.

▲ Spaces, which was added to Mac OS X 10.5, allows you to easily switch between applications as you work.

iPhoto

iPhoto is a superb way to manage your photos, and if you've mastered iTunes then you'll be up and running within minutes, since it uses Apple's familiar interface design and concepts like Smart Albums. It's more than just a photo library though. There's a whole range of tools to help salvage photos from common flaws such as red-eye. When you're ready you can share photos, send them via email, publish to the web, or showcase your photographic skills by publishing your own photobook or calendar.

We've reached a point in consumer electronics where you're probably carrying a digital camera as part of your mobile phone, even if you've never purchased a dedicated camera. Over the years, even a casual snapper will build up a sizable collection of photos of friends and family. It's important to keep them organised, but you could do that with folders. So why use iPhoto?

If you take photos of a many different people and places, iPhoto gives you the ability to attach keywords to each photo in the library so you can quickly find the one that you want at a later date. Make a habit of doing this from the start and it'll be easy to find the photos that you want many years down the line. There's no need to pore through photo albums by hand, as you'd have to do with printed photos. Make good use of your Mac's ability to process information quickly and let it do the hard work of weeding out a handful of photos from hundred or thousands of others, leaving you with a much easier job of pinpointing the exact photo that you want.

iPhoto's selection of editing tools is just right for the majority of us, addressing common flaws like red-eye, tilted images where a camera wasn't held level, and incorrect white balance where a camera's automatic mode has failed to live up to expectations. The basic tools are complemented by a range of special effects and adjustment tools.

One of the standout features is the ability to make your own photobooks, calendars and cards, and to have them printed and bound professionally. iPhoto provides a great deal of control over the look of each page, with plenty of alternative

page layouts, cropping and scaling of photos on the page, and captions to annotate events or other details for a photography portfolio. They make wonderful gifts and a superb creative outlet to make you proud of your handiwork.

The first of our workthroughs details how to make a web gallery that only family and friends can see. It also demonstrates one of the excellent benefits of hosting your website on Apple's .Mac service: other people can contribute their own photos to the gallery. The second workthrough shows you how to create a calendar featuring your photos; the same skills can be used to create books and cards.

The iLife Media Browser lets you use any photo from iPhoto in iWeb, iMovie and iDVD. Don't forget to check out the workthroughs for those applications that cover other ways to share your photographs.

ALSO CONSIDER...

APERTURE 2
apple.com/aperture
Apple's professional equivalent of iPhoto costs a modest £129 and it integrates with the Media Browser so your photos can still be used in the other iLife applications.

PHOTOSHOP LIGHTROOM
adobe.com/lightroom
Lightroom carries the Photoshop brand name. It also provides extensive tools for managing large photo collections and improving the look of your photographs.

▲ Editing in full-screen mode gives a lot more room for manoeuvre, with tools hidden off the bottom of the screen until needed.

INTERFACE

1 Flag photos if you want to reorganise them into a new event (Events > Create Event From Flagged Photos) or to keep track of shots that need work – such as colour correction – before they're usable. Flag a photo by selecting it and choose Photos > Flag Photo.

2 Items deleted from the library aren't really gone for good. iPhoto has its own trash can, and photos sit here until you either restore them to the library or select Empty Trash Can on iPhoto's application menu.

3 Events display a range of dates during which photos were taken, and a count of how many photos are visible and hidden. Hide and show their contents by clicking on the triangle next to their names. Change the size of thumbnails by dragging the slider at the bottom right.

4 Photos belong to one event, but can appear in as many albums as you choose. This button adds an album. Hold Alt while pressing the button to create a Smart Album that uses keywords, ratings and other information to gather photos, such as your favourite ones.

5 This group of buttons lets you create a web gallery or email selected photos. Choose the quality at which they're sent; print photos with optional titles, borders and other presentation features; and order prints of your photos through the online Kodak Print Service.

6 Click on the magnifying glass next to the search box to choose whether to search on photos' dates, keywords or ratings, or all data including event and photo names. Just type in the box and the photos shown are updated to only those matching your criteria.

Creating a private .Mac web gallery

▲ **STEP 01 IMPORTING PHOTOS** Save people downloading large email attachments with a password-protected gallery on .Mac. Friends and family can upload their own photos using a web browser or via email. If you haven't already done so, import some photos into iPhoto, and make any necessary corrections such as red-eye removal, blemishes and colour enhancements.

▲ **STEP 02 ADD TITLES** If you want to publish photos with a title, press the information button at the bottom left to show a panel where the title can be changed. Select View > Titles to preview them in the library and check for mistakes before uploading. Once you've selected the photos to upload, press the Web Gallery button; in future, you'll email photos to the gallery.

▲ **STEP 03 ADD A PASSWORD** Protect your site by adding a password. Click on the first option to choose who can view the album: everyone, just yourself or a specific username. Select Edit Names and Passwords, then the + button and enter a new username and password; these are needed to view the web page and the RSS feed. Go back to the first page and choose the new user.

▲ **STEP 04 UPLOADS AND DOWNLOADS** Here we've allowed users to upload via email. Since visitors need a username and password, there's no harm publishing the email address on the page itself. Check the relevant box under advanced settings then click on the Publish button. Keep an eye on the progress indicator shown next to the gallery name.

▲ **STEP 05 VIEW IN A WEB BROWSER** Select your web gallery in iPhoto's left pane. Near the top of the window is the gallery's address and email address for uploads. Click on the address to visit the page. Above the photos are links to upload photos and to subscribe to the photo feed. Viewing options below the photos include the trendy Cover Flow-like carousel.

▲ **STEP 06 UPLOAD PHOTOS** Email people to let them know about the gallery. As well as the address, don't forget to supply the username and password, and tell them how to upload by email. All they have to do is create a regular email and attach a photo. .Mac creates photo titles from the subject header, so it's best to upload just one photo per email.

Publishing a calendar

▲ **STEP 01 CREATE A CALENDAR** Select some photos in the library, then press the Calendar button in the toolbar and choose a style for it. Calendars can be between 12 and 24 months. National holidays can be added along with birthdays from Address Book and iCal calendars. Turn these off for now as we'll concentrate on the look of the calendar before personalising it.

▲ **STEP 02 ADD PHOTOS** A pane containing your photos is shown alongside the calendar's cover page. Drag a photo to the placeholder on the cover. Click on the photo on the page to display a toolbar. The slider zooms in and out, and the hand repositions the photo within its frame. If you run out of photos to use, drag more from the library onto the project in the left pane.

▲ **STEP 03 CHANGE PAGE LAYOUTS** Add photos to the rest of your calendar. Press the layout button to choose a different page style. Some have a second version with space for a caption. Don't worry if your photos don't match the orientation of boxes; iPhoto tries to rearrange them. Photos are also easily swapped between placeholders just by dragging one to another box.

▲ **STEP 04 ADJUST PHOTOS** Beware of double-clicking a photo on the page, which edits the original in the library. Press the Adjust button to show a panel for changing saturation and other settings. Changes made here affect only the instance on the page. Keep an eye open for alert icons on photos. Those photos are low resolution and may not print well at the size chosen.

▲ **STEP 05 PERSONALISE DATES** Switch the page view to a single page instead of a full spread, then to a calendar page. Add iCal calendars, holidays and birthdays through the Settings button, or add information directly by clicking a date. If you want to highlight some events, select their text and press Command-t to show the fonts palette to customise colours and more.

▲ **STEP 06 BUY OR PRINT A CALENDAR** The Buy Calendar button purchases professionally printed copies of your calendar, photobook and card projects. Proofread your project first to avoid any embarrassment. iPhoto doesn't let you do this in full-screen mode. For a bit more room, select File > Print and save to a PDF file and open it in the more streamlined Preview. ✪

iTunes

The iPod is undoubtedly a work of engineering genius that has made Apple a household name, but its success owes plenty to iTunes, which is an integral part of the experience. A digital music library means no more searching through a stack of CDs, just type in its name to find the track you want. Rediscover long-forgotten classics using Smart Playlists and Party Shuffle. Abandon physical music altogether in favour of the iTunes Store, where you can pick up tracks for 79p each.

iTunes is far and away the best known iLife application. Apple released a Windows version a few years ago for iPod users on that platform and as a taster of the Mac experience. In unison, the iPod and iTunes have drawn some people to switch from Windows. Anyone doing so will be relieved to know that iTunes has the same look and feel on the Mac as it does on Windows. The majority of features on iTunes, such as ripping CDs, buying music from the iTunes Store and transferring music to an iPod, all work in the same way.

However, you may already have a large iTunes library on a PC. Our first workthrough shows you how to transfer it to the Mac using an external hard disk. There are also some essential tips on ripping CDs and browsing the library for absolute beginners. Adding genres, ratings and other details to tracks in the library lets you harness the power of Smart Playlists to find your least or most popular music, and automatically create mix CDs for long car journeys.

That's just the surface of iTunes; it's more than just a music library. Our second workthrough demonstrates the power of playlists. You'd be forgiven for thinking that they're just a convenient way to make your own compilations. iTunes can do more than just play their contents thanks to a nifty feature called an iMix.

By the end of this article you'll know how to share playlists with other music lovers by using the iTunes Store's handy iMix feature to publicise your favourite tracks. iMixes can be published on the iTunes Store for everybody to see, and they're easily added to a website, complete with links

back to the store, so that others can preview the tracks and purchase them.

Publishing iMixes as a widget on a website or as an RSS feed is much more exciting for visitors than a static page that talks about your favourite tracks of all time. iMixes are dynamic; even after a playlist has been published to the iTunes Store, its contents can be updated and republished. If you're a .Mac subscriber, put an iMix on a blog entry to encourage visitors to discuss your selection, making for a much richer website with two-way interaction. These two dynamic features will keep visitors flocking to your website as they'll feel involved.

Music is the perfect subject matter to make your website a hub of interesting conversation. After all, who doesn't have an opinion about music?

ALSO CONSIDER...

LAST.FM
last.fm
This social network is for dedicated music fans. The free software publishes your listening habits to your profile. It's all about bringing together people with similar tastes, and it's a great way to learn about new artists and bands.

EYETV
elgato.com
The iTunes Store has a limited range of TV shows. Get an EyeTV digital tuner to watch TV on your Mac. The accompanying software also puts shows on your iPod.

▲ The iTunes Store offers over 6 million songs and thousands of podcasts, audiobooks and TV shows from the likes of the BBC.

INTERFACE

1 The Library is divided into several categories. Unless you own an iPhone, ringtones are irrelevant. Likewise, iPod Games won't be of interest to everybody. Open iTunes preferences and you'll find options to show or hide categories under the general settings.

2 After signing up for an account, you can purchase music from the store. Purchases are made with a single click, or you can switch to a shopping cart system in preferences pane. The Store can also be disabled under the parental controls settings.

3 Regular playlists (shown with a blue icon) are a good way to make your own compilations, while smart playlists (with purple icons) offer a refined version of Party Shuffle to help you become re-acquainted with long-forgotten friends.

4 In List and Album views, the button marked with an eye shows and hides three columns: Genre, Artist and Album. With a well-categorised music library, these columns make it very easy to find music to match your mood. The other button here simply ejects a CD, if one is present.

5 The view buttons switch between a long list, tracks grouped by album and Cover Flow. Clicking on these buttons changes the area below the view. Here Cover Flow is shown, whereas the other two views would show columns for selecting Genre, Artist and Album.

6 The search box works like any other in Mac OS X. Clicking the magnifying glass lets you search by album, artist, composer, song or everything. Just click in the box and type what you're looking for. The areas below immediately changes to show only matching tracks.

▲ **STEP 01 TRANSFER YOUR PC'S LIBRARY** Use an external hard disk to transfer an iTunes library from a PC. Ensure there's enough free space (library size is shown in the status bar) then create a new folder. Select Edit > Preferences then Advanced > General. Set the library location to the new folder then press OK. Select Advanced > Consolidate Library to gather all items.

▲ **STEP 02 IMPORT ON THE MAC** Disconnect the hard disk from the PC and connect it to the Mac. When it appears on the Mac's desktop, open iTunes and make sure the option to copy imported files to the library is enabled (Preferences > Advanced > General) then choose File > Add to Library and point at the folder on the external disk. Wait while the library is imported.

▲ **STEP 03 CHANGE IMPORT SETTINGS** Press Command-comma to open iTunes' preferences and select Advanced > Importing. AAC plays on iPods and some other devices, but MP3 plays on a wider range of non-Apple hardware. If yours has limited capacity, choose a lower quality like 128Kbit/sec to fit more tracks onto it, otherwise you can choose a higher quality.

▲ **STEP 04 RETRIEVE CD DETAILS** Insert an audio CD and it appears under Devices. iTunes will retrieve information about CDs from the Internet. This can be switched off in preferences under Advanced > Importing. Sometimes there will be several possible matches. If the wrong one is selected, choose Advanced > Get CD Track Names to try again, or enter them manually.

▲ **STEP 05 MANUALLY ENTER CD DETAILS** The cursor keys move between tracks and Enter on the keypad edits names and confirms changes. Press Command-a to select all tracks and Command-i to edit common information such as the album title. Save others the bother by selecting Advanced > Submit CD Track Names then press the Import CD button.

▲ **STEP 06 ADD ALBUM ART** In List and Album views, Command-b shows genre, artist and album columns. Columns on the right are affected by selections to their left. Select Advanced > Get Album Artwork to download artwork for the whole library. Copy artwork to the clipboard from a website, then edit the tracks, click the artwork field and press Command-v to paste it.

5 out of 5 cats prefer Fish

Madasafish has a long tradition of supporting Mac users, including complete support for OS X 10.5 Leopard, as well as all the other big cats as far back as Puma. All of our support technicians are Mac experts, our Online Support Centre is packed with Mac articles and our free wireless router is fully Mac compatible. We won't charge you a premium either. Madasafish Broadband starts at **just £9.99 a month.** Visit **www.madasafish.com** today for broadband with bite but no hidden claws.

£9.99 a month for the first 6 months. £14.99 a month thereafter.
Non-cable line required. 12 month contract and usage limits apply.
Connection speed will depend on line quality and distance to local exchange.

▲ **STEP 07 CREATE A SMART PLAYLIST** Press Alt-Command-n to create a smart playlist. Set the first rule to Last played is in the last and 7 days. Click on the + button at the end of the row to add a rule and choose Genre is not and type Podcast. Create additional rules to exclude the Books & Spoken and Audiobooks genres. The playlist shows songs played in the last week.

▲ **STEP 08 LIMIT THE PLAYLIST'S LENGTH** There's no limit on how many items our smart playlist contains. Ctrl-click it and edit it. Beneath the rules, you can limit the playlist using various criteria. Tick the adjacent box and set the options to 10 items selected by most often played. This short list of the most popular songs will look more presentable on a website.

▲ **STEP 09 PUBLISH AN iMIX** Playlists can be shared on the iTunes Store and a website. Sign into an iTunes Store account, then select File > Create an iMix. Enter a title and description. Tracks may be missing if track information doesn't accurately match an item in the store or it's unavailable. Click on Publish. An email confirmation will arrive when the iMix is available online.

▲ **STEP 10 SHARE ON THE WEB** Click on the arrow next to the playlist and choose View. At the store page, press Publish to the Web. On the web page, choose a size for the widget, select the code, and press Command-c to copy it to the clipboard. Make a blank page In iWeb. Select Web Widgets > HTML Snippet and paste the code into the floating toolbar. Click Apply to preview it.

▲ **STEP 11 SHARE BY RSS** Click on the arrow next to the playlist and click View again. Further down the page is an address to an RSS feed that can be read in Apple Mail. FeedDemon (*newsgator.com*) is a free reader for Windows. Email the address to your friends and they'll be able to preview and buy tracks from the iTunes Store, and they can always share their own iMixes too.

▲ **STEP 12 KEEP YOUR iMIX UP TO DATE** iMixes can contain up to 100 tracks and can be updated too. Add some new tracks to the playlist then click on the arrow next to it. Click Update in the window. Check the changes are okay, and click Update to submit them. The iMix takes a while to update, but the widget and feed update without intervention, keeping friends up-to-date. ✖

iWeb

There's nothing quite like the thrill of seeing your own website live on the Internet. Technical jargon and difficult-to-use tools put many people off the idea, long before any pages have even been designed. iWeb takes away the pain of website creation by hiding technical details so that you can concentrate on the important details of designing a site and filling it with compelling content such as a blog, photo galleries and podcasts. Make your mark on the web without going through hours of frustration.

So you've already got a profile on a social networking site, and you're sharing photos in an online gallery. Maybe you already have a blog too, but have you got your own website that keeps all of this information in one place and makes it easy for everyone to keep up to date with all the interesting things that are happening in your life?

iWeb comes with a range of themes and page templates that help you to create an attractive website that visitors will want to keep coming back to over and over again. The tools it provides genuinely make a pleasure of adding new information to your site because you can rest assured that iWeb is taking care of the technical side of things in the background. Of course, you're not limited to the existing page layouts. It's possible to create your own and add text and photos and arrange them however you want.

Subscribers to Apple's .Mac service get a few extra features, such as a searchable blog and the ability to make private pages that are protected by passwords. But you don't have to subscribe to .Mac to benefit from the really important features that will

impress visitors, such as beautiful photo galleries that look and feel like a professional website, rather than something that looks and feels outdated.

Our workthrough covers building all of the essential types of page. You'll see why iWeb is the ideal application for building your first website and you'll want to keep using it because it's such a doddle. Integration with other iLife applications makes it easy to add photos to a page using drag and drop, then crop and adjust them to fit the website using simple techniques that don't require you to jump back and forth between applications.

Although it buries technical details out of sight, don't think iWeb is too limited. We'll also show you how to use widgets – HTML code – from sites such as Google Maps and *last.fm* to integrate compelling web applications into your site. If you're concerned that no one will visit your site then send your friends a link to it. They can subscribe to your RSS feed, which iWeb also builds on your behalf – so Apple Mail users (and other RSS readers) are kept informed every time you update the website.

▼ To add photos to a page, just drag them from the Media Browser. Enter keywords, ratings or other information stored in iPhoto into the search box. The browser makes it easy to find exactly the right photograph.

◄ The Inspector contains a lot of tweaks for your website's appearance. You can set how many blog postings are shown before they're archived, add links to other websites, and control what can be downloaded from your online photo galleries.

INTERFACE

1 The left-hand pane shows your website's structure. Pages that haven't yet been published to the web appear in red, while blue pages have already been published to the web. Cream pages – like the blog and podcast archive – are automatically kept up-to-date by iWeb.

2 Press the + button to add a new page to your website. A panel displays the available themes and page templates. The page's placement in the left-hand pane is reflected in the site's navigation bar. Click and drag a page in the list to change its order in the bar as well.

3 As well as adding photos by dragging them from the Media Browser, you can add shapes and boxes for text by clicking these buttons. Add other interesting elements to the page, like Google Maps, Google Adsense and HTML snippets (also called widgets) from other websites.

4 Objects on the page can overlap, so use the Forward and Backward buttons to choose the order in which they're stacked. Photos appear without a mask when they're dropped onto the page, so click on the Mask button and edit the mask to show only part of the photo.

5 The Adjust button lets you tweak a photo's appearance on the page. It provides the same controls as iPhoto, allowing you to adjust exposure, contrast and other factors. This lets you tweak images so they fit with the tone of your page. Changes made within iWeb only affect the photo on the page, not the original.

6 The Colors and Fonts buttons bring up the standard Mac OS X dialog boxes for controlling the appearance of text. Although you can use any font on your Mac, other people won't see them unless they have they are installed on their computer too.

▲ **STEP 01 CREATE A PAGE** Open iWeb and choose the Darkroom theme, then create a Welcome page. It's automatically added to the navigation bar, which appears throughout the site. Double-click page names on the left to rename them there and in the bar. Open the Inspector (Alt-Command-i). Pages can be excluded from the bar and it can be turned off too.

▲ **STEP 02 CHANGE TEXT** Click once on text to resize and move its box on the page. Click again to edit the text. Press Command-b and Command-i to add bold or italicised text, respectively. If you've prepared text in another application, Edit > Paste and Match Style keeps the template's style. iWeb creates the code behind the site. Replace all of the text on this page.

▲ **STEP 03 ADD AND REPLACE IMAGES** Select View > Show Media Browser to use media from other iLife applications. Go to the photos tab to see your iPhoto library, which can be searched using keywords, ratings and other information. Drag a photo to the page to add it, or onto a placeholder to replace its contents. Add some of your photos to the boxes on the page.

▲ **STEP 04 CHANGE SIZE AND POSITION** Delete all but the largest placeholder. Drag a photo from the media browser onto it. To better fit the page's width, click on the placeholder and select Edit Mask on the toolbar. Drag its right handle until a blue line cuts through vertically. On the toolbar, drag the slider to resize the photo. Click and drag it to reposition within the frame.

▲ **STEP 05 CREATE A GALLERY** Select File > New Page and create a Photos page. Replace its text and drag photos to the grid. Click it to customise the thumbnail size, number of columns and more. The floating toolbar's 'i' button shows the Inspector, which lets you choose whether downloads are allowed, publish an RSS feed and, for .Mac subscribers only, invite comments.

▲ **STEP 06 CREATE AN ALBUM** Add a new page and select the My Albums template. In the left-hand pane, drag the gallery inside the album. Click on the albums grid and the toolbar again lets you tweak the layout. Create and drag more photo galleries into the album. Change their names on the left and they change in the album too. Drag galleries in the grid to reorder them.

▲ **STEP 07 ADD A BLOG** Add a blog page this time. Three pages are added to the site: the blog summary and Entries and Archive pages. On the entries page, a list of them appears at the top of the window. Double-click a title or date to change it, which allows entries to be written retrospectively. Replace the entry's text and images, then add more entries and do the same.

▲ **STEP 08 CHANGE THE BLOG SUMMARY** Select the main blog page. Change the text and photo at the top of the page, then click on the list of blog entries below. A toolbar appears, as in the photo gallery. Open the Inspector and select the RSS button. Choose how many excerpts appear – between five and 10 is reasonable. Older entries will be available through the archive link.

▲ **STEP 09 ADD GOOGLE MAPS** Add a Google Map to blog entries that talk about places. Create a new blog entry, click on the main text box and make it narrower. Click on Web Widgets and select Google Map. When it appears on the page, click and resize it. Enter a location in the address bubble and hit apply. The location shown will appear when someone visits the page.

▲ **STEP 10 ADD HTML SNIPPETS** The iTunes workthrough shows how to add iMixes from the iTunes Store. HTML snippets aren't limited to Apple's own services though. Widgets (HTML code) can be used to embed video from YouTube or use a site like *last.fm* to show what you've just listened to in iTunes. Here we've added one that shows our most played artists.

▲ **STEP 11 VIDEO PODCASTS** Add a podcast page; it's structured like a blog. Edit a movie in iMovie and share it in the Media Browser. In iWeb, drag it onto the entry's placeholder. In the Inspector, choose RSS then Podcast to set details of the series or individual episode. Podcasts can be submitted to the iTunes Store from the File menu, though they are reviewed before going live.

▲ **STEP 12 PUBLISH YOUR SITE** .Mac subscribers only need to select File > Publish to .Mac to upload a page. For other website hosts, use the Publish to a Folder option and save to your hard disk. Your hosting company will provide details of how to connect and upload to their server. Many use FTP (File Transfer Protocol) and you just need to drop the files onto the server. ✖

iMovie

iMovie is a great application for editing movies, whether they've been recorded on a DV camera, the iSight camera built into some Macs, or one of the new generation of AVCHD video cameras. It handles the technical side of video while you concentrate on the creative part. It's much simpler to use than professional applications, but don't be fooled into thinking that equates to poor results. With a little effort, you'll be able to publish superb video podcasts and DVDs that are far from amateurish.

iMovie 08 is a radical departure from earlier versions. Its interface has been given a visual overhaul to make it easier for non-professionals to edit movies. All of the essential tools for producing video podcasts and movies for the web and DVD are provided – and there's little fuss or scope for confusion along the way. That's not to say iMovie is just about basic editing tools; it's crammed with features that produce stylish and impressive movies.

The baggage of professional applications is stripped away, leaving a clear view of your projects. Video, audio and other elements on the timeline are colour coded in a single timeline that is always uncluttered and easy to understand.

When it comes to finding footage, just roll the mouse cursor over a video and a preview is continuously updated in the viewer; it's much faster than dragging a playhead around a timeline.

▲The Video Adjustments panel contains controls for adjusting the look of a video clip. So if your video is underexposed, press 'v' to call up the panel and try to improve the situation.

The changes introduced in this version were controversial for some existing users of previous editions of iMovie, but rest assured that they are intended to make life much easier for you. iMovie 08 delivers great results.

Our workthrough shows you how to add footage to the timeline and put together a cut of your movie. Most movies include titles of some sort, so you'll also find out how to add them to your project. They're essential for documentaries, podcasts and any movie that needs end credits. Apple provides a solid list of common titles that can be customised with different font styles to suit the movie's subject matter. Along with transitions, they're key to making an eye-catching production.

On the audio side, there are plenty of options. iLife's Media Browser gives access to music from GarageBand, allowing budding musicians to build their own score. There's also a library of sound effects in the iLife and iMovie effects libraries and, most excitingly, there's the opportunity to follow in the footsteps of all good documentary makers by recording a voiceover. Again, iMovie's simplicity betrays excellent features that mimic professional productions, like the ability to lower background audio while your spoken commentary plays.

The workthrough also covers using Ken Burns-style effects on still images. This adds subtle but effective motion to otherwise static photos to keep the viewer's interest. It's an essential technique whether your project is a fully-fledged documentary or a simple commentary about holiday snaps.

There's one thing iMovie 08 is poor at – it can only place DVD chapter markers at a specified interval, which means messy results when a marker is added mere seconds from the end of a scene. Luckily there's a fix for this, but you must be happy with your edit before sending it to GarageBand and, ultimately, to iDVD. This extra work is worth the effort. It puts an end to amateurish DVDs that fail to show you in the best light. When people receive your DVD, they'll be impressed by your film-making and DVD-authoring skills. They probably won't guess that it was produced with software that came free with your Mac.

INTERFACE

1 This button switches the position of the Project and Events libraries. Give yourself more editing space by placing the Project Library on the bottom half of the window. Use shortcuts (Command and a number from 1 to 4) show and hide the Media Browser, titles and transitions panels so they don't get in the way too.

2 The Events Library shows footage that has already been imported from a camera onto your Mac. Portions of this footage can be selected in the timeline on the right. Click and drag several pieces of footage to assemble a cut of your movie.

3 With a selection made in the Event Library, these three buttons let you mark a clip as a favourite, mark a piece of video as a reject, and clear videos of marks. At the bottom of the library, you can then choose which videos you want to show. Like iPhoto's ratings, it lets you find the footage you're looking for more quickly.

4 The Project Library holds multiple projects, each with its own timeline for combining video, audio, titles and transitions into a movie. Projects can be organised into folders (File > New Folder). The button at the bottom left hides the list of projects, giving even more editing space.

5 The viewer shows a preview of your video, including titles, transitions and video adjustments. Hold down the Command key and press a number from 5 to 7 to change its size. At its smallest size, it lends more space to editing your project.

6 These four buttons call up essential tools for polishing the look and sound of your movie. The first calls up the voiceover recording panel; the second crops video in the view; and the other two let you adjust various aspects of the audio and video.

▲ **STEP 01 IMPORTING VIDEO** Create a new project and choose the aspect ratio that matches your material – iMovie's help file details how to capture from specific types of camera, such as DVD, hard disk and DV tape. During import, you can add clips to one or more events. Footage already added to a project's timeline has an orange bar along its bottom.

▲ **STEP 02 ASSEMBLE AN EDIT** Clips that make up an event appear as a series of thumbnails from the video. Roll over the clips to see a larger preview in the viewer. Click on a clip and a yellow box appears. Drag its left and right edges to set in and out points. Click inside the box and drag to the timeline to add it. Keep adding clips until you've assembled a rough edit.

▲ **STEP 03 TRIM CLIPS** To trim a clip on the timeline, roll over it and press the clock icon that appears on top of the clip. The timeline switches to trimming mode; drag the left and right handles to trim. Allow some footage either side of these handles as this is needed for transitions. If you trim too much, drag the handles outwards to reinstate footage.

▲ **STEP 04 ADD TRANSITIONS** Press Command-4 to reveal a list of transitions. Drag one between two clips; a green bar shows where it'll be inserted. Ctrl-click the transition and choose Set Duration. Choose whether to apply the duration to just this one or all in the project. Replace the transition by dragging another on top. The duration will remain unchanged.

▲ **STEP 05 ADD TITLES** Press Command-3 to show a list of title styles. Drag one on top of a clip to superimpose it, or between clips to act as a title slate. Add one between two clips for now and, in the viewer, click on the text to change it. Click Show Fonts to change the font, its colour, add drop shadows and strokes so that text remains readable over the top of video.

▲ **STEP 06 TITLE DURATIONS** Titles are marked by a blue bar above a clip. Changing their duration works differently to clips. Click and drag their left and right edges to adjust the duration. Click and drag on the middle to adjust where the title begins and ends. Overlap a title between clips or a transition to produce subtle effects, like fading text out as the next scene fades in.

▲ **STEP 07 ADD MUSIC** Press Command-1 to display the music and
sound effects browser. iLife has a range of useful sound effects such as
ambient noise, or make your own using GarageBand. Drag some music into
the timeline. If you add more than one track, Ctrl-click the green background
and select Arrange Music Tracks to change the order in which they play.

▲ **STEP 08 KEN BURNS EFFECTS** Press Command-2 and drag a photo
from the browser to the timeline. Click on the clip then press the crop button
on top of it, then the Ken Burns button in the viewer. Green and red boxes
mark the motion of the effect. Move and resize them by clicking and dragging.
Press play in the viewer to see how this dynamic adds to photos in movies.

▲ **STEP 09 VOICEOVERS** The microphone button shows the Voiceover
panel for recording a commentary. Select your Mac's built-in microphone (or an
external one) and run some tests to tweak volume and noise reduction levels.
Wear headphones if you need to refer to existing audio. Click where you want
to record audio; iMovie counts down. Click away from the clip to finish.

▲ **STEP 10 EDIT AUDIO** Voiceovers appear in the project as purple bars.
Close the Voiceover window then click on the purple bar. Drag and trim it in
just the same way as for titles. Press 'a' to show the Audio Adjustments panel,
where other audio can be ducked (lowered) while the voiceover plays and
reduce the distraction. Fade audio in and out for smoother results.

▲ **STEP 11 EXPORT THE MOVIE** iDVD can only place chapters at a set
interval, but that can be worked around. Select Share > Export using QuickTime
and choose Movie to DV Stream. Use the following settings: DV, the same
format and aspect ratio as your iMovie project, interlaced scan mode, and
48,000kHz for audio. Save to the Movies folder for use within GarageBand.

▲ **STEP 12 ADD CHAPTERS** In GarageBand, create a new podcast
episode. Reveal the Media Browser (Command-r) and drag your movie to the
podcast track. When asked, convert it to a movie track. Position the playhead
above the track and press 'p' to add a chapter. Choose Share > Send Movie
to iDVD when done. The movie and a chapter menu are automatically created. ✖

iDVD

You've already created a masterpiece with iMovie and posted it on the Internet so that family and friends around the globe can enjoy it. However, a physical gift will be much more appreciated, and this is where iDVD comes in to action by helping you to make a professional, slick-looking disc that your loved ones can play in their living room DVD player. iDVD gives you all the essential tools to make DVDs that feature chapters, extras, menus and photographic slideshows.

iDVD is the perfect companion to iMovie, so it comes as no surprise that they are both part of the iLife suite. Publishing movies on DVD allows your friends and family to enjoy them in stunning quality on their television in their living room, rather than huddling around a computer to watch them online.

There's a huge selection of menu themes bundled with the application. Apple has built this collection with each release of iDVD over the years so that you have dozens of stylish designs at your fingertips. Many of them are customisable by dropping photos and videos into drop zones to tailor the menu's appearance to your content. Some of the more recent templates include motion graphics that create a subtle mood for themes like wedding discs.

Adding content to a disc couldn't be easier. Once you've prepared a movie in iMovie, open the Media Browser and drag it onto a menu to add a button. iDVD automatically links everything together. Photos from iPhoto or Aperture can be made into slideshows in the same manner, and menus are enhanced by adding music and ambient sounds from GarageBand, which is also part of the iLife suite.

DVDs are much more personalised gifts for friends and family. If your website goes down or if they don't have access to the Internet, they'll be unable to view your movies, while a DVD is always to hand when the recipient wants to look back at happy memories. A physical disc elicits a better reaction.

Best of all, making discs doesn't require hours of painful, intensive work to get brilliant results. That's because iDVD uses the Media Browser to make it easy to gather media from other iLife applications.

Follow our workthrough to learn the basics of adding menus and movies. It also covers the advanced features like adding slideshows and photo galleries, and adding other files to the disc, such as high resolution copies of photos.

Authoring a professional DVD isn't just about flash menu graphics, though. That's why we've also covered a few essential tips that will save you the hassle of burning duff DVDs. By the end of this workthrough, you'll know how to make good use of the huge capacity of space available on a DVD. Despite it being free with every Mac, iDVD still makes the most of the format to produce brilliant results.

▲ iDVD's map view shows how the various parts of your DVD are linked together. If you want a movie to play as soon as the disc is inserted, switch to this view and drag it to the first box. Drag the slider beneath the map to shrink the boxes and see more of your disc's structure.

▼ The Project Info window (Command-Shift-i) shows a breakdown of space on your DVD. By default, iDVD encodes movies in the background as you work. You can check how it's progressing here.

INTERFACE

1 The largest area of iDVD's window shows your DVD menu in all its glory, with menu effects like reflections and motion graphics conveniently animated without the need to burn to a disc. Press the loop button beneath it to preview the menu.

2 Use this to reveal the floating Inspector window. Its contents change depending on what is currently selected. For buttons, it shows font options. Click on a menu background to change its duration, background audio and the colour of button highlights.

3 The DVD map is a tree-like overview of the DVD's structure. It shows how all of your menus, movies and slideshows are linked together. You can see where work is needed as broken links are highlighted with a clear alert symbol.

4 The play button takes you to a live preview of your project, as it will appear on a disc. Details like transitions aren't visible in iDVD's editor, so use this to check that they're correctly set and that you're happy with their appearance before burning a disc.

5 The right column in iDVD provides a wide range of menu themes and button designs. It also encapsulates the Media Browser so that you can gather photos, music and movies from other iLife applications.

6 Click on the burn button when you're ready to write your disc. iDVD checks for problems with your project, such as unlinked buttons on menus. That saves on the unnecessary waste of burning a disc only to discover that a simple mistake means redoing the work.

▲ **STEP 01 CREATE A NEW PROJECT** Create a project and choose the aspect ratio that matches your footage. Open iDVD's preferences found under iDVD in the menubar and ensure the video mode matches your camera (Pal for the UK). Changing this setting requires you to create a new project – TVs in some countries use NTSC. Your disc will play on computers worldwide.

▲ **STEP 02 CHOOSE A THEME** The column on the right will already show DVD themes. Each consists of main menu, a chapters menu and an extras menu. You don't have to add the latter two but the main menu always exists. From the list at the top of the window, we've chosen 5.0 Themes and then Travel Cards.

▲ **STEP 03 ADD A MOVIE** iDVD's media browser is integrated into the main window. Press the media button and find a movie you've prepared in iMovie, then drag it onto the menu. iDVD creates a button and links it to the movie. Click on the button and open the Inspector to change font settings; don't use thin ones as they will flicker on a TV. Click again to edit the text.

▲ **STEP 04 FILLING DROP ZONES** Click on the Edit Drop Zones (the box with an arrow pointing inside it) button to see all the Drop Zones. Drag some photos into a box beneath the menu to set a drop zone's content. Click on the box to see the drop zone in the animated menu. Open the Inspector, then click on menu background to change options like duration.

▲ **STEP 05 CHANGE A MENU'S AUDIO** Prepare some music or record a voiceover in GarageBand, then select Share > Send Song to iTunes. In iDVD, select Media then Audio and locate the track. Open the menu's Inspector by clicking on the 'i' button and drag the track to the audio box. When making audio, take into account the menu's duration, as audio will stop briefly when it loops.

▲ **STEP 06 ADD A SLIDESHOW** Select two photos in the media browser and drag them to the menu. The new button links to a slideshow. Double-click it to add more photos or movies. Drag items up and down the list to reorder them. Set a uniform duration at the bottom of the window; five seconds is a good starting point. Fade Through Black is one of the more tasteful transitions.

▲ **STEP 07 ADD AUDIO TO YOUR SLIDESHOW** Drag an audio track from the media browser onto the speaker icon beneath your slideshow. The slideshow's duration is adjusted to match the audio. Press the play button to check the pace of the slideshow and the music. If it's not right, just drag the track out of the box or drag another one into the box to replace the existing track.

▲ **STEP 08 ADVANCED SETTINGS** Click on the Settings button. You can add copies of original photos to the disc, so recipients can print a high resolution copy. Choose whether to loop the slideshow indefinitely, and include photo titles and comments. Adding navigation arrows gives manual control of the slideshow; don't use them with a soundtrack as this will skip when moving between photos.

▲ **STEP 09 ADD OTHER FILES** The Advanced menu has an option to add other files to the disc. Slideshow photos shown here can only be removed in the slideshow's settings. In iMovie, prepare an iPod version of your movie (Share > Export Movie) to include on the disc. It's easier to gather files and folders in the Finder than adding folders here and adding the files individually.

▲ **STEP 10 PREPARE MENUS FOR TV** DVD menus are visible all the way to the edge on a computer, but TV sets cut off the border. All text on a menu needs to fall within the TV safe area. On the View menu, turn off the crop area option, then turn on the TV safe area. The grey area outside the red line is likely to be cut off on a TV set. Move all text inside this area on all of your menus.

▲ **STEP 11 CHECK FOR ERRORS** Switch to the Map view. If any alert icons are shown in the map, roll over them to see what the problem is. It could be an empty slideshow or empty drop zones on a menu. iDVD will also warn you if a button on a menu isn't linked to anything. Menus also need at least one button. Fix these issues before attempting to burn a disc.

▲ **STEP 12 BURN A DISC** To burn multiple copies of a DVD, choose File > Save as Disc Image. Wait a while for iDVD to compile the DVD. When it's finished, browse to Applications/Utilities and open Disk Utility. Drag the disc image into the pane on the left. Click on the image in the pane and press the Burn button. Once it's done, press the Burn button again to make another copy. ⊗

iWORK

iWork

You don't need to spend a fortune to buy an office suite for the Mac. Apple's excellent iWork family comprises a word processor, spreadsheet and presentation application, which are called, respectively, Pages, Numbers and Keynote.

They boast excellent compatibility with Microsoft Office, the leading suite on both the Mac and PC, and go further than the de facto choice in many areas by enhancing its layout tools to greatly simplify the task of creating attractive, effective documents.

Over the next 20 pages, we'll walk you through each application in the suite, and show you how you can step beyond the basics to produce persuasive output that will really impress.

Pages

On every new Mac you'll find a copy of iWork, and part of that is Pages, Apple's word processor. It replaces the much-admired equivalent in Apple Works, but expands greatly on its feature set to offer basic page layout tools. They may not rival the kind of software used to design newspapers and magazines, but for home users who need to knock up a quick birthday card, poster or invitation they are both flexible and easy to use. We take a look at Pages' key features and show you how to use its styling tools.

Pages is Apple's word processor. It's not quite a full replacement for Microsoft Word on the PC, but the two do share many common features, such as the ability to track changes, check your spelling and format documents. However, while Pages may be lacking some key Word features – and by default uses its own file format – it boats some impressive features that put it ahead of its competitor, such as a desktop publishing (DTP) style layout mode that performs many of the same tasks as Microsoft Publisher.

Pages looks and works very much like an application from iLife. A large, simple toolbar at the top of the interface gives you access to its most common features, and an Inspector palette (accessed by clicking the blue 'i' on the right) lets you make changes to your document and pull in resources from iPhoto, iTunes and so on.

It is a highly organised application, which works on the basis of applied styles. Styles are collections of attributes, such as text colour and size, font, alignment, spacing and so on. While you can change each of these individually – you can pick a new font using the drop-down menu on the toolbar, for example – it is much more efficient to either tweak the editing styles or define new ones of your own.

You can see this in practice by opening a new Pages document (Command-n) and clicking the circular blue button on the far left of the toolbar. It looks like it has a back to front P in it (actually a paragraph mark). This opens up the Styles drawer. Now type a few words in your document, and then pick a new font from the toolbar's menu.

Notice how the downward-pointing arrow beside Normal in the drawer, which was once black, is now red to indicate that you have made some

changes. Click it and select Redefine style from selection. Your previously-entered text will change to your new font, and any other text styled up as Normal elsewhere in your document will also be changed.

If a plain typed document is just a bit too bland for you, there is a wide range of pre-defined layouts already built in. Click File > New from Template Chooser… (Command-Shift-n) and all of the available templates will be displayed, ready for you to pick one.

These are divided by type, and cover everything from envelopes to reports. Some of them will be pre-populated with important information, such as your name and address, which is drawn from your own card in Address Book (see page 41 for more on setting this up). Be wary, though, that some forms will be US-orientated, and you may want to think carefully before using something like a standard CV template (or resume, as it calls it) to apply for a job.

Once you have completed your document, you can obviously save or print it from the File menu. You can also send it to iWeb for use on a web page. Be aware that when saving, though, Pages uses its own file format by default, and so if you want to share your documents with other people – especially those on a Windows PC – they may have some trouble reading them. The answer is to export them rather than save them. Choose File > Export… and then pick PDF, Word, RTF or plain text from the menu that pops up. Plain text is the most compatible of all, but you'll lose all of your formatting. To both retain your formatting and maximise compatibility, choose RTF (Rich Text Format). For Word-native files, pick Word, and for use on the web, pick PDF (Portable Document Format).

▲ The look and feel of your documents is controlled by the Styles palette, where you define how text should appear.

▼ It's often missed, but Pages includes an impressive word count tool. To use it, open the Inspector and click on the first tab, followed by Info.

INTERFACE

1 The Pages panel shows you thumbnail views of the pages in your document, allowing you to quickly skip back and forth between them.

2 The Paragraph Styles drawer organises the various typefaces used on your pages. They can be defined by changing the instance on the page and then updating the saved style.

3 Images are held in boxes, which define where they appear on the page.

4 The slider enlarges or reduces the size of the image inside the box, showing more or less of it in the available space.

5 Shapes added to the page can be dragged to new positions, and used either as containers for text, or as masks for images.

▲ **STEP 01** Pages gives you the opportunity to create new documents from a template, saving you a lot of work. In iWork 08, Pages' templates are split into two sections for plain word processing and laying out more complex documents. Pick Flyers > For Sale Flyer and click on Choose.

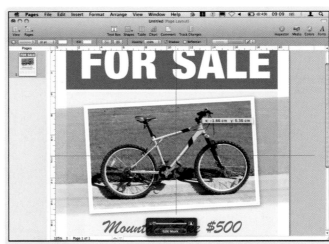

▲ **STEP 02** Pages may be a word processor, but it includes some sophisticated tools. The bike photo, for example, is much larger than the section you see, but masked out so that only the part in the frame is visible. Double-click and drag it to reposition it within the white border.

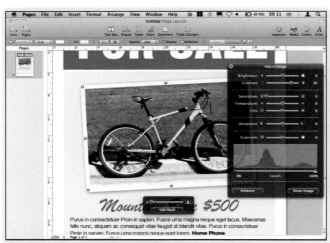

▲ **STEP 03** Now we'll change the look of the photo. Click on the Image Adjustments button on the toolbar (sixth button in) and use the head up display that appears to reduce the level of colours by dragging Saturation all the way to the left. Increase the contrast by dragging its slider to the right.

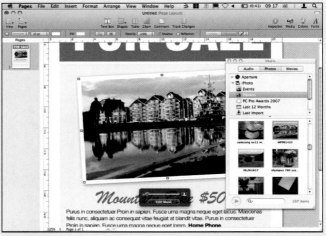

▲ **STEP 04** But of course you're not restricted to using Apple's photos. Click on Media in the toolbar and use the panel that pops up to browse through the photos on your Mac. Once you've found the one you want, drag it out of the media browser and drop it on the page in place of the bike.

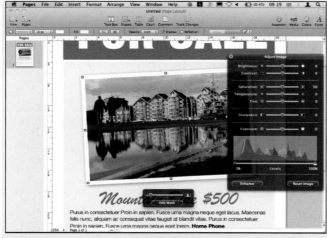

▲ **STEP 05** Notice how even if you used a colour photo it will be converted to black and white when dropped on the page. That's because the settings we applied to the bike photo are attached to the frame holding it. To get your colours back, click on Reset Image on the Image Adjustments panel.

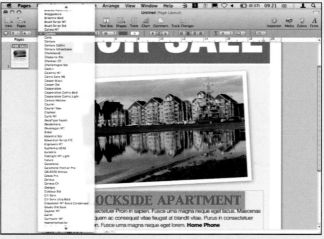

▲ **STEP 06** We're not selling a bike any more, so change the text under the photo to something more appropriate, then choose a suitable font from the drop-down menu on the toolbar. You have now performed the most fundamental tasks in the layout mode, so it's time to look at plain word processing.

▲ **STEP 07** Close the Flyer and pick File > New from Template Chooser…
Pick Letters > Modern Letter and Pages will open a far plainer document than
the Flyer we have just been working on, ready for you to edit. Here we'll take
you through character styles, which are used to format text on the page.

▲ **STEP 08** Select the recipient's address, then click on View > Show Styles
Drawer. This opens a panel through which you can manage the look of your
document. Click on Address to change the recipient address font to match the
one used on your own address at the top of the page.

▲ **STEP 09** Without deselecting the address on the page, use the drop-down
menus below the toolbar to choose a new font and size, such as Arial, 10pt.
When you apply them they will change only the selected text, but in the next
step we'll automatically apply them to our own address, too.

▲ **STEP 10** Notice how the arrow to the right of Address in the Styles Drawer
is red. This indicates that you have made changes to a piece of text that uses
it. Click on the arrow and select Redefine Style from Selection, and see how,
because this style has now changed, your own address at the top of the page
matches the recipient address.

▲ **STEP 11** When you click on the main body of the letter, all of the text
is highlighted. This is because it is only there as a placeholder and used as
guidance. Start typing your letter and you'll see that as you press the first
character all of the text is removed. Templates are a very speedy way to
create documents in Pages.

▲ **STEP 12** Once you have finished your letter, you can obviously print it from
the File menu, and save it by tapping Command-s. However, you can also save
it as a Microsoft Word document. Do this by choosing File > Export > Word.

Numbers

If you want to work with numbers, you need Numbers. Well, that's what Apple would like you to believe. It's a spreadsheet application, and it took a long time to make it into iWork. A radical departure from other spreadsheet tools, it lets you work on several tables side by side on a single sheet, so you can directly compare your figures and make references between them for more dynamic and meaningful analysis. Here we'll show you how to create and style your tables and charts.

The best-looking spreadsheet application on any platform – bar none – is Numbers. It took a long time for Apple to add a spreadsheet to its office suite, but once it arrived it was well worth the wait. It has great layout tools, produces the smoothest, most engaging charts, and lets you put more than one table on any sheet. This last feature is the ace in its hand. It's not until you've used it and then switch back to something like Excel that you realise how innovative and useful it is. Why did nobody think of it before?

The first time you start Numbers, you'll be presented with a blank spreadsheet. To the left is a column showing the number of sheets in the document, and the tables in each sheet, and below that the styles that can be applied to the sheets. You'll see that there are grey cells running across the top and down the left-hand edge of the current active table – which takes up the whole of the sheet.

The easiest way to understand the relationship between sheets and tables is to right-click on Table 1 in the sidebar and select Delete. The cells will disappear, but you'll see that Sheet 1 stays active in the sidebar.

▲ The range of colours and styles that can be applied to charts is impressive, and includes realistic marble and wood finishes.

Click on the Tables button in the toolbar and select Basic to insert a new table into the sheet. By default it will have 10 rows and four columns, but you can make it larger or smaller by dragging the fat corner handle at the bottom right. Click on Tables again and select Sums Checklist. A new table will appear in the same sheet, this time with checkboxes that let you mark off different items in a list. Note how both tables can exist side by side and you can work on them both at once. You can't do this in Excel.

Add some details to columns B and C in your new spreadsheet, and then check a few of the boxes to the left. Note how the total at the bottom of column C doesn't start to rack up until you have checked the boxes in column A. This is an example of the pre-defined functions Apple has built into Numbers.

Try moving your tables around by dragging the dimpled area above row one and to the left of column A. Notice how blue guidelines appear to help you line them up with other tables and elements on the Sheet, making Numbers one of the best spreadsheet applications for laying out attractive sheets of data.

To add new tables on a separate page you need a new Sheet. Right-click in the top half of the sidebar and select New Sheet to create one. You can now click backwards and forwards between them, with each one showing only the tables it contains.

Elsewhere, Numbers works in a similar way to Excel, and if you have any familiarity with Excel's formulas, you should have no problem making the switch. =SUM(D3:D9) would add together all of the cells between D3 and D9. =SQRT(C2) gives you the square root of the value in cell C2. =AVERAGE(B1:B4) will give you the average of those cells. A trick for checking the validity of your functions as you type them is to always use lower case, and watch how the case changes as you type your opening bracket. Thus =average(will jump to upper case, showing you the function is correct. =avg(will remain in lower case, indicating a problem you need to resolve.

▼ Highlight a range of values and Numbers performs these quick sums in the sidebar. You can drag them into cells on your spreadsheet.

☐ Blue Headers	
☐ Blue Fill	
sum	340
avg	85
min	70
max	100
count	4

33	
34	
35	
36	
37	
38	
39	
40	
41	
42	
100%	

INTERFACE

1 The Sheet panel holds all of the pages in your spreadsheet. Each sheet can contain several tables and charts, allowing you to present diverse data side by side.

2 The Styles panel lets you quickly format your spreadsheets. However, as this is a context-sensitive area, which changes depending on what you have clicked in the spreadsheet, it can also show quick automatic calculations if you have selected a range of numbers.

3 The formatting toolbar above the working area works in the same as at that in a word processor, allowing you to change font and sizes, and background colours.

4 The input bar is where you input the data to be displayed on the spreadsheet.

5 Guide lines help you to line up the edges of tables and charts with other elements on a spreadsheet page.

6 Turn to the toolbar to perform the most common tasks in creating a spreadsheet, including adding charts, shapes and notes.

▲ **STEP 01** The first thing you see in numbers is an empty spreadsheet. We're going to use it to track some spending, so enter the months January to June in the grey boxes at the tops of columns B to G, and Food, Car, Leisure, Rent in the grey boxes down column A, from rows 2 to 5.

▲ **STEP 02** Enter some numbers for each category and month so that you have a total of 24 values on your spreadsheet. The first thing we're going to do is total each month. Click in the cell below the numbers in column B and type =sum(B2:B5) then press return.

▲ **STEP 03** Numbers adds up the values for January and puts the answer in cell B6. Do the same for the remaining columns, noticing how the case of 'sum' changes to capitals to indicate that Numbers understands the command.

▲ **STEP 04** Now click in cell H2 and type =sum(and rather than finish off the sum, click on cell B2, then with the mouse button held down drag to H2 to highlight every cell in the Food line. Type the closing) and hit return and Numbers performs the calculation without us typing the formula.

▲ **STEP 05** We'll use that formula again for the other categories, but without typing at all. Click on H2 again and then on the small circle in the bottom-right of the cell. Keep the mouse button held down and drag this circle down to H5. As you move it, Numbers fills in the totals spent on Car, Leisure and Rent.

▲ **STEP 06** Let's make a graph. Click and hold the mouse in cell A1, then drag it to cell G5 to highlight all of our values and category names, but not the totals. Now click on the Charts button in the toolbar and pick the fifth chart down in the left-hand column. Numbers puts a line chart under the data.

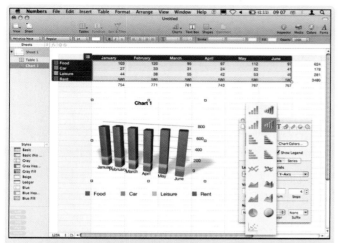

▲ **STEP 07** Notice how the categories are given colours to match the lines on the chart. It will also have opened an Inspector palette, which we'll use to customise the chart, starting by changing the chart type. Click on the large square button to the left of chart colours and pick the style shown one down in the right-hand column.

▲ **STEP 08** We now have a 3D bar chart. Click on Chart Colors and pick a new colour scheme by clicking on the drop-down menu and choosing from the list that comes up. Press Apply all to apply the colours to your chart. Try a few colours, including Wood, which gives a realistic veneer.

▲ **STEP 09** Close the colours palette and click on the Inspector's 3D scene button. Here you can change the 3D depth of the chart. You can also swivel it around by clicking on the circular blue button to the left and dragging it in various directions. Try this.

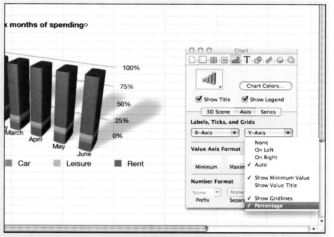

▲ **STEP 10** Our chart is simply called Chart 1, which would be no good in a presentation. Click this in the chart itself and change it to 'Six months of spending'. Now click on the Inspector's Axis button, then Y-Axis, and pick Percentage from the menu that pops down.

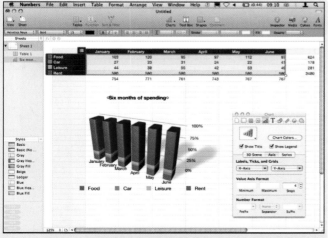

▲ **STEP 11** All of your bars now extend to the full height of the chart, allowing you to see what proportion of your total spending for each month went on each category in our spreadsheet, helping you identify your major cost areas.

▲ **STEP 12** Close the chart Inspector. It's time to save our spreadsheet. You could simply press Command-s to save in Numbers' native format, but for maximum compatibility, you should save as Excel. Do this by picking File > Export... > Excel.

Keynote

Apple's CEO, Steve Jobs, is well known for his stunning presentations. Relaxed and casual, he steps up on stage twice a year to announce the company's new product offerings, against a backdrop of smart, impressive graphics. It was obvious he wasn't using industry-standard PowerPoint, so when Apple came out with Keynote the world was impressed, but not surprised. Since then it has matured to become one of the best, easiest presentation composers you could ever hope to use.

If there is one thing for which Apple CEO Steve Jobs is famous, it's his keynote addresses every January and September. At these he steps up on stage with the minimum of props, always wearing his trademark blue jeans and black polo-neck jumper, and announces what products the company will be launching in the next six months. His only prompts are a series of impressively slick slides that pop up behind him as he prowls the stage.

For years, it was obvious that he was not using PowerPoint, Microsoft's industry-leading presentation software, so it came as no surprise when the company finally released Keynote, a rival Mac-only presentation package.

Keynote is a gift for anyone lacking design experience. It ships with 36 pre-designed themes, each of which can be created in one of five different screen sizes. The themes boast a wide variety of master slides, allowing you to drag different designs onto pages you have already produced to change their layouts. If you change your mind about the theme altogether, you can even switch themes half way through, and Keynote will re-layout all of your sides to match the new design.

Keynote takes the best of Pages and Numbers, giving you access to first-class layout tools and powerful graphing features. It also integrates chunks of your iTunes and iPhoto libraries, allowing you to directly place media within your presentations, and can even incorporate QuickTime movies to create some truly compelling output. These are controlled by the Inspector palette which, as in Pages and Numbers, is split into different areas, each of which focuses on a specific task, such as changing fonts, adding tables and changing the size of images.

Beyond this, the most important button of all is the View menu found on the toolbar. This lets you skip between slide creation and navigation modes, a light-table on which you can re-organise and re-order your slides, and the essential presenter notes view. Presenter notes are additional points you write for yourself to help you through your presentation. They only come into play if you're running your presentation on two monitors, or a monitor and a

projector. The slides will be shown on the projector for your audience, while the presenter notes will be shown on your own screen, along with a preview of the next slide.

As with any presentation tool, though, the rule by which you should live when creating your slides is to keep them simple. Don't be tempted to put so much content on your slides that you end up reading them out wholesale when you come to make your presentation, make sure your text is large enough to be seen from the very back row of your audience, and if you can ever use a picture instead of words, do so. Let it illustrate what you're saying while you speak the words yourself.

You should also avoid using too many transitions. We would suggest sticking to just two wherever possible; a subtle motion from one slide to the next, and a more obvious choice, such as the rotating cube, to move between sections or groups of slides. Combine these with slide builds to introduce the various parts of a single slide in succession and you'll quickly build an engaging presentation that holds your audience's attention from beginning to end.

▼ **The easiest way to start a new presentation is to select a template from the Gallery that pops up when you start the application. This includes a blank template if you're feeling creative.**

INTERFACE

1 The Master Slides panel contains all of the pre-set style layouts in your chosen theme. You can drag them onto blank slides to create quick layouts.

2 The Slides panel contains your work, and shows thumbnails of every slide in your presentation

3 The Inspector controls every aspect of your slides and their contents, including images, text and transitions.

4 Use the Effects menu to choose a transition style, allowing you to apply fades and motion to the switch from one slide to the next, as well as introduce a little bit of interactivity to your presentations.

5 The main part of the screen is taken up by your working space, which is where you'll do the work of the layout of your slides. This slide contains two text boxes and a single image box.

6 The Toolbar gives you quick access to the most common tasks you'll need to perform, such as adding a chart, placing a shape, building a table or defining a text box. All text must be placed inside a box.

▲ **STEP 01** Every time you start Keynote, you'll be given the opportunity to choose a pre-defined slide type. Scroll down the list until you find Formal, which we'll use as the basis of our presentation. Click it and then click Choose.

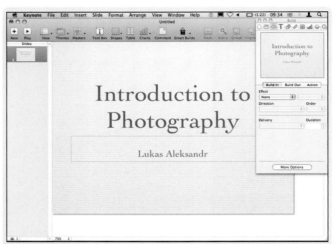

▲ **STEP 02** Keynote creates your first slide. Double-click where indicated, and replace the main headline text with the words 'Introduction to Photography'. Double-click the line below and replace it with your name to give yourself a credit.

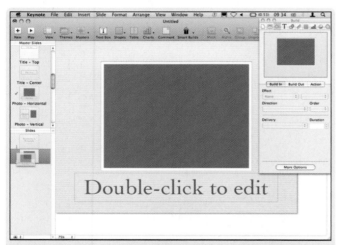

▲ **STEP 03** Time to add another slide, by right-clicking in the Slides pane on the left, and picking New Slide. Click on the View button on the toolbar and select Show Master Slides, then scroll down the list in the panel that appears and drag Photo Horizontal down onto your new slide.

▲ **STEP 04** Notice how your new slide changes its appearance. Open the Media Browser from the View menu and scroll through any existing photo libraries on your Mac. Pick an image you like, and drag it into the large grey square to place it on your slide.

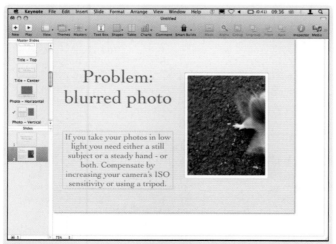

▲ **STEP 05** Give your photo a caption using the space below. Now let's imagine we need more space for a secondary caption explaining our point. Drag Photo – Vertical from the Master Slides pane and notice how the slide's layout automatically reformats. Use the new space to expand your caption.

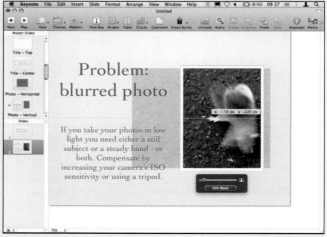

▲ **STEP 06** Changing the slide's layout means our photo no longer fits its holder. Clicking and dragging moves it around the box holding it, but double-clicking shows a ghost of its full contents, allowing you to drag these around to re-centre the image on the main focus – in this case, the squirrel.

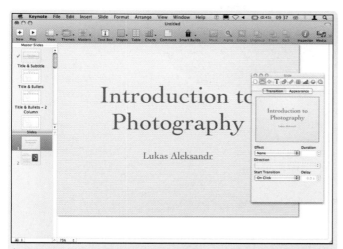

▲ **STEP 07** Try playing your presentation and you'll see that the slides make a straight switch. Not very exciting. Spice things up a bit by clicking on your first slide, then in the Inspector, click on the Slide button (the second one along the button bar, with a blue square on it).

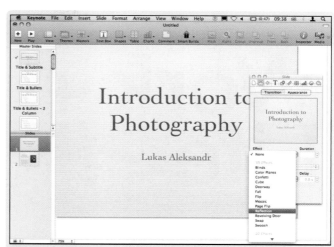

▲ **STEP 08** Use the Effect menu to choose a transition style you like, remembering that you should only choose two for your whole presentation: a low key one to take you between slides in the same section of your presentation, and a more impressive one to transition between distinct sections.

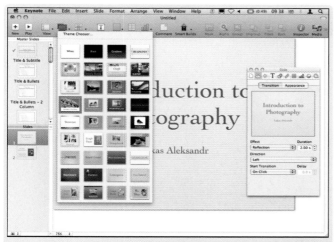

▲ **STEP 09** Nice though this theme is, you might think it doesn't quite work for our chosen subject, photography. It's a bit too formal and over-designed. You can change this quickly, by clicking on Themes on the main toolbar and picking a new one. Try Vellum or Modern Portfolio.

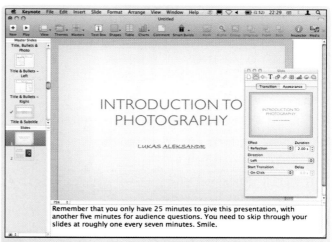

▲ **STEP 10** Continue building your slides until the presentation is complete, then click on View in the toolbar and select Presenter notes. This opens a small pane at the bottom of the interface, where you can type notes to which you can refer when making your presentation. These will show up on your screen, but not the one seen by your audience.

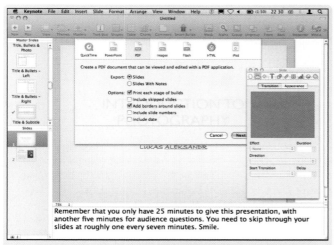

▲ **STEP 11** It's time to save your presentation. Rather than clicking on Save, go to File > Export, where you can choose a specific format, including PowerPoint, PDF or HTML, for outputting your slides for the web. This allows you to publish presentations for viewing when you're not around.

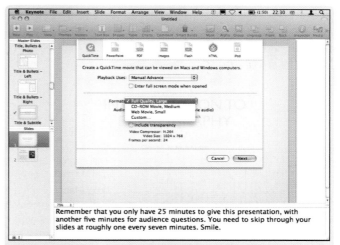

▲ **STEP 12** The most advanced presentation type is QuickTime. Compatible with both Macs and PCs, it is rendered as a small movie that can be played back in the QuickTime application, embedded in a Web page, or used in another Keynote presentation.

iWork + iLife PRO

Apple's iLife 08 and iWork 08 are inexpensive software suites aimed at home and small-business users. But with a little knowledge and a couple add-ons, they can become very powerful workhorses. Over the next eight pages we'll uncover the hidden gems within the applications in these bundles and tell you which plug-ins and add-ons are worth your time and money.

iLife 08

iPhoto

Photography Danny Bird

WORKING WITH MULTIPLE LIBRARIES

You can browse iPhoto albums and events in iLife's Media Browser but storing photos in separate libraries keeps it running smoothly. Holding down Alt when launching iPhoto will prompt you to create or choose a

library. iPhoto Buddy works as a hub for all iLife applications; combinations of Ctrl and Alt keys make the selected library active before launching iWeb, iMovie or iDVD. It also lists the contents of each library, including a count of albums, photos and so on. A thumbnail can also be set for each library by dragging it from iPhoto onto the corresponding library. And you can set the path to each iLife application, so iMovie 08 won't cause problems if you prefer to use

the previous version. Until backup software is updated to handle incremental backups in an iPhoto library, this also helps to make backing up more manageable.
URL *iphotobuddy.com*
Price Free

HIGH DYNAMIC RANGE IMAGES
Making HDR images doesn't require Photoshop. There are cheap alternatives available for even the most budget-

conscious cameraman. First up is Qtpfsgui, though it's not as slick-looking as iLife apps, then there's PhotoMatix, which comes with a short tutorial and good tips on HDR images.
URL *qtpfsgui.sourceforge.net* **Price** Free
URL *hdrsoft.com* **Price** £51.20

PANORAMIC PHOTOGRAPHY
Panoramic photographs can look stunning but there's no way to make them in iPhoto. Step forward Hugin, a front-end for the

Panorama Tools library, which is an open-source product.

Hugin can stitch photos of different perspectives into a single image, or build full-blown panoramas. Making the latter requires a fair amount of detail to be input such as lens type, focal lengths and lens distortion, as well as setting control points for each overlapping area between photos.
URL *hugin.sourceforge.net*
Price Free

⊖ MIGRATING TO APERTURE

As your skills develop, you can comfortably switch to Aperture. It lets you import your iPhoto library and more importantly, it integrates with iLife's Media Browser. That means there's no need to worry about the prospect of any hassle when showcasing your work, with other iLife applications.

◄ **Aperture integrates with the Media Browser so you can use it with other iLife applications.**

PLUG-INS

There is already a range of third-party plug-ins, including upload plug-ins for Facebook, Flickr and other sharing sites. Dedicated sites like *wheezersociety.blogs.com/iphoto_plugins* also keep track of the latest iPhoto plug-ins.

Apple has already released a plug-in SDK through the Apple Developer Connection, so if you're skilled in that area too why not make life easier for yourself and other iPhoto users.

▲ **The Facebook plug-in for iPhoto is just one of many, even allowing you to attach captions to points of interest.**

▲ **Plug-ins like Photon allow for quick and easy posting of photos to blogging platforms such as WordPress.**

▲ **iMovie 08 is takes a different approach than previous versions and is only suitable for simple movie-editing jobs.**

iMovie

WHICH VERSION TO USE

The anticipation of complaints about the radical changes to iMovie 08 led Apple to make the previous version available for download. However, there are useful benefits to the new offering: it's ideal for making short online videos such as video podcasts, for example, while Intel Mac owners can use it with AVCHD cameras.

G4 Macs are unsupported though and we recommend using iMovie HD 6 if you're editing longer movies. This is especially so for DVD because it gives more refined chapter creation at the editing stage without having to jump into GarageBand. The older version runs on G4 Macs and works with most kinds of camera, such as DV, HDV and Mpeg-4.
URL *apple.com/support/downloads/imovieHD6.html*
Price Free

MANAGING YOUR TAPE LIBRARY

If you're using a DV camera, iDive is an excellent way to organise your tapes. It offers a library much like iPhoto, with the ability to assign keywords to tapes and individual clips for quick retrieval later. It can store thumbnails or compressed QuickTime files of tapes, providing a preview of what's on them without having to find and scrub through the original. Although iDive is a very competent piece of software, it's not suitable for all workflows.

▲ **Save time looking for tapes by logging them in iDive. Look up tapes, and even individual clips, using keywords.**

EFFECTS

iMovie HD 6 shipped with a range of effects such as motion blur and bloom. Other firms, such as Stupendous Software (*stupendoussoftware.com*) and GeeThree (*geethree.com*), have provided creative and practical extensions but support for these has been ditched by the latest version – another reason to step back to iMovie HD 6 if your ambitions go beyond stitching clips and adding transitions.

▲ **iMovie 08 is missing most of the Video FX, so you'll need to have iMovie HD 6 to use them.**

BROADCAST SAFE

Professional tools like After Effects and Final Cut Pro will ensure that colours in a movie are acceptable for television.

This effect could be replicated in older versions of iMovie, using a plug-in such as GeeThree's Slick Transitions and Effects Volume Six whose colour correction filter includes a broadcast-safe option.

FLASH VIDEO

iMovie 08 lets you share movies on YouTube with minimal fuss. Using ffmpegX to encode Flash Video (FLV) files gives control over typical settings such as data rates and frame sizes. Unlike YouTube, these can be made to keep widescreen movies as such instead of being letterboxed.

The ffmpegX program uses the open-source ffmpeg encoder, but is itself inexpensive shareware. The application is simple to use and the website provides a guide to encoding FLVs, using the built-in preset, plus chapter and verse on how these can be embedded into a page.
URL *ffmpegx.com*
Price $15 (about £7.50)

▲ Flash Video can be encoded and hosted on your own website at very little cost and effort.

TV SAFE AREAS

Unlike iDVD, iMovie doesn't provide guidelines for the TV safe area, which is unhelpful to say the least if you want to add titles to your DVD. But there is a way of getting around this and that is to make an image that marks the outer area as unsafe.

Use Afloat to add transparency settings to the Window menu of many applications. Open your safe area template in Preview and set the window to semi-transparent before positioning it over the iMovie window. Setting iMovie to show the video at full resolution may also help.

The result won't look as neat as iDVD's built-in safe areas, but it should save you the disappointment of burning a disc only to find out that a title overflows the safe area and is cropped on some TVs.
URL *millenomi.altervista.org*
Price Free

iDVD

CHAPTER MARKERS

It's natural to want to place chapter markers at scene breaks – the movie industry has been doing that for a decade, after all.

The best that iDVD 08 can do though is to place them at a specified interval in minutes but fortunately this shortcoming can be worked around.

Either use iMovie HD 6 to place markers on exact frames during editing or share your movie in iMovie 08 so that it can be opened in GarageBand.

Drag the movie from GarageBand's Media Browser into the Podcast track and you can add a marker at the playhead by pressing P or through the Edit menu by selecting the Add Marker option. When you're finished adding chapter markers to your movie, export it, open iDVD, and drag it into iDVD.

TV SAFE AREA AND CROP AREA

To ensure that important parts of your menu appear on a television, be sure to take the TV safe area into account. iDVD provides an option to show it in the View menu. Use this indicator to prevent vital navigation from being hidden or cropped on a TV.

The complementary option to show the standard crop area marks the visible area on 4:3 TVs that crop 16:9 content rather than letterboxing it. However, though you can check against safe areas for menus, iDVD doesn't let you do the same for movies – see the iMovie tips to get round this.

▲ GarageBand lets you add accurate chapter markers, though you can do the same with iMovie HD 6.

MAKING DVDS WITH VIDEO AND FILES

Most of us use iDVD for putting movies on to DVD. If you're a professional using its simplicity and elegant themes to showcase your own creations, you can include files such as higher resolution images or MP3s on the disc as well.

The Edit DVD-Rom Content item in the Advanced menu caters for this. You can structure the content in the Finder, then drag and drop them to quickly add to your project.

PROJECT THEMES

It's possible to customise themes in iDVD and save them as templates but there's no official Apple SDK or guidelines on how to build your own iDVD themes to utilise animation and drop zones. Unfortunately the theme packages require a detailed knowledge of Apple's developer tools such as Quartz Composer, so the best way to find out about new developments is to register for a free ADC online membership at *developer.apple.com*.

▲ If you don't take TV safe areas into account you run the risk of some viewers not seeing everything as intended.

iWeb

BACK UP YOUR WORK

Though you should make backups of any essential data, it's most important to do this when using iWeb's domain file on a regular basis – preferably whenever you make changes to your website. Should it become damaged, it can't be reconstructed easily from the online version as iWeb uses its own format and flattens it into HTML only when the site is published.

Save hours or even days of reconstruction work by using Automator to back up the domain file. Add the Get Specified Finder Items action to a new workflow and add the folder containing the domain file to the action; by default, this is in your home folder under Library/Application Support/iWeb. The second step should be either to burn

▲ Backing up your iWeb site is vital. A simple Automator script is enough to save rebuilding your entire site.

a disc or to copy the files to a secure location. .Mac users can use their iDisk's Documents folder for an off-site backup, otherwise an external hard disk or network drive is a good option.

WORKING WITH MULTIPLE SITES

While iWeb lets you maintain multiple sites in one file, it's best to keep sites for separate domains in their own files. First of all, open your home folder and browse to Library/ Application Support/iWeb and drag this folder into the sidebar for quick access later.

If you have built a site in iWeb already, it is stored in the solitary Domain file. Make a backup copy of this file before proceeding.

Move the original file to the trash and empty it, then launch iWeb. It will prompt you to create or choose a domain file. Create one and when asked where to save it, make a folder called New Domain in the iWeb folder and save it there. iWeb will open and ask which template to use. Cancel this window and iWeb will close as well.

Don't work in this new file. To work on a new website, make a copy of the new folder and rename it. Double-clicking a domain file opens it in iWeb, which, if launched directly, conveniently remembers the last domain file opened. .Mac users need to be particularly wary when publishing sites to ensure that you don't accidentally replace your own .Mac site. You should remember to publish to a folder and upload manually.

▲ It's not just .Mac users that can invite user feedback. iComment can add the necessary code to add this functionality to any site.

INVITING COMMENT

As long as you're publishing to a .Mac account, iWeb can insert page counters and enable site visitors to add comments. If you're publishing elsewhere, iComment (*web.mac.com/cbrantly/iWeb/Software*) can reproduce this functionality.

Once you've set up accounts with HaloScan and StatCounter, it's very easy to add these features to a page.

The first thing to do is to create a new text field on a page and type one of the special keywords that will tell iComment where content such as comments or page counters should be inserted.

Publish your site and run the iComment application. It can be set to process a single folder or all nested folders, which makes it very easy to add these features across your whole site.

GarageBand

MORE INSTRUMENTS AND LOOPS

Apple's Jam Packs for GarageBand are a great way to add thousands of loops and instruments to the application. They're the most obvious choice to expand your repertoire. There is plenty of free and commercial third-party content available

too – search for Audio Units and GarageBand loops to find sites such as *siliconbeats.com* and *platinumloops.com*.

CONTROLLERS

A mouse isn't the most intuitive way to control GarageBand; its interface replicates the functionality of physical controllers. For real control you should use a specialist device such as M-Audio's iControl (*maudio.co.uk*). MacUser magazine was so impressed, it awarded it five out of five. While it's still quite pricey in the UK, it is USB powered so shop around online

◄ Get more involved in your music by using a physical Midi controller, otherwise opt for GarageRemote with the configurable controls on your Midi keyboard.

▲ Apple's own Jam Packs are just one source of extra instruments and loops for GarageBand.

for a better deal. If your Midi keyboard has its own programmable transport controls, GarageRemote is a small freeware application that lets you configure them for GarageBand.
URL *muratnkonar.com/otherstuff*
Price Free

MIGRATING TO LOGIC EXPRESS AND PRO

If you practise a lot, chances are you'll want to shift to Logic Express or Pro. Audio Units work across Apple's range of audio applications, allowing you to keep on using GarageBand's loops and instruments.

iWork 08

Numbers

REUSING TABLES

Numbers' ability to create polished-looking tables is unmatched in any other spreadsheet application. But once you've created your masterpiece, you can also store it and use it as a base for other tables.

Once you have resized a table and defined columns and rows, choose Format > Advanced > Capture Table. Name the table and you can then access it at any time from the menu of predefined tables in the Tables toolbar.

MORE TEMPLATES

Numbers' basic list of pre-built templates will get you started but more and more users are adding attractive templates for common spreadsheet tasks such as mileage logs and net worth calculators. The most frequently updated site *numberstemplates.com* offers tips and tricks alongside templates.

FREEZING COLUMN TITLES

One perceived weakness of Numbers is that it doesn't offer Excel's ability to freeze cells so that as you scroll through a document, its header columns or rows remain fixed in place.

There are a couple of workarounds. To see column titles in a large spreadsheet, select View > Show Print View. When you scroll this way, the table's headers will be repeated at the top of every page.

Another option is to copy a table's headers into a new, single-row table above it. Align both tables and as you scroll through the one below, the headers in the new table, will remain in view at all times.

LINKING TO OTHER TABLES

Numbers' unique use of tables might serve to confuse Excel migrants. How can you access data from one table and use it in another? Simply refer to the source table

▲ Switch cell formats briefly to text – that way you can see underlying formulae in a table.

name in the function. For example, to copy data to a table called Table 2 from cell 'A1' of 'Table 1', you would enter '=Table 1 :: A1' in the relevant cell in Table 2.

CREATE CHARTS FROM NON-CONTIGUOUS COLUMNS

There's no obvious way to create a chart from data in columns A and C of a table, while missing out the data held in column B. But some lateral thinking will get you round it. Just create a new table that copies the data from columns A and C into two new,

adjacent columns. You can now create a chart from this.

SHOWING FORMULAE

When troubleshooting large documents, it's useful to be able to reveal the formulae behind the numbers. In Excel, it's simple – just press Ctrl + ~. There's no similar short cut in Numbers but there is a quick way to view formulae. Click and drag over the table area whose functions you want to view and with the Cells Inspector active, select Text from the Cell Format menu. This displays

▲ Plan your life by picking up a project planner – it's one of many easy ways to use templates for Numbers.

WORK PLANNER

Numbers is much more than a spreadsheet program. For example, it can even double as a useful work scheduler. Thanks to the free DIY Planner template, Numbers creates one-page-per-day calendars for a whole month. It's easy to keep up to date too. You just need to update a single cell at the start of month and the entire worksheet will repopulate with that month's data.

URL *diyplanner.com/node/4667*
Price Free

all formulae as text. Remember to select File > Undo before adding any more information to the table.

AUTOFILLING

Numbers has an 'autofill' feature that you can use in the same way as Excel, however, you have to be careful how you use it. To autofill content from one cell to a range of adjacent cells, drag the Fill handle in the lower right corner of the first cell over the cells into which you want to paste the content.

SECOND BIGGEST NUMBERS

Numbers includes easily added formulae for finding the minimum (Min) and maximum (Max) values in a range of numbers. But you can also retrieve the second or third biggest values as well, using the Large function. Its second parameter selects the ranking of a value within a range, so Large (A1:E1, 2) returns the second-largest value in the range A1 to E1. Change this second parameter to '3' and it will pick up the third-largest figure.

Keynote

EXTENDING INSTANT ALPHA

Keynote 08's instant alpha feature makes it easy to render transparent image backgrounds just by dragging a selection over areas containing similar colours. It's easy to create good results with this masking technique and you can paste the resulting image into the other components of the iWork suite with transparency intact. But to transfer the transparent image to an application such as Photoshop requires an extra step.

In Keynote, draw a shape above the transparent image. Set its Fill and Stroke to None. Group the shape and the transparent image behind it and select File > Copy. Now paste the selection into an empty Photoshop document and the masked image will appear on its own layer, complete with transparency.

EMBEDDING OTHER DATA

You can extend Keynote's power significantly through a third-party plug-in that offers support for Linkback, a technology that lets you share content between other similarly enabled applications.

With the plug-in installed, you can add content from a small but growing list of Linkback-capable programs including Nisus Writer, Omnigraffle, OmniOutliner

and the excellent vector editing program, Lineform. Double-click on the content in Keynote and it reopens in its originating application. When you save the changes, they are automatically updated in Keynote.
URL *commons.ucalgary.ca/~king/projects/ keynoteplugins/linkback/*
Price Free

ADDING SPECIAL CHARACTERS

Adding special characters, such as mathematical, artistic or scientific symbols, can be awkward. You need to choose Edit > Special Characters, find the character and then double-click to add it to your document. But there is a quicker way to regularly add symbols.

In Keynote's Preferences, select the Auto-Correction tab and make sure that

the box for Symbol and text substitution is checked. Here you can add short cuts to symbols by entering a short-cut phrase and adding the special character in the usual way to the Replace with field. The time saved can be significant.

CREATING HTML PRESENTATIONS

Yes, you can export Keynote files to iWeb, but how can you generate native HTML presentations easily? The solution is to export HTML slide shows through third-party tool, KeyWebX.

First, export your presentation as a PDF or QuickTime movie, then by using KeyWebX you will be able to slice it into separate images with HTML navigation.
URL *keywebx.com/keywebx.html*
Price $10 (about £5)

▲ Keep transparency effects added in Keynote when you transfer the images to third-party applications – this can really enhance your presentation. And to achieve it, all you have to do is add a keyline around the image. So simple.

▲ Keynote can export directly to YouTube – a great place to host your presentations, even if you don't want to make them available to the public.

SENDING TO YOUTUBE

One of iMovie's trumpeted new features is the fact that it can export your movies directly to YouTube, the popular online video-sharing service. What is surprising, though, is that few people seem to have

cottoned on to the fact that Keynote offers the same ability.

The truth is that this is a great way to share rough drafts of presentations with remote users who may not own Keynote – and the YouTube resolution of up to 640 x 480 should be good enough to handle most of the uses you ask of it.

If you already have a YouTube account, select Choose File > Send To > YouTube. Enter the presentation's title and description along with any tags, which will help people find the content.

One particularly convenient aspect is that, if you prefer, you can specify that your presentation is for private consumption only. This will ensure that your creation is kept away from the public's gaze.

VIEWING KEYNOTE FILES ON A PC

While Keynote offers a PDF and PowerPoint export option, what happens if you're on the road and have access only to your native Keynote file? All isn't quite lost, at least if you remember to choose the Include preview in document option when you save your Keynote file. Do this and you can view the document in PDF format on any Mac or PC that can read PDF files.

The Keynote file appears as an ordinary folder with the suffix .key on a PC. If you open the QuickLook folder inside this, you can double-click on the Preview.pdf file and open it in Acrobat Reader. On a Mac, control-click the Keynote document's icon and select Show Package Contents from the pop-up menu, then open the QuickLook folder and open the Preview.pdf file.

Incidentally, exactly the same technique can be used with Numbers spreadsheets as well as with Pages documents.

CREATING AN INDEX

Pages has a table of contents feature, but you can sort lists too. Paste your list into a table and Pages will create a new row for each line. In the Table Inspector, click on

▲ Here's how to shrink your images quickly – simply use iPhoto to compress them, then just drag them from a Mail window into the document you're working on.

SHRINK FILE SIZES

Unlike high-end desktop publishing applications, Pages embeds images added to it rather than merely referencing the originals. The downside of that approach is that Pages file sizes balloon even if you scale the images. The trouble is that on the face of it, there's no way to adjust their resolution.

A neat way around this problem is to open the image you want to add in iPhoto. Select the Email option from the bottom of the iPhoto window and choose one of the smaller file sizes in the dialog box. This will see to it that the image is posted into a new Mail window.

Now drag that image, without saving it, into a Pages document. This adds the smaller, resized image to the document. You can then close the Mail document.

NUMBERING LINES

Pages doesn't provide built-in line numbering but you can cheat your way around this. Create a narrow text box to the left of your main text area on a page, and add sequential numbers to it so that each occupies its own line. Select Format > Advanced > Move Object to Section Master. Now the numbers will appear on all pages, although they will start from the beginning on each one. Choose File > Save as Template to store the page as a template.

Edit Rows & Columns. Choose Sort ascending to list the table alphabetically. Deselect the Header Row checkbox and remove the cell borders. Now it looks like a simple list and as you add new words to the bottom of your 'index', re-run the Sort command to preserve the alphabetical order.

WYSIWYG MENUS

Missing a Wysiwyg menu in Keynote? Stone Design's FontSight could be your saviour. It places a menu that previews fonts in Keynote – or any other Cocoa-based application.
URL *stone.com/FontSight*
Price $19 (about £10)

Pages

EMBEDDING SPREADSHEETS

The arrival of Numbers means you can embed complex tables directly into Pages documents. Simply drag a table from Numbers to turn it into a Pages table. Although some special functions of cells unique to Numbers – such as sliders or steppers – are lost in the translation, functions remain active. This means that if you adjust the imported table in Pages, total values will be recalculated. And there's no need to worry that your spreadsheet and your Pages document will be permanently out of sync. The translation goes both ways – you can copy the table in Pages and paste it back into Numbers.

A SMARTER WORD COUNT

A word count feature is a must-have for writers. Happily, Pages offers a basic counter – in the Document Inspector's Info tab where the document and selection statistics are shown. So here's a tip to count words up to wherever the cursor is positioned: click on Shift + Home. This selects all the text up to the cursor and displays the number of words in the Inspector.

BETTER TEMPLATES

The built-in templates in Pages are adequate, but sparse. Pages Templates collects 20 high-quality, professional templates that range from menus to portfolio templates. They're not free, but they save a lot of time if you need good results quickly.
URL *umsoft.com*
Price $39 (about £20)

MEDIA PLACEHOLDERS

You can automatically create placeholders that size and position images added to Pages. Just drag an image file to the document window, move and resize it, then choose Format > Advanced > Define as Media Placeholder. Dragging media over this placeholder replaces its content.

MERGING DOCUMENTS

You can merge two Pages documents by selecting View > Show Page Thumbnails in each, and copying and pasting between their Thumbnail panes. To copy only part of a document, create a section break (Insert > Section Break) between them. The sections can then be individually selected in the pane.

LINK TEXT BOXES

Flowing text across multiple pages in a document is standard fare in XPress and InDesign. To do it in Pages, click on the blue arrow at the bottom right of the first box, and then click with the cursor anywhere on the second box. To link new text boxes, create a text box, click on the blue arrow and then draw another text box with the cursor anywhere in the document.

MORE WYSIWYG MENUS

In addition to using FontSight in Pages to work around an absent Wysiwyg font menu, you can opt for the Styles menu which has a preview function. Open a blank document and create styles named after the font and point size – Times 12, say. Save this as a template in the program's preferences and choose it as the default for all new documents.

▲ A quick way to preview the fonts you may wish to select from is to include them in the Styles drawer.

SOFTWARE

Software for the Mac

Whoever said the Mac doesn't have a wide range of software clearly never used a Mac. Many of the key applications on Windows, including Microsoft Office, Photoshop and Dreamweaver also run on the Mac. So, come to that, does Windows itself, assuming you have a fairly up-to-date machine.

But how do you know what is the best application to meet your needs? And what should you do with it when you've installed and launched it for the first time? Those questions can be tough to answer for the novice Mac user.

Here we'll walk you through the task of choosing the best software for your Mac, and then installing and using Microsoft Office, web development applications, messaging clients and even Windows for those times when you simply can't find a Mac-native application to meet your needs.

Windows on the Mac

Just because you've bought a Mac, it doesn't mean that you are only limited to applications specifically built for the Mac. By using emulation software or Boot Camp, you can turn your Intel Mac into a Windows PC to run Windows software. Why would you want to do that? Because regardless of how wide the range of software you can run on the Mac might be, there are some notable exceptions that are PC only. And besides, you may just want to test a website you've designed on both platforms.

Much as you may love your Mac, there may be times when you have to run an application that is only available for Windows. Perhaps this is because you still need tools like Visio and Access that simply don't run on a Mac (although there are Mac equivalents that you should try), or maybe it's because you need to check that a website you've designed works across all platforms and browsers. Either way, you have two choices: you either hang on to your old PC, or you install Windows on your Mac.

Since Apple started using Intel processors in its Macs, it's been making some of the most versatile computers on the market. They are the only machines that can simultaneously run three operating systems: Mac OS X, Windows and various flavours of Linux, both natively and in so-called virtualisation mode.

Virtualisation is a means of poking a virtual hole in the Mac's main operating system, Mac OS X, so that other operating systems, such as Windows, can share the hardware inside your computer.

Before this was possible, you had to run a third application called emulation software, of which Microsoft Virtual PC was the most popular. This ran on top of Mac OS X, and Windows ran on top of Virtual PC. Virtual PC would then capture every instruction sent by Windows and translate it into a language understood by Mac OS X, rather like a translator, and the Mac operating system would then perform the necessary function.

As you can imagine, it was a slow, tedious and unpleasant way to work, which is why virualisation has proven such a boon. Microsoft is no longer actively developing Virtual PC for the Mac.

A CHOICE OF TWO
There are two leading contenders in the virtualisation market: Parallels and Fusion. Both works in pretty much the same way and in terms of performance, for everyday tasks, there's little to choose between them. Once installed they will walk you through the steps necessary to install Windows, leaving you to go off and do something more productive in the meantime.

Under both systems, Windows applications can be made to act as though they are native Mac OS X software, appearing in their own distinct frames, rather than being trapped inside a Windows environment, which in turn is inside a Mac window of its own. If you prefer, however, you can minimise the impact of Mac OS X and running two operating systems at once by running Windows in full-screen mode, with OS X in the background. Performance will be noticeably improved.

Parallels ships in two editions: Desktop (£49.99) and Desktop Premium (£59.99). Both let you access your Windows files without starting Windows, open Mac files with Windows applications (and vice versa), offer support for Windows games, let you run Windows and Mac applications side by side in a single environment, and have a snapshot tool for saving known working configurations of your Windows machine, effectively freezing it in time so that you can come back to it at a later point.

Opting for the Premium edition adds in Kaspersky virus protection, Acronis Disk Director for adjusting the size of the Windows portion of your hard drive if you find it's too small, and Acronis True Image Home, which backs up your whole Windows installation, including all of your settings so that should it all come crashing down at some future point you can recover the lot. It's well worth the extra £10.

▲ **Boot Camp comes with Mac OS X 10.5 Leopard and it allows you run a version of Windows on your Mac.**

▲ **Windows Vista appears in a window on your Mac when its run under emulation. Here we've used VMware Fusion.**

VMWare ships only one version of Fusion, which costs £44. It boasts many of the same features as Parallels, allowing you to run PC games with support for DirectX 9, and the ability to run Mac and Windows applications side by side. It will also detect Boot Camp installations, and let you run their copies of Windows without rebooting, which brings us to Apple's solution to the question of running Windows on the Mac...

THE APPLE OPTION

There is a third option for anyone running Mac OS X 10.5 Leopard, called Boot Camp. This isn't quite the same as virtualisation, as rather than simply poking a hole in the Mac's native operating system, it pushes it out of the way altogether, allowing Windows to have 100% of the Mac's hardware resources.

It is by far the most efficient way to run Windows on the Mac, but does require that you reboot your machine every time you want to switch from one operating system to the other. The benefit is that with Boot Camp there is only ever one operating system working at once, so no need to share resources, unlike running Windows full

screen in either Parallels or Fusion, which may occasionally feel a little bit sluggish because the Mac is still having to devote resources to its own native operating system at the same time.

The Boot Camp Assistant, which helps you install Windows on your Mac, is found in the Applications > Utilities folder. It examines your hard drive, identifies the necessary free space for installing Windows, and then partitions off a section to keep the two operating systems separate.

You next insert your Windows disc and, once that's finished installing, re-insert your Mac OS X 10.5 Leopard DVD to install all of the drivers for your Mac's internal hardware. This is much easier than installing Windows on a PC, where you may have to spend time trawling the Internet for the necessary drivers for your computer's components.

It is important to note that whatever technology you choose to help your run Windows on your Mac – Parallels, Fusion or Boot Camp, you'll still have to buy a fully-licensed copy of Windows to go alongside it, as none of these applications come with a bundled copy. You'll also have to activate it, which means you can't use a copy you've

already installed on a PC somewhere, or indeed on another Mac using the same copy of Parallels or Fusion. Windows treats every instance of virtualisation software as a new virtual machine, so you'll be subject to the same restrictions as anyone who was foolishly hoping to buy one copy of Vista and install it on a dozen PCs.

Fortunately, it is now possible to use any version of Windows Vista with each of these three methods. Previously, Microsoft would only licence the more expensive Ultimate and Business editions for use under Parallels or Fusion.

Combined, these three ways of running Windows – or pretty much any other modern operating system – on the Mac makes Apple hardware far more versatile than a PC, contrary to most peoples' expectations. PCs may let you run various editions of Windows, Linux and Unix, but they don't open up the world of small developers available to Apple users, and they don't give you access to what many people consider the world's best, most stable operating system – Mac OS X. ⊕

Windows on the Mac

You have chosen a Mac, but there are times when you need to run Windows, be it for testing purposes or to be compatible with PC-using colleagues. But you don't need a PC to do so, as it's easier than ever to install and run Windows on a Mac, as we explain here.

When you buy a Mac, you've chosen
more than just your hardware, as it comes
bundled with the world's best operating
system. For most people, that's as much
of a draw as the computer itself.

Yet sometimes you have to test your
work on alternative operating systems. While
we may believe the Mac is the best platform
for web design, failing to check that your
pages display properly in a PC browser can
be commercial suicide. And while we may
love the Mac and be perfectly satisfied with
the range of software at our disposal, there
are times when a client may send you
something that just won't run under Mac
OS X. It's at times like these that you have
no choice but to run Windows, but rarely will
investing in a PC be a cost-effective option.

Fortunately, now that Apple builds its
machines around Intel chips, it's easier than
ever to install Windows – or Linux – on
Apple hardware, as we'll show you here.

Hardcore fanboys aside, traditional
Mac users should welcome this
development with open arms. It brings
to the Mac the ability to run applications
that are developed only for Windows.
As well as creatives who can take
advantage of the benefits we've outlined
above, IT professionals should also take
note, not just because it means Macs can
now access hitherto denied corporate
applications such as Access and Visio, but
also because it means the decision over
whether to buy Mac or PC hardware is
much simplified: buy Mac, because it can
run both operating systems.

This is particularly true when buying
hardware for hotdesking or other sharing
techniques – the stereotypical designer can
boot up the Mac into OS X, while 'the office
worker' can boot into Windows.

And PC users? Well, they get access to Apple's beautiful hardware. It's not just about aesthetics with Macs: it's about care and an attention to detail, plus a certain panache.

In this feature, we'll explain the different ways in which you can install and run Windows on a Mac, highlight each approach's strengths and weaknesses, and walk you through the process of installing the latest version, Vista.

One important thing to remember before we begin, however, is that you should ensure you're properly licensed. Installing Windows on a Mac is no different to installing it on a PC – literally as well as conceptually – and Windows will have to be activated as it is on a PC. Note, too, that you'll need full versions of the operating system; upgrade discs won't work, and while OEM install discs are likely to work in practice, using them would contravene your End User License Agreement (EULA).

CHOOSING THE RIGHT SOFTWARE

When it comes to installing Windows onto a Mac, you essentially have two options.

One comes from Apple, and it's the company's Boot Camp utility. More on this later, but for now you just have to be aware that this works by partitioning off a chunk of your Mac's hard disk for a fresh Windows install. If you want to run Windows, you have to boot the Mac from this partition, and Windows completely takes over the computer. Boot Camp comes free with Mac OS X 10.5 Leopard, previously it was only available as a beta and has now ceased to be available as a standalone tool for anyone running Mac OS X 10.4.

The alternative to Boot Camp is virtualisation. Here, the Mac boots into Mac OS X, but you can run Windows and

▲ Boot Camp lets you create a Windows partition on your drive to install the operating system.

its applications alongside the host operating system. The advantage here is that you can move seamlessly from one operating system into the other, without having to reboot. If you're a web developer working in Dreamweaver on the Mac, for example, you can check how your site looks in Internet Explorer 7 simply by pasting a URL into the Windows browser.

To enable virtualisation, you'll need to get hold of some third-party Mac software. Parallels Desktop for Mac was the first solution available to allow this (£50 from *avanquest.co.uk*), but virtualisation giant VMware has now thrown its hat into the ring, recently releasing the second beta of its Fusion software for the Mac.

Virtualisation has the advantage of flexibility and convenience, but what it lacks is the power to run Windows natively. One obvious reason for this is that if you're running a virtual guest operating system alongside the host operating system, the hardware has to allocate resources across both at the same time. (Indeed, you can run many more than one guest operating system concurrently, compounding the problem at the same time as giving you more flexibility.)

More importantly, though, we have to understand the difference

01 Virtualisation software can take advantage of one or both cores.

02 Windows Task manager lets you monitor how it is utilising your Mac's resources.

03 PCs boot using a bios – Macs don't have one.

INSTALLING WINDOWS UNDER PARALLELS

▲ **STEP 01 CHOOSE INSTALLATION** Pick your Parallels installation type. Express asks you for the serial number for Windows XP or Vista, and it will do the rest, picking default options for hardware configuration and dumping the virtual hard disk and configuration file in ~/Library/Parallels. Typical is similar, but gives you more control over where your virtual machine is stored. We'll pick Custom.

▲ **STEP 02 ALLOCATE RESOURCES** Specify how much of the Mac's resources you want to allocate to the guest operating system. Here, we're creating an expanding hard disk. It will start of at zero bytes in size and grow as the guest operating system makes demands of it, all the way up to the size specified, 32,000MB. You can store it anywhere, even on an external disk.

▲ **STEP 03 CHOOSE INSTALL DISK** When you come to pick the disk to install from, you can simply slot in the CD or DVD, but you'll find the install process works much more quickly if you work from a virtual disk image. Roxio's Toast on the Mac creates appropriate ISO images. Actually, they're .toast images, but you can rename them .iso and everything will be fine.

▲ **STEP 04 INSTALLATION** The installation process will begin, and the length of time it will take depends on the complexity of the operating system you have chosen. This process is usually fully automated, but some operating systems require you, for example, to eject the install CD manually following installation. If you're using an ISO, click the CD icon at the bottom right of the window.

▲ **STEP 05 INSTALL PARALLELS TOOLS** Once the install process has completed, you have to install Parallels Tools to activate such features as copying and pasting between host and guest operating systems. With newer versions, this should happen automatically, but if it doesn't, simply pick Install Parallels Tools from the Actions menu.

▲ **STEP 06 WINDOWS SECURITY** The drivers that allow network sharing and the like are unsigned. Under Windows XP, the installer can optionally suppress the warnings, but Vista's more robust security model insists on clearing every component's installation with you before going ahead. Remember to follow normal Windows patching and updating procedures.

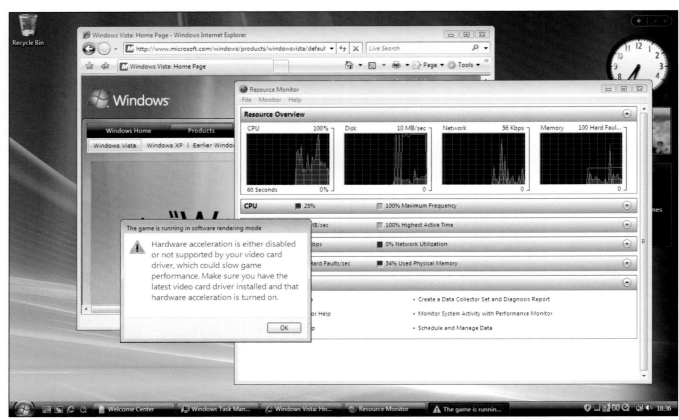

▲ Due to a lack of drivers for some Mac hardware you may find some incompatibilities under Windows Vista.

● between emulation and virtualisation, and the limits of the latter. This is covered on the following page.

As such, the bottom line is that using Boot Camp to boot the Mac hardware exclusively into Windows will give you the best performance – although the Boot Camp drivers are still not perfectly optimised – while using virtualisation provides most convenience. Mac users in a corporate environment, for example, might choose to use Mac applications within OS X most of the time, but have Outlook running under Windows for richer Exchange integration than is offered in native Mac tools.

The good news is that you don't have to plump for one approach to the exclusion of the other. When Parallels was first launched, it followed the traditional approach for guest operating systems – that is, it generated a small configuration file, and created a ring-fenced, virtual hard disk not by partitioning the physical volume but by creating a virtual

hard disk document (you can still opt for this approach, as it makes backup and restore very simple).

Now, though, it can also use a partition created by Boot Camp. This has two advantages. Most significantly, it enables you to boot the Mac into Windows when you want to give all the system resources to Windows, or to boot back into Mac OS X when you want to run the two side by side. Second, it can allow more complete access to the Windows partition. Formatted as Fat 32, Mac OS X can read and write to this partition with no difficulties, but if you decide to format the Boot Camp-created partition as NTFS, the Mac can only read the data that's held on it. Parallels, running from this partition, can give Mac users the ability to drag and drop to and from it.

And Parallels has one last trick up its sleeve: Coherence. 'Trick' is the right word, too, as it's just a sleight of hand, but a damned good one. Along with Full Screen and OS Window – the latter constraining the guest operating system within a window, say, set to 1024 x 768, or on a secondary screen – Parallels supports Coherence mode for the guest operating system, in which windows floating within the guest operating system environment are effectively cut out and stuck alongside windows from the host operating system. You can access the Start menu from Parallels' Dock icon,

and Windows applications can be added to and launched from the Dock. All it does is mask out the Windows desktop.

ADDING LINUX
There are many Linux distributions that can run natively on older PowerPC Mac hardware as well as Intel hardware. Dual-boot systems (and more) are possible, too, although these require a little more mucking about in the command line than many users will be comfortable with.

A simpler option is to use virtualisation software to run a Linux OS alongside Mac OS X. This is very easy indeed, as most distributions are offered as downloadable ISO images, and both Parallels and VMware can install directly from ISOs on the Mac's hard disk without them first having to be burned to optical media.

Technically, any x86 Linux build will run under virtualisation. Parallels, for example, provides presets for Red Hat, Debian, Fedora, SuSE, Mandriva and Xandros, along with Other Linux kernel 2.4 and 2.6, and the über-generic Other Linux. You also have options to run even less mainstream operating systems, including Solaris, OS/2, FreeBSD and Dos.

Under Parallels, the experience isn't as rich in the Linux builds we've tried as when

MAC OS X ON A PC
Of course, this is all well and good if you want to run Windows on a Mac, but if you'd rather install Mac OS X on your PC, well, you're rather out of luck. It's not so much that it's impossible, rather that there are so many legal and technical hurdles in the way that it's just not worth it. Various projects – among them the well-known tutorials at *tinyurl.com/y7z3cf* – can walk you through the process, but it's simply not a practical option at the moment.

running Windows: the Parallels Tools set of utilities that, for example, allow you to sweep the mouse pointer across from the host into the guest operating system and out again aren't as fully featured for Linux. Basics such as shared networking are provided, but you don't get the same abilities in sharing files or changing screen resolution, and you certainly don't get Coherence mode.

Things are a little more consistent with VMware Fusion. However, as Coherence is a Parallels trick, you don't get it here, either.

There's little stopping you mixing and matching as many virtualised operating systems as you like. On a test 2GHz MacBook with 2GB of Ram, we've had Windows 98SE, XP Pro, Vista Ultimate, Ubuntu and Red Hat Linux running simultaneously under Parallels, plus XP Pro and Ubuntu running using Fusion. We're not claiming that performance was even particularly usable at this stage, but the Mac was taking it quite happily, and the only reason we stopped there was that boredom started to set in.

Indeed, the only real problem we've experienced of running any virtualised operating systems is when we flick from the Mac OS X user that's hosting the running instance of Parallels, either to another user or to the login screen. More often than not, we've successfully come back to the host user account smoothly, but it has occasionally hung.

THE LIMITATIONS

Emulation – the technology for running Windows on pre-Intel Macs – translates instructions from one processor architecture to another. In the case of PowerPC Macs running software such as Virtual PC, it was translating instructions given to the emulated Intel chip to the real PowerPC chip.

▲ Even when it's running on a Mac, Windows Vista requires that a valid activation code is entered on installation.

Virtualisation software, however, can dip into the processor and pass instructions to and from it directly, bringing commensurate performance. For virtualisation to work, however, it has to be supported in the hardware, as it is with the Intel Core chips that power the Mac line. Every other piece of hardware has to be emulated.

This is most evident with graphics performance. Support for DirectX is limited – and you can forget about getting Vista's Aero interface running under Parallels – and we strongly recommend against attempting to run any modern 3D games under a virtualised operating system.

That said, Parallels and VMware do a cracking job of network and USB support. Parallels, for example, gives you the option of bridged networking where the guest OS negotiates its own connection; shared, where it uses NAT to piggy-back onto

the Mac's connection; or host-only, isolating the guest OS from the network. Both Parallels and VMware support USB 2.

VMware Fusion is ahead in some respects here. It allows for the guest operating system to access more than one of a multi-core Mac's cores, and already has experimental support for DirectX 8.1. Additionally, while Parallels can only virtualise 32-bit operating systems, Fusion enables you to install 64-bit versions on Core 2 Duo and Xeon-powered Macs.

Because Windows can't natively read or write the Mac's default disk format (HFS+), you have no access to the data held on the Mac partition when running Windows courtesy of Boot Camp without installing third-party applications such as MacDrive from *mediafour.com*.

This could be a good thing, mind you, as you're not making the data held on your Mac's hard disk vulnerable to attack through sloppily configured Windows installations. Mac data is held on a different (and differently formatted) partition in the case of Boot Camp, and in an entirely different way – a virtual C: drive rather than an actual volume – in the case of virtualised solutions.

You should be aware, too, that the EULA for Windows Vista prohibits its use with virtualisation software except with the Business and Ultimate editions; other versions will install fine, but you'll be contravening your licence agreement.

Finally, remember that if you install Windows using Boot Camp, you'll get no technical support from Apple, and may find it trickier to get support from software and hardware developers on the Windows side. ✪

WINE

There's a third option if you want to run Windows applications within Mac OS X, and it's very cheap – you don't even have to pay for a copy of Windows. That's because the applications designed to run under Windows are recompiled to run natively under OS X. This is achieved thanks to Wine, a project that allows Unix-like operating systems such as OS X to execute Windows applications via the X Window System. Install discs for OS X also contain X11 to provide this X Window System, so all you need is a copy of Wine.

We should state clearly that the Wine system, originally designed to allow Windows applications to run under Linux, should be regarded at best as a beta software experience; it's not usually for the faint-hearted.

There are many concurrent Wine projects for the Mac as well as for other operating systems – among them Darwine, porting the Wine libraries to the Darwin layer that underpins Mac OS X; and Cider, a developer-only tool from TransGaming

Technologies to begin to enable Windows games to run under Mac OS X – but the most end-user-friendly of these is CrossOver Mac from *codeweavers. com*. This $59.95 (about £30) piece of software will allow you to run many Windows applications within Mac OS X, and while our testing suggests that it's a feasible alternative for low-power and office applications, it's not without its flaws.

The company is commendably up front about this, however: in a statement from its CEO giving feedback on its real-world experiences of using CrossOver Mac, it says: 'If you decide to purchase CrossOver Mac [even without reading about these experiences], and feel that you did not receive a fair value, we will refund your money, no questions asked.'

You can check how well certain Windows applications fare at *codeweavers.com/compatibility*, but remember that if an application doesn't appear on the list, it just means that the company isn't aware of it, and hasn't yet tested it.

Adobe Creative Suite

The Mac is the computer of choice for many professional designers. In part this is because in the earliest days it was the only affordable machine to sport a graphical interface controlled by a mouse, and because it sported an excellent range of creative software. Today that's also true of the PC, but the Mac has nonetheless remained a key choice for arty pros. A lot of that is thanks to the continued existence of Creative Suite on the platform. But what exactly is it, and what does it do?

ADOBE CREATIVE SUITE 3

If one company – other than Apple – can be said to have ensured the continued production of Macs, it's Adobe. As the owner of Photoshop and page layout application InDesign, it has ensured a healthy stream of high-quality software that has made the Mac the computer of choice for creative users.

Of course, these applications are available on the PC, too, and Adobe sells more Windows editions of its software than it does for Mac OS X, but the continued availability of Creative Suite is key to the continued existence of the Mac.

Creative Suite 3 includes various applications covering design for print and the web, or movie creation.

PHOTOSHOP

Photoshop is unquestionably the headline application. It is a powerful image manipulation application with an extensive set of tools that cover everything from adding a heading to airbrushing out exes from photos. It used to ship with a separate application called ImageReady, which was largely designed to create compressed editions of your images for use on the web. These features have now been rolled into the regular Photoshop application, giving you direct web export options.

Photoshop can open an enormous range of file formats, including many native camera file types, allowing you to import your photos without first translating them using the software that came bundled with your camera. It also works with external peripherals, such as graphics tablets, and is extendable, allowing you to download or buy additional features from third-party publishers.

You can't deny that to get the most out of Photoshop you need to spend some time

learning its features. However, there are some jobs for which it is not the best tool. Despite the fact that Creative Suite ships with a management application called Bridge, first-time users will find iPhoto better suited to storing and cataloguing their photo collections; particularly with the addition of Events in iPhoto 08.

It is also not so hot on vector graphics, either. These are made up from specific coordinates, and lines and curves drawn between them, which is very different to photos, which are made up from a grid of coloured dots. Photoshop can offer some vector-style drawing features, allowing you to draw shapes, lines and so on, but depending on your version of Creative Suite you may also have a copy of Illustrator, which is built specifically to handle these types of files.

INDESIGN

It's a long time since the only choice in high-end desktop publishing was QuarkXPress. At one time that application was used to lay out pretty much every newspaper, magazine, flier and newsletter you read, but then Adobe came along with InDesign and things changed for good.

Over the years many users have accused Quark of being slow to react to change and have criticised its price tag, and although this has changed in recent years you can't deny that it must have contributed – in some part, at least – to the speed at which Adobe found an audience for its rival application.

InDesign may be overkill for low-end home use, but if you do a lot of design work then you will find it a far more suitable application than Pages, which offers

▲ **InDesign is Adobe's heavyweight desktop publishing application and is commonly used to design magazines.**

rudimentary layout tools for creating text boxes and positioning images.

Adobe also sells a companion application to InDesign called InCopy. This works in a similar way to a word processor, giving content creators a simple interface through which they can concentrate on writing the words without having to think about the look and feel of the page.

DREAMWEAVER

The majority of websites designed by professional web developers are built using Dreamweaver. It wasn't originally an Adobe application, but the company acquired it when it bought rival developer Macromedia. Before Adobe's acquisition of its rival, the company had its own web design tool called GoLive.

Dreamweaver lets you work in two ways: either code-based, where you directly type in all of the HTML underlying your pages, or design-based, in which you draw boxes on your pages like you would in InDesign, and then style them up to your own particular requirements.

Dreamweaver understands a wide range of online languages, can connect to the most common database types to create interactive sites, and has excellent error checking tools to make sure that the pages you create with it are compatible with the widest possible range of browsers.

However, it is a very high-level application, and its most powerful features are beyond even some of the most advanced users. As such, first-time web

▲ Most professional web designers favour Dreamweaver and it is used for the vast majority of commercial websites.

designers would do better to use an application like Real Mac Software's RapidWeaver (see page 108). Not only is this application inexpensive, it is very well supported by an active user community, and it works on the basis of templates, allowing you to create new pages in no time at all, and change their look in even less time.

We would not recommend Apple's own iWeb application as even in its second iteration it is an immature application that needs some work to bring it up to what we would call competent standards.

FLASH

One of the most important technologies on the Internet is Flash. It was the basis of YouTube's original incarnation, where it was used to encode all of the videos in its library, and in many cases still is.

It's also the video mechanism that underpins the BBC's iPlayer, and it is the animation tool that we must thank for those countless addictive online games that waste many a Friday afternoon.

However, if Dreamweaver is a high-end application for professional users, this is in a different league entirely. It's easy to create new Flash files and put some shapes on the page, and even to make them move around on screen, but to do anything… well, 'flash' with it you need to understand a complex coding language that can take months to learn to any competent degree.

While it is bundled with many versions of Creative Suite, therefore, and is a tempting tool, it is beyond the reach of many inexperienced users on any platform.

PREMIERE

Adobe was once a big player in video on the Mac, and then along came Apple's own Final Cut, and Premiere disappeared from the platform. For a long time. But now it's back. On the PC it remains the leading application in its field, but on the Mac it's going to have an uphill battle to build itself a market. Again, it's a high-end application that will appeal to very few first-time users, who will naturally be drawn to iMovie, which ships as part of the iLife suite.

▲ Photoshop is a high-end application that is mostly used by professional photographers and graphic designers.

RapidWeaver

All new Macs ship with iWeb, a sophisticated tool for developing personal websites. The results are impressive, and by calling on features that form part of the .Mac hosting service, it can perform some pretty cool tricks, rivalling applications many times its price. However, it's not entirely friendly, and getting the best out of it can require jumping through some hoops. Fortunately, there is an alternative in the form of RapidWeaver, an approachable, powerful, template-based designer for everyone.

Unless you want to learn a powerful, complex tool like Adobe Dreamweaver, the best tool for consumer web design on the Mac is Real Mac Software's RapidWeaver. It may have a similar name as Adobe's high-end software, and it may perform the same function – designing pages for the web – but that is where the similarities come to an end.

It makes no assumptions about your knowledge of web design, allowing you to create everything using a series of templates, into which you then put your own words and pictures. It ships with a wide selection of templates in the box (or, more accurately, in the download package) and extras can be downloaded – usually for a fee – from both the Real Mac Software site and those of third-party developers.

When you first open RapidWeaver, you're presented with a very clean interface. There's a welcome screen in the middle and an empty column on the left. Clicking the '+' button at the bottom of this column creates a new page, allowing you to pick from a wide range of page types, such as a blog, a photo gallery or styled text, which gives you a word processor-like page into which you can enter your own content.

As you work on your pages you have a choice of three environments: Code, Edit and Preview. Code is used simply for inspecting the underlying HTML and can be largely ignored by novice users; Edit is where you do the work of creating your page; and Preview is the pane through which you can see the fruits of your labours.

If they don't look right, you can quickly change their look and feel by clicking on the arrow button on the bottom row of the interface to call up the templates chooser. Here you can see thumbnail previews of every installed template, and click on a new one to apply it to your page. You'll see right

▲ **RapidWeaver is a powerful tool for designing websites, yet it is not as complex to learn as Adobe's Dreamweaver. The application comes with a wide selection of templates to choose from and creating web pages is very and simple.**

away that the content you have created is immediately slipped into the new styling without any extra work from you.

Some elements of your pages can't be edited through the usual page creation interface because they're integral to the design, such as the name of your site and its slogan, which appears in a prominent position on your pages, along with your name and various copyright notices. These are changed through the Inspector, accessed by clicking the button marked 'i' on the bottom bar.

iWeb, which ships as part of the iLife suite, performs a similar function to RapidWeaver, but to our mind it doesn't do it nearly as well. For one thing, iWeb is very skewed to publishing on Apple's . Mac service, and although you can publish

to your own domain you lose some of the smartest features. At least with RapidWeaver you know from the very beginning that whatever the design of your website then it will be compatible with pretty much any web host.

You will obviously need to sort out your own hosting deal before you can publish your pages with RapidWeaver, as web space is not included in the package price. We would recommend doing this after you have finished designing your pages so you know whether you need any specific features as part of your hosting deal, such as the language PHP, which is required to host RapidWeaver's contact form pages. Many hosts include this as part of their standard package, but some charge extra for it as an option. ✖

Fusion...Great Speed. Great Value.

Switch between Windows and Mac apps without rebooting

Run Windows Vista, Windows XP and Mac OS X simultaneously

Minimize Windows apps to the Mac OS X Dock

Switch between Windows and Mac apps using Exposé

Share data between OSes by dragging and dropping files

VMware FUSION

Seamlessly run Windows applications on your Mac!

The power of multiple operating systems and the ease of quickly switching between them. That's the power of VMware Fusion!

Fusion allows you to easily launch your Windows applications and switch between Windows and Mac applications without rebooting! With support for Windows Vista Business, Enterprise, Ultimate, Windows XP, Linux, Solaris and more than 60 supported PC operating systems, Fusion lets you customise toolbars, share data easily between OSes by simply dragging and dropping files or with Shared Folders, and much more.

VMWare Fusion gives you the best of both worlds - your favourite Windows applications on your Mac!

£49.98
RRP INC VAT

Messaging clients

Like sending text messages on your mobile, instant messaging is a convenient way of having a conversation with a friend or colleague over the course of a day. Apple bundles an instant messaging client, iChat, with Mac OS X. This allows you to chat, have voice conversations, and even video conferences, but only with people on the Aim network. If you want to talk to friends on Yahoo! or MSN, you'll need to look further afield. Luckily there is a variety of clients available, so we take a look at the options available to you.

Instant messaging, once the preserve of teenagers who couldn't bear to be out of contact with one another for more than a few minutes at a time, is fast becoming a seriously useful tool for a variety of communication functions. These include video conferencing, voice over IP telephony, and sending and receiving files.

Although instant messaging clients have been around for more than a decade, it still has the feel of a technology in its infancy. For example, much like the early days of email, there's no standard protocol. And applications which use different protocols can't communicate with each other, with one or two exceptions. In some cases, protocols are proprietary, for example, both Microsoft and Yahoo! use their own protocols. Others, such as Jabber, are open.

Things are improving. Microsoft and Yahoo! clients can now talk to each other, although functionality is limited. And Google's adoption of Jabber for it's Google Talk application may encourage more organisations to adopt existing systems rather than use their own.

iChat, the instant messaging client that comes with Mac OS X and which was pre-installed on your Mac, uses AOL's Instant Messenger protocol. This means that as well as chatting with other Mac users on iChat, you can chat to PC users who have AOL's Instant Messenger.

That would be fine if most PC users had Instant Messenger as their instant messaging client of choice, but they don't. Most use either Yahoo! or Microsoft's Messenger systems. In order to talk to them, you'll either have to install the Mac versions of these two applications, or one of the multi-protocol messaging applications available for Mac OS X, such as Adium. Whichever route you take, you'll need to set up an account with the provider whose service you want to connect to.

There are other options. One is web messaging. These services work like Adium and its contemporaries in that you can connect to multiple services from one place. And like Adium, you'll need an account with each service you want to connect to. Web clients are particularly useful if you use

different machines in different locations as you can elect to save chats on the host's server and have them available whenever you log-in through a web browser. Using a web client is also a useful way of connecting to an instant messaging client in a location where a firewall prevents you from using a desktop instant messaging client.

The final option is to access an instant messaging client from a mobile device, such as a phone, rather than your Mac. Sadly, the iPhone doesn't yet have an iChat client, but Yahoo! and Microsoft both have versions of their clients that work on mobile phones.

If you have friends or business contacts who use a number of different systems, you can choose to download and install an application for each and log into them separately each time you go online. This would mean you would have to launch and sign in to iChat, Yahoo! Messenger, Microsoft Messenger and Google Talk, and have windows for each application on your screen if you wanted to chat to different people on these networks during the course of a day.

▲ **Yahoo! Messenger (left) and Microsoft Messenger (right), are the most commonly used instant messaging clients and each will need you to open a separate account to use.**

▲ Adium is a multi-protocol client that will allow you to log on to various systems.

▲ Meebo is a Web-based instant messaging client that you can use on any computer.

The advantage of this approach is that you have access to the latest features of each system as soon as the application is updated and that you have more control over settings for each service. And you can be sure of having access to all the functionality of each system.

The disadvantage is that you have to log in to each account separately and then have multiple contacts windows cluttering your screen. If you choose this approach, the best option is to use the free applications available from the service provider, that is Yahoo! Messenger for Yahoo! and Microsoft Messenger for MSN or Windows Live as it is now called.

There are other clients available for these systems, but by using the official client, you ensure the best chance of compatibility with the people you chat to and will always have the latest available features for the system.

YAHOO! MESSENGER 3 BETA
Yahoo! Messenger 3 for Mac OS X is currently available as a beta download. This means that the program is not finished and is still being tested.

There are a few features missing from Messenger 3 when compared to its PC counterpart. The most obvious of these is the lack of voice chat on the Mac version. While the PC client allows you to make free voice calls to contacts in your list, just like iChat, the Mac client doesn't. You can, however, share video from a webcam and swap files. You can also tab conversations in Yahoo! Messenger 3, and its Dock icon displays the number of unread messages.

Message archiving is also listed as a feature, although we couldn't archive messages in our tests. You can also add contacts from Microsoft's Messenger and chat to them from Yahoo!.

MICROSOFT MESSENGER 6.0.3
Like Yahoo!'s application, Microsoft Messenger 6.0.3 lags behind its PC counterpart in a number of ways. However, you can exchange files, archive conversations and chat to contacts from both Microsoft and Yahoo!'s systems.

So far, so Yahoo!. But Microsoft's client also integrates with its Office suite of business applications. So if you're working on a Word document, you can use Messenger from within Word to share the document with a contact as well as have a Messenger conversation from within Word.

GOOGLE TALK
The desktop application for Google's Talk messaging service is currently Windows-only. However, Mac users can use the systems from within Gmail, Google's web email service. You invite contacts to chat, in a similar way to iChat and you click on a contact's name in the Gmail sidebar to chat to them. A small window opens up in the bottom-left of the Gmail window, allowing you to converse with the contact. If a contact is offline, that is not logged in, when you send them a message, it's stored like an email in a folder within Gmail called Chats.

ADIUM AND PROTEUS
Adium and Proteus are both multi-protocol clients. This means that you can log into all the systems for which you have accounts from one interface with all your contacts listed in one window, along with an icon which denotes the system they are connected to.

By setting Adium or Proteus to log in automatically on start-up, you can log into all your accounts simultaneously with one double-click. Although you still need multiple accounts, one for each system, this approach does take away much of the pain of incompatibility between protocols.

The downside is that if, for example, Yahoo! released the next version of Messenger tomorrow and it had the ability to make Mac-to-Mac voice calls, you'd have to wait for it to be implemented in Adium or Proteus before you could use it. And because both are made by small developers, there's no guarantee of a regular flow of updates.

MEEBO
Web-based instant messaging clients allow you to log into your account from any computer with a web browser — great if you are travelling or are away from your main computer. They are also useful if you want to chat on a computer on a network that is connected to a company firewall. Many companies set their firewall to block the ports used by instant messaging clients and so chatting using the client application is impossible.

Yahoo! Messenger has its own web messaging client, but there is no equivalent for the likes of iChat or Microsoft Messenger. Step-forward Meebo. An online messaging and chat application in its own right, Meebo also allows you to chat on most other protocols. So, by entering your log-in details for iChat, Microsoft Messenger and Yahoo! Messenger, you can connect to all three systems simultaneously and chat using your web browser.

Meebo supports avatars and emoticons and allows you to archive chats on its servers. It has all the usual functions you'd expect of an instant messaging client, such as the ability to exchange files and add contacts. There's also a Firefox plug-in that allows you to keep track of contacts and conversations in a browser sidebar. ❌

Online video

The Internet is alive with audio and video content, with everything from teenagers miming to their favourite tracks on YouTube to the latest news bulletins available for viewing. Yet to the uninitiated, watching streaming content can be complex process. It needn't be, though. With the help of a few additional applications and plug-ins watching video, whether it is streamed or downloaded, is a simple as doing anything else on your Mac.

Watching video on the Internet used to be a frustrating experience. Postage stamp-sized clips, poor video and audio quality, and long download times made it a pastime for only those with bags of patience to spare. Add to that the various different formats for viewing downloads and streaming content and its little wonder that for most of the web's lifetime video has been little more than a curiosity.

Things have changed dramatically in the past couple of years however. YouTube has changed the streaming video landscape and made it possible for anyone with an up-to-date computer and an Internet connection to view and share video clips. Every news site worth its server space has it's own video content to accompany text and images, and you can view and download high-resolution movie trailers on your Mac. The BBC's iPlayer allows you to catch-up on up to seven-days worth of BBC TV content, and you can buy or rent movies and TV shows to download and watch on your Mac.

The most significant technological shift in video on the web, and the one which has

allowed this video revolution to take place has been a de facto standardisation of formats. Just as MP3 became the standard for downloading audio, Flash has done the same for video.

The FlashPlayer, owned by Adobe, is bundled with Safari and Firefox, meaning that you don't have to download additional software to view content on YouTube or iPlayer. The only exception is when Adobe upgrades the FlashPlayer in between browser updates. However, in this instance a dialog box will open on your Mac and you'll be invited to download the latest version.

Sadly, not all video on the web is as easy to view, and there are still a number of different formats around. Many of these are viewable on the Mac without the need for additional software, while others need the help of browser plug-ins or QuickTime add-ons to work. The two most common are Real Media and Windows Media.

We'll deal with Windows Media first. Until recently, to view Windows Media content on a Mac, you needed the Mac version of Microsoft's Windows Media Player. That was

problematic, because the Mac version was way behind the Windows version in the development cycle and suffered compatibility problems as a result. In addition, it meant you had to use the hideous Windows Media Player interface. Now, though, Microsoft has abandoned the Mac version of Media Player altogether and instead licensed a utility from Flip4Mac that allows you to view Windows Media video content in QuickTime Player. It's not perfect, and can be a bit sluggish, but it's a workable solution.

To download Flip4Mac, go to *microsoft. com/mac* and click on Other Products. Click on the third item down, Flip4Mac, and on the next page, click on Download Flip4Mac for free. Click Free Download on the next screen, and download on the screen after that. Double-click on the disk image which mounts on your desktop when the software has downloaded and follow the instructions. You'll now be able to play Windows Media format movies in QuickTime Player.

Although you can now play WMV files, you can't export them in a different format, or create WMV files from other video

▲ To view DivX movies, you first need to download its player from *divx.com*.

▲ Flip4Mac allows you to play Windows Media content in the QuickTime player.

formats. To do that you'll need WMV Player Pro and WMV Studio, which cost $29 (about £15) and $49 (about £25) respectively. To find out more, go to *flip4mac.com*.

Real Media is a different story. A pioneer in streaming audio and video over the web, Real has steadfastly clung to its proprietary format and although fewer and fewer sites stream content using Real, it's still used on high profile websites, such as the BBC. The basic RealPlayer plug-in is pre-installed with Safari and Firefox, so if you do come across a site that uses it, and there's no alternative, you should be able to view the content in a browser window.

To find out more about Real Player, go to *real.com*. Click on Download Free Real Player and install it. You will now be able to watch and listen to Real video and audio in a web browser or dedicated application.

These days most streaming and downloadable video content is encoded in Mpeg-4 (think of it as MP3 for video). That would be straightforward if there was only one version of Mpeg-4, but unfortunately for us, there are several. The two most common variants are H.264, Apple's preferred video format, and DivX, a format that gained significant support until the advent of H.264.

Apple encodes all the video downloads in iTunes, including movie trailers and the new video rentals in H.264 and so, unsurprisingly, support for the format is built into QuickTime.

Support for viewing and encoding DivX files doesn't come as standard with QuickTime, but can be added easily. Go to *divx.com* and click on the Free Download button. Once it's downloaded, installation will begin automatically. The free download allows you to watch DivX movies, and will install trial versions of software which will allow you to convert other movies to DivX.

As an alternative to the DivX player, particularly if all you want to do is watch

▲ To get the best quality when importing audio tracks, you adjust the bit rate – the higher the bit rate, the better quality.

DivX movies in QuickTime Player, download Perian. Perian is an Open Source QuickTime component which adds support for a whole host of file formats to QuickTime. It's free, takes only a few minutes to download and install and has been known to come up trumps when nothing else works. Go to *perian.org* to find out more and download it.

AUDIO FORMATS

Playing audio is almost as complex as video. The de facto standard for downloaded music is MP3. However, most of the major download stores don't use MP3. Apple uses another open standard, AAC, and a variant called protected AAC on iTunes, and many other download stores use a protected form of Windows Media Audio.

Some download sites, like Emusic, use MP3. If you have an iPod, your music must be either MP3, AAC or protected AAC. The iPod doesn't support Windows Media Audio. Similarly, MP3 players from other manufacturers, such as Creative, don't support Apple's protected AAC format. Microsoft's Zune has yet another proprietary audio format. For the widest possible compatibility, you should encode any

CDs you import to iTunes as MP3. However, AAC offers higher quality audio at lower file sizes and is widely compatible. If you buy tracks from the iTunes Store, opt for the iTunes Plus version where available. This is a non-protected file and so will be playable on any device which supports the AAC format.

If you want to listen to radio programmes from the BBC's website, either live or using it's Listen Again service, you can choose between Real Audio and Windows Media Audio. As with video, whichever you opt for, you'll need to have the relevant plug-in installed in your browser.

When you convert audio CDs to play on your Mac or record your own audio, a good rule of thumb is the higher the bit rate, the better the quality of the resultant file. However, high bit rate files take up lots of room on your hard drive so you need to compromise between file size and audio quality.

The first thing to do is make sure variable bit rate is switched on. In Preferences in iTunes, click on the Advanced button, then the Importing tab. Select either MP3 or AAC and in Setting, select Custom. Tick the box labelled Use Variable Bit Rate Encoding and experiment with different bit rates to see which is the lowest that is acceptable to you. Variable bit rate encoding uses the maximum bit rate in passages where it is needed and where its not, uses a lower bit rate, keeping down the file size.

The sheer number of video and audio formats used on Macs and PCs can seem daunting. Gradually however, standards are emerging and by following these guidelines you should be able to play any audio or video file on a Mac.

▲ RealPlayer is one of the preferred methods for streaming video on the BBC website.

Microsoft Office

The lack of software compatible with Windows PCs is one of the most cited reasons for not switching to the Mac. Yet with the release of Microsoft Office 2008 for the Mac, this argument has little bearing in today's business environment. Office has been a key application in the Mac's software line-up for two decades now, and today it's stronger than ever. But is Microsoft's choice of business applications the best option for non-Windows users? In many cases, the answer is a hearty 'yes'.

One of the reasons people give for not switching to the Mac is that they can't get the same applications as they use on their Windows PCs. They worry about compatibility, but really they shouldn't. Why?

Because as we've already pointed out, Macs can run Windows on those rare occasions when you can't find a compatible equivalent on this platform. In addition, there are often direct translations of Windows software that are available for the Mac. Microsoft Office is a prime example. It was originally a Mac application that later made the switch to the PC, so in some ways you could argue that it wasn't the Mac that was made compatible with the PC, but the PC that was made compatible with the Mac.

The latest version for the Mac is Office 2008, and although it lacks some key features of the Windows edition, such as Visual Basic scripting, it does boast excellent file compatibility, ensuring the Mac and Windows users can share documents with ease. That should calm the worries of the Mac's biggest detractors, and may yet be enough for some business users to make the switch.

Yet there are some key differences, the biggest being the omission of Access, Microsoft's business and consumer database for Windows, from the Mac version. Fortunately, FileMaker, a wholly owned Apple subsidiary, produces two excellent products to plug the gap: FileMaker Pro for business users, and Bento for home users running Mac OS X 10.5 Leopard.

But it works both ways. Windows users have no built-in equivalent of Project Centre, the low-end project management tool built into the Mac version. Neither do they have access to My Day, a floating toolbox that keeps track of your appointments and tasks for the day ahead.

THE DRAW OF COMPATIBILITY
Word and Excel remain the world's most important word processor and spreadsheet. Their native file formats, .doc and .xls, are used by a wide range of other applications. While other formats such as plain text, rich text (RTF) and comma-separated values (CSV) may be more widely used, you can't play an active role in document sharing if you can't read .doc and .xls, particularly in business and academia. Simple as that.

This is complicated slightly by the fact that Microsoft changed its file types for its latest Office suite when it introduced the Office Open XML format. However, that still doesn't mean that you have to invest in Word or Excel to keep up with the Joneses of the business world. Pages – part of iWork – can read and write Word 2008 documents and Numbers can read and write files for Excel 2008. Other applications such as Nisus Writer Express do an excellent, although not quite perfect job of interpreting older Word files, offering you an inexpensive way into the format for simpler documents.

For those who choose to follow the crowd and stick with the Microsoft solution, though, here's a run-down of the suite's most salient features.

MICROSOFT WORD
Microsoft is selling Word, in part, on the basis that it simplifies creation of DTP-style documents. It ships with a wide range of templates on which you can change the default frame sizes, swap out images and re-style text. You can flow text into boxes, which moves from one box to the next as you edit it; you can drag images onto the page and, once they're there, re-size them.

◄ If you've ever worked in an office environment then the chances are that at some point you will have come across Microsoft's spreadsheet application, Excel.

The 2008 edition is far better at doing this than any previous edition, as there is now a dedicated layout mode to complement the regular writing mode, so for home users there will be little to choose from here between Word and Pages.

One feature missing from Pages is the notebook view that Microsoft introduced with Office 2004. Used for taking notes with associated recordings, this has had a revamp, so you can now colour-code the pages it contains and create to-do items while you're taking notes. Word also has excellent outlining features, allowing you to quickly structure a document's outline, which you then flesh out later. For anything other than low-grade DTP or plain document writing, then, Word is the way to go.

MICROSOFT EXCEL

The world of business spreadsheets is ruled by Excel. Nothing else comes close. It took over from Lotus 1-2-3 on the PC a couple of decades ago, and has remained the dominant force ever since. If you want to use a Mac rather than a PC in a business environment, Office is a sensible move. However, it's no longer necessarily the best.

Since the removal of Visual Basic from Office 2008, which impacted compatibility, Microsoft has done much to dent its appeal, and you should be asking yourself whether switching to another third-party tool such as Mariner Calc, which also offers good, although not perfect, compatibility would be a financially astute move. Or, if you're feeling brave, make the switch to an online tool like Google Spreadsheets (*docs.google.com*).

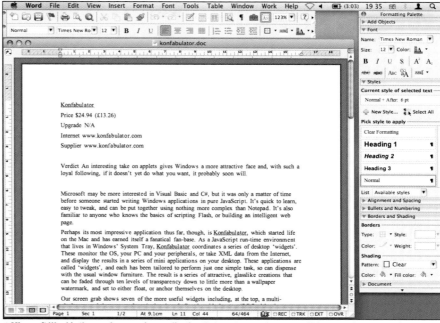

▲ Microsoft Word is the word processing application that most computer users will have used at some point.

However, if most of your spreadsheets are destined to be printed and used as evidentiary documentation, we'd recommend using iWork's Numbers. It's much easier to create a good-looking spreadsheet in Apple's own office suite than it is in Microsoft's offering, which could be just enough to swing a business proposal in your favour.

MICROSOFT POWERPOINT

PowerPoint is the industry standard for presentations, so it was a shame that the Mac version lagged behind Apple's Keynote for so long. Microsoft has rectified that with

this release, which boasts improved transitions and better slide designs. However, as many users take their own computers to a presentation and plug them in before they speak, there's now little to choose between PowerPoint and Keynote since the latter became so well established and compatibility is now less of an issue.

MICROSOFT ENTOURAGE

Entourage offers the best compatibility with corporate email systems currently on offer. Microsoft's Exchange server technology dominates many businesses, and while Apple's own Mail application does offer good compatibility, it's not up to the standard of Entourage, which will see you running both server and client software from the same vendor.

Entourage doesn't have the contact and appointment sensitivity of Mail, but it does boast excellent tools for working with shared calendars and, thanks to its links to MyDay, it enables you to keep an eye on your appointments without launching your full-blown communications tool.

MICROSOFT MYDAY

MyDay is a Mac-only application for showing your appointments in one unified interface that floats within the Mac environment. If you want a constant reminder of what you should be doing next, rather than relying on iCal alarms, it's a neat solution, although there's a choice of Dashboard Widgets that will do the same for you by hooking into Mac OS X's centralised calendaring database. ⊗

▲ Industry standard for presentations, PowerPoint for the Mac is now on a par with the Windows edition.

.Mac

It's not cheap, but Apple's online service, .Mac, really does help you to get more out of your machine. It's an excellent, pain-free way to share data between several machines, to get your photos and web pages up online, and to back up your files and keep them safe. As an added bonus, it also throws in calendar sharing and email features, and a steady stream of free software. So what exactly is this service that Apple tries to foist upon you the first time you switch on your Mac? And is it worth it?

Pronounced dot-Mac, .Mac is Apple's online service for Mac users. It is closely integrated with many features of Mac OS X, and you will have been given the opportunity to sign up for it when you were first setting up your Mac. Note that it's not a free service, and you will have to pay an annual subscription to keep it running, but despite this it is a feature-packed, worthwhile service that will make your Mac far more useful – especially if you have more than one.

SHARING DATA

.Mac is by far the easiest way to share data between several machines. Address Book and iCal are built from the ground up to synchronise their contents with a .Mac account and, as you can sign in to an account from an unlimited number of Macs,

you can use it as an easy way to keep your calendars and contacts at home and at work perfectly matched.

Synchronisation is set up through System Preferences, and here you can specify how often data is swapped with your .Mac account (we recommend hourly) and what should be included. As you'll see, it goes well beyond contacts and appointments, even offering to back up your browser favourites, your Dashboard Widgets and your email account settings.

Once set up on every machine that you want to synchronise, you should not need to do anything else. Each Mac will take care of updating itself at the specified intervals and passing back any changes you have made to its records to the .Mac servers.

Occasionally, however, there may be a conflict when, for example, you have made

two sets of changes to a particular record on two machines between synchronisations. In this case, iSync will throw up the Conflict Resolver, highlight the differences between the two adjusted records and let you choose which one to keep.

PUBLISH WEBSITES AND GALLERIES

The Mac is often seen as a creative computer, so it is only right that Apple should provide some means of publishing your work online. .Mac integrates well with iPhoto, iWeb and its professional photo processing application, Aperture, allowing you to upload websites and photo galleries to your public webspace on the .Mac servers for all to see.

If you only made use of .Mac for publishing web pages, it would be an expensive solution to a fairly simple problem, but when this feature is bundled in with everything else that the service offers, it's an added bonus – particularly when you see the quality of the galleries it produces.

Because Apple controls the hardware, the software and the online service, it is able to make sure that they all work together flawlessly, so .Mac photo galleries are among the most impressive you could ever hope to browse. Even better, if you have an iPhone, you can post photos taken direct to your .Mac gallery, meaning that even before you get home your friends can see what a great night out you've been having.

BACKING UP FILES

Mac OS X 10.5 Leopard may ship with Time Machine, a high end backup system for copying your changed files to an attached hard drive, but it suffers from two fatal flaws. First, it doesn't run on anything earlier than Leopard, so if you're not running the latest operating system you're out of luck.

▲ A key feature of the .Mac account is the ability to synchronise applications on one Mac with those on another.

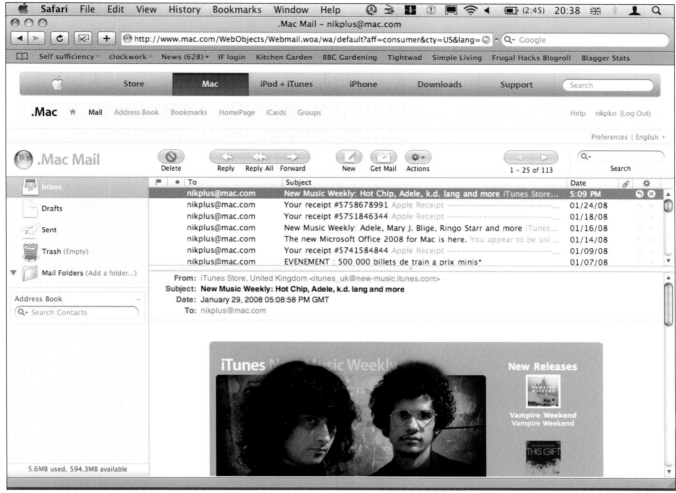

▲ As part of the .Mac account you will receive a web-based email account, which can be accessed from any Mac and is synchronised with your Address.

Second, as your backup drive is connected to your Mac, your backups will probably be kept on the same site as your original files. Think what this means if you have a fire; not only will you lose your originals when your Mac goes up in smoke, but you'll lose your precious backup copies, too.

Fortunately all versions of Mac OS X include a backup application called, not surprisingly, Backup, and found in the Applications folder. This lets you set up various backup sets – groups of files – that can be backed up to the iDisk on your .Mac account. This is just a storage area in which you can keep files that you want to either have access to from multiple locations, or keep copies of off-site.

To simplify matters still further, it includes presets for backing up your important data and settings, such as addresses and calendars, or your iTunes library. To see these, simply launch Backup and press the '+' button at the bottom of the interface to start a new backup set. If none of them meets your needs, pick Custom from the list of available options and you'll be able to pick the precise files you want to back up.

AN ALWAYS-AVAILABLE CALENDAR

As well as backing up your appointments, .Mac will publish your calendar online, so that even if you access it from a Mac not yet registered to your .Mac account (or indeed from a PC, which is not compatible with .Mac) you'll still be able to get a quick fix on where you're supposed to be, and when. This is a boon for business travellers who may need to quickly borrow some airtime on someone else's corporate network, or log in at an Internet café, to check which appointment they should be attending next.

To publish a calendar online, open iCal and right-click (or hold down Ctrl while clicking) on its name in the left-hand sidebar. Choose what you'd like to publish from the dialog box that pops up. We recommend checking the box to publish changes automatically, which is left empty by default. In this way, every change that you make to the calendar, such as adding, deleting or altering an entry, will automatically be sent to the server.

Click on Publish and iCal will send your calendar to the .Mac server and show you the address, giving you the option of visiting it directly or having the address emailed to you. Click on the button to see it right away (you can always come back and have the address sent on) and you'll be taken to an address starting *ical.mac.com*, where a replica of your calendar should be on display.

FREE SOFTWARE

The final bonus of .Mac, which is forgotten by many users, is a periodical supply of free software. It's not massively generous by any means, but if you use GarageBand in the iLife suite it's a good place to go for free loops to add to your library, and it's also the place to look for updates to the Backup application.

The free software can be found by opening a new Finder window (click the square face on the left-hand side of your Dock) and then navigating to iDisk (in the left-hand pane) and then Software. The applications and add-ons are organised here in individual folders; to download them to your own Mac, drag them out of the Software window and onto your Desktop before installing them in the appropriate folder, which is usually Applications.

FEATURES

Features

Want to uncover the coolest tools for your Mac? How about the most useful tools for your business? Do you want to become a Google power user, or build a website in a weekend?

All of these things – and many more – are possible with a Mac. All you need is a little bit of time, and a little bit more know-how. We may not be able to do the former, but in this section, we'll set out to do the latter, and include our ultimate tips guide to fast-track you from novice to know-all on the Mac.

Leopard Books

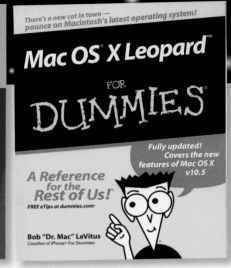

We review five books that are designed to help you make the most of all those mouth-watering features in the Leopard armoury.

Brilliant Mac OS X Leopard

Price £11.89 (RRP £16.99)
Author Steve Johnson
Publisher Pearson/Prentice Hall
ISBN 0273714408
Contact *pearson-books.com*
Available from *http://books.macuser.co.uk/ leopardbooksbrilliant*

Mac OS X Leopard for Dummies

Price £10.49 (RRP £14.99)
Author Bob LeVitus
Publisher Wiley
ISBN 0470054338
Contact *eu.wiley.com*
Available from *http://books.macuser.co.uk/ leopardbooksdummies*

Leopard has more features than any previous version of Mac OS X and whether you're a beginner or a more experienced user, you could almost certainly do with a helping hand when it comes to making the most of them.

The fact that Apple doesn't include a comprehensive manual with Leopard means that we have to turn to third-party books for help. Luckily, there are plenty of them on the market. From pocket-sized, monochrome productions to larger, more extravagant, full-colour publications, the titles covered here represent a broad, though by no means exhaustive, sample of those available in your local high street stockist and online.

Whether you need an author to hold your hand as you take your first steps with a brand new Mac or just want a reference book to dip in and out of occasionally, we're sure you'll find something here to meet your needs. The five publications reviewed range from £6.29 to £11.89 and are all available on *MacUser*'s online bookstore.

This is the only book here in colour and it's visually appealing. Tasks are presented as step-by-step guides down the side of the page, with crisp, annotated screenshots opposite. There's a brief discussion of each task, although it doesn't lend itself to the broader conversation found elsewhere.

The range of topics includes using TextEdit as a word processor and a description of what .Mac has to offer. But more specialist aspects, such as running Windows applications, aren't afforded much depth, with Boot Camp being the only proffered description. Uninstalling software is unfortunately simplified to just trashing the application – and some descriptions leave a great deal to be desired, being unhelpfully self-referential.

This isn't the book for those looking for in-depth discussion or hidden secrets, and keyboard shortcuts are a little thin on the ground. It's more suited to outright beginners who don't need these; those with intermediate skills should look elsewhere.

Living up to its name, this For Dummies title offers descriptions of the most basic terms – such as point, click and double-click – that only a total novice will find useful. On that level, it even provides a detailed walk-through of the system's Save dialog box.

In the page margin are markers to draw attention to tips and Leopard features. There are groan-inducing puns too, though talk in the third person is more off-putting. Nonetheless the language is suitably chatty to attract reticent technophobes who need easing into the subject matter.

In spite of this, the book admirably teaches a useful range of keyboard short cuts and provides a tear-out sheet of common ones. And when it comes to backups, coverage isn't simplified and biased towards Time Machine. Alternative applications and regimes are there as well.

Patience with the writing style is rewarded with a good introduction to the Mac. But those wanting to cut to the chase should seek a straight-laced option.

accepted Zip, GZip, BZip2 and 7-Zip formats, with or without encryption, and a Rar plugin is available separately.

A big attraction is that it can open and decompress 25 different formats from ARJ to Comicbook Zip, the only significant omission being StuffIt's newer .sitx archives, for which you will still need StuffIt Expander. Its preferences allow you to make BetterZip the default application to handle each of these formats should you wish. This is a nice touch that makes it a strong candidate to be your primary compression utility. For good measure Windows-using friends will thank you for moving away from proprietary .sit and .sitx formats.

▲ BetterZip can compress to Zip, GZip, BZip2 and 7-Zip, making it suitable as your primary compression tool.

03 Buzzword
URL *virtub.com*
Price TBA

For many developers, the future lies in Office over Internet (OoI) services, although current market expectations are almost certainly overinflated. Mobile users are most likely to be core customers who should end the year settled with the OoI service of their choice; the rest of us may dabble for a while then return to traditional local application suites.

Buzzword, from Virtual Ubiquity, has caught Adobe's eye sufficiently to be snapped up before a single product was shipped, and looks well positioned to deliver one of the better OoI experiences. For a start it makes few compromises in features despite running in a browser. Documents are fully styled, typographically respectable as you might expect from Adobe, and flow around embedded graphics, tables and other rich content.

Buzzword aims to match the versatility of powerful word processors. Imagine Pages running through your browser, and you can see how attractive this could be, while a matching spreadsheet tool could be a killer app.

▲ Buzzword allows text to be fully styled and flow around embedded graphics to create stylish documents.

04 F-Script
URL *fscript.org*
Price free

Although AppleScript and Automator remain powerful tools for integrating applications, AppleScript Studio (part of the high-end Xcode development system) has not armed the scripter with easy access to Mac OS X's Cocoa interface. F-Script is an open source development environment that provides a lightweight scripting interface to Cocoa. With it you can write your own applications as well as interface with those that support F-Script scripting, such as Colloquy (chat client), Daylite (business productivity suite), and Event Horizon (3D first-person game).

▲ F-Script provides a lightweight scripting interface to Cocoa and enables you to write your own applications.

▲ Google's sophisticated Web Toolkit is one of the best ways to build Ajax applications for interactive pages.

▲ Thanks to Hostal you can block advertisements, pop-ups and porn sites very conveniently.

Uniquely you can inject F-Script code into existing Cocoa applications – such as most modern Mac software – to explore and extend them as you wish. F-Script is also an excellent interface to Cocoa for those using other scripting languages such as Python. For the ultimate in Python, try the free add-on PyInjector tool – this injects F-Script and a complete Python interpreter into a running Cocoa application. With its Smalltalk-like syntax and powerful object browser, F-Script is everything a Mac geek needs.

05 Fluid
URL *fluidapp.com*
Price free

As web applications become increasingly popular, it can get messy having to open new windows or tabs in your browser, then rummage through them to catch up with your friends on Facebook. Mozilla Labs' Prism project aims to allow users to encapsulate a browser tied to a specific website into a discrete application.

Fluid is a Mac equivalent. Arm it with the URL of the site that you want it to take you to, an application name, destination and icon (which can be based on the site's favicon), and it will create a 1.3MB browser application dedicated to that site. You can then have your Facebook, *MacUser*, Gmail, Buzzword and other applications running at the same time, switched through the Dock or even spread over different Spaces under Leopard. It also helps you switch contexts cleanly and avoid confusion.

▲ Fluid quickly creates a 1.3MB browser application dedicated to the site that you want to work on.

06 Google Web Toolkit
URL *code.google.com/webtoolkit*
Price free

Unless you're a professional web developer your personal website will probably consist of static pages generated using an application like iWeb or Freeway and pulling no punches. If you want to stay in the vanguard, you need to make your pages interactive rather than flat, preferably with asynchronous JavaScript and XML – Ajax.

This makes them quicker to load and update, more attractive to the visitor and opens many new capabilities for you to harness their interaction. Few are geeky enough to be able to hand-roll the requisite XHTML, CSS, JavaScript, XML and content, so you need a toolkit and development platform to smooth your transition. One of the best ways of building Ajax applications is Google's sophisticated Web Toolkit, which has extensive help, documentation and examples embedded in it. You will still need to test your site out, using a range of different browsers and platforms, but this toolkit should prove an excellent aid for authoring stunning sites.

07 Hostal
URL *northernsoftworks.com*
Price $8.99 (about £4.50)

In the early days of networking and the Internet, mapping domain names to IP addresses and vice versa depended on the hosts file on each system. It is poetic justice perhaps that now we want to block advertisements, pop-ups and sites with inappropriate content such as porn, one of the best ways of doing so is through the same good-old fashioned hosts file.

Hostal provides a very convenient and helpful way of maintaining your local hosts file, so that adverts and adult sites are blocked. If you are getting fed up with persistent pop-ups enticing you to view pornographic matter and the other irritating dross that has become so obtrusive on the Internet, give Hostal's old hosts trick a try. Its single window is split into three tabs.

The first offers fairly traditional access to host definitions, which you can use to ease connections with local computers for instance. The second tab comprises a long list of blocked hosts offering adult content, while the third consists of a huge listing of all the major advertising addresses that you can block as you wish.

08 HoudahGeo
URL *houdah.com/houdahGeo*
Price £23.11 (£19.67 ex VAT)

As long as the clock in your camera is correctly set, every digital photo that you take will be perfectly orientated in time. But just where did you take all those pictures? Some will be at recognisable locations, while others may remain a mystery even when you have tried to work out where you were at that time on the given day.

HoudahGeo helps you keep your images orientated in space, either from GPS data recorded when you took the photos, or by finding each location in Google Maps. Import a block of images that you want to work on, then add positional info (latitude, longitude and altitude). Even if you don't have these from contemporary GPS records, you can zoom in and out of a Google Map window to place a cross where the photo was taken; HoudahGeo will then calculate the latitude and longitude for you. Finally you can export the geocoding data as Exif metadata to each image, export to Google Earth or publish the whole show in Flickr.

▲ With HoudahGeo, you'll always know the exact locations of the photographs you've taken.

09 Loop Editor
URL *audiofile-engineering.com*
Price free

GarageBand and Final Cut Studio's more technical Soundtrack Pro thrive on large libraries of audio loops. Although you can edit the content of loops in editors such as Amadeus Pro, looping aspects normally require a special tool. Apple Loop Utility is free and better than nothing for editing your own loops but is limited in features.

Enter Loop Editor, available in free unlicensed form or enhanced to its Plus version for $50 (£25): you can now work with any sample rate, bit depth or number of audio channels, edit during playback, and edit loop points with nudge and zero-cross controls. Additional features of the Plus version include detailed property editing, detailed visual slice editing and automatic slice creation.

Loop Editor also has powerful controls for customising keyboard shortcuts, which

▲ Loop Editor enables you to perform just about everything when it comes to editing audio loops.

will be especially appreciated by those working on their next DVD-full of commercial loops. If you use GarageBand or Soundtrack, Loop Editor is an essential companion.

11 Movable Type 4
URL *movabletype.org*
Price free

You don't actually need much in the way of tools to maintain your own blog, but using a

▲ Movable Type 4 comes in very handy when maintaining an unlimited number of blogs.

full-featured professional blog-authoring system can certainly help yours rise in the ratings. When Six Apart released Movable Type as a free product in December 2007, it ensured that every blogger could afford the best and most sophisticated tool in town.

Hewn in Perl and needing MySQL or a similar database to store content and data, it can maintain an unlimited number of blogs for those who are unrepentantly garrulous. Page generation can be static, in which you have to upload each updated page – or dynamic, in which the server assembles blog content from the dynamic content in its supporting database or any combination of the two.

For those with corporate interests, features, such as LDap management, can be particularly attractive. It was the first authoring system to include TrackBack that, along with its other innovative features, has been adopted by competitors. At last you can use the real thing for free.

10 MobileLocate
URL *mobilelocate.co.uk*
Price from £1.47 monthly per phone

We are going through a revolution in the availability and use of geographical information. GPS devices have become popular in sports such as running and cycling, and can be accessed by tools such as HoudahGeo to geocode your digital photographs (see page 124).

Mobile phones can also be used to work out where someone is as long as their phone is switched on. Whether based on a GPS device connected via a phone or iPhone, or on phone location alone,

tracking services can be used for a wide range of purposes from the tagging of children or partners to ensure that they do not stray, to the mundane commercial.

MobileLocate is one such service now available – expect others of even greater sophistication and lower cost in the coming year or two. Instead of your associate or partner having to send you garbled texts as they wend their way through our congested transport system, you will be able to monitor their progress on maps on your Mac or iPhone. Thankfully this should not be so precise as to distinguish whether they were stuck in a tailback or a tavern…

12 Picnic
URL *objectpark.net/picnic*
Price $29.95 (about £15) per user

All the permissions and security trappings of Mac OS X made one thing harder than in Mac OS 9: distributed filesharing. Unless you run Mac OS X Server there is always something to get in its way – this despite advances such as Bonjour, which enables you to identify locally networked Macs without the awkwardness of raw IP numbers.

Picnic builds on Bonjour to automatically synchronise designated folders on each Mac in your network. Gather together your collection of reference documents, project information or finished work, then keep each system up-to-date with the latest changes and additions. It deals intelligently with laptops and other Macs that may be removed from the network, syncing back any changes made once the portable system is reconnected.

Its only real limitation is that you should not try syncing iTunes or iPhoto libraries, mailboxes or similar because of their

▲ MobileLocate pinpoints the exact location of a partner or colleague. But is he or she stuck in traffic – or a bar?

▲ Picnic automatically syncs designated folders on each Mac in your network.

complex structures. The trouble is that this makes it unsuitable for keeping whole home folders synchronised, a task that is still best accomplished, using a real server.

13 Purify
URL *hendricom.com*
Price $29.95 (about £15)

Spam is one of the certainties of online life, afflicting everyone with an email account. Unless you run your own mail server or trust your ISP to block junk email before it even reaches you (not the brightest of ideas), you need a spam filter that is as adaptable and versatile as those who perpetrate the stuff.

The tools from *audiofile-engineering.com* are all very well when carefully trained but spammers are constantly looking for ways to outwit the popular filters. Purify provides belt, braces and loads more tricks to trap spam, using several different techniques. Among these are a trainable, statistical Bayesian system, filter by country of origin and user-defined phrases in content, friends lists, images and addressing errors.

Fully scriptable, it works with all mail protocols such as Pop and Imap, as well as most mail clients including Mail. Although of more questionable value, Purify provides single-click abuse reporting to ISPs. The latest versions offer forwarding of filtered mail to iPhone accounts, or to any accessible SMTP server. While it may not succeed in making Spam go away completely it should give you the wherewithal to keep the unwelcome pest at bay.

▲ Purify may not trap and block all the spam out there, but it will prevent a great deal of it from getting through.

▲ Remote Presenter… tantalising glimpse of future business presentations to clients without leaving your desk.

14 Remote Presenter
URL *soundscreen.com/presenter*
Price TBA

As roads and public transport become more congested, and we grow more conscious of the carbon footprint of business travel, it is far better to stay put and instead project your presence to anywhere that the Internet can reach. There's always videoconferencing of course, except that the system remains kludgy and hardly conducive to compelling pitches or presentations.

So cue Remote Presenter, which, though still a concept, is surely the future.

15 Skim
URL *skim-app.sourceforge.net*
Price free

Acrobat PDF documents are an ideal platform for comments and annotation. Unlike printed books and papers, which are irrevocably altered when you write notes in the margins, PDFs store added comments and markings separately from their main content. Skim is a PDF annotation and reader tool designed primarily for those who referee and study academic papers and other publications.

It mirrors Adobe's Acrobat Professional but is lighter in weight – and free. In addition its display options include a full-screen mode to make study easier. It can be used for presentations, includes bookmarks and searching, and can convert PostScript print to file output into PDF. It can also capture a document in a given state to a snapshot. Skim is an excellent replacement for Preview irrespective of the content of your PDFs.

Crafted in QuickTime with XML, using LiveStage Professional for authoring, it can combine live audio and video with pre-recorded media, slides and more.

An alternative approach available today would be to control Keynote remotely, using AppleEvents (AppleScript), and add live sound via VoIP. The trouble is that this would require punching a hole through the remote Mac's firewall – and that could be exploited by an intruder. It lacks Windows support too. So watch for products that work over VPN to spare you hours of travel for that brief presentation, coupled with iChat or Skype for live audio linkage.

16 The Issue
URL *theissue.com*
Price free

If you know where to look you are bound to find the right information or opinion in a blog. But gaining any sort of coherent view over the blogosphere can take a lot of time and browsing. As with any other content the only solution for busy people is to find someone to collate and edit the disparate material into

▲ The beauty of Skim is that it's lighter in weight than Adobe's Acrobat Professional – and it's free.

▲ The Issue breaks new ground by drawing together material from more than 50 blogs. It's a good read too.

▲ The multi-functional TinkerTool System still occupies the leading edge now that Apple has released Leopard.

▲ In addition to storing text, images and passwords, Webjimbo gives Internet access to your Yojimbo library.

a coherent whole. This is exactly what The Issue aims to do.

As one of the first attempts to draw together material from more than 50 different blogs, it is treading new ground that others will undoubtedly follow. Perhaps inevitably it reflects a US-centric view, but it does have some excellent coverage from world-wide correspondents. Book reviews are very strong, while a WEHT (What Ever Happened To…?) feature looks back at a topic that has been heavily featured in the media in the past but which has recently faded from view. Contributors are volunteers, and finances seem dependent on Google advertisements and private donations, which perhaps cast doubt on it surviving the year.

17 TinkerTool System
URL *bresink.com/osx/TinkerToolSys*
Price €8.33 (about £4.20)

Multi-function utilities like the excellent shareware Cocktail have proved both popular and numerous – and there is every sign that they will continue to find a place on most Macs. However, one in particular has consistently supported more and better features than any other – Marcel Bresink's TinkerTool System.

Not to be confused with TinkerTool, Bresink's free utility for tweaking hidden options, this shareware tool offered the first graphical interface to Access Control Lists (ACLs) as well as extended permissions introduced with Tiger. Moreover it continues to occupy the leading edge following the release of Leopard. At the last count, it can comfortably replace System Profiler, Console, cache cleaners, file and folder cleaners, attribute and permissions editors, most panes in System Preferences, uninstallers and a fair bit of Disk Utility.

For good measure it gives ready access to dozens of features that are otherwise quite tricky or obscure when it comes to finding them. If someone suggests that you should fix a problem by repairing the help viewer or verifying your login items, then this is one of the few tools that can do the lot.

18 WaterRoof
URL *hanynet.com*
Price free

One of the persistent disappointments in Mac OS X has been its software firewall, ipfw. There is nothing wrong with the firewall itself but, despite public criticism of its facile if not misleading GUI controls, Apple has not seen fit to provide a decent control interface even in Leopard.

WaterRoof is one of several tools that write script configuration files for ipfw. It is free, open source, full-featured and accessible. Its many configuration windows give superb insight into the sophistication of ipfw: here you can add static and dynamic rules to filter network packets, manage bandwidth permitted for given types of network traffic, control the Nat daemon to map external IP addresses to internal ones, watch and block active network connections, and use some basic network tools. A configuration wizard can walk you through the basics of setting up ipfw in a few minutes. Or you can try the more basic NoobProof from the same author, Hany El Imam.

19 Webjimbo
URL *webjimbo.com*
Price $29.95 (about £15)

Yojimbo (see page 131) is a personal information organiser from Bare Bones Software that has attracted quite a following. Although perhaps not quite as slick as the hypertext-based Voodoo it can store a wide variety of different classes of information,

including text, images, passwords and serial numbers, PDFs and web page archives. Add Webjimbo and you have easy Internet access to the contents of your Yojimbo library.

Away from your desktop you simply connect your laptop or iPhone via Safari. Inevitably you will need to punch a hole through your firewall to allow the incoming connection but Webjimbo endeavours to make this as secure as possible. It can get a bit messy to work with the firewall and other features of AirPort Extreme base stations, but once your configuration is working you won't need to repeat the setup wizard again. Webjimbo makes the already attractive Yojimbo completely compelling.

20 Zfs
URL *sun.com*
Price free with Leopard

For far too long we have lived with the association of logical volumes with physical hard disks: each disk can contain one or more volumes but a volume can't span two or more disks. Sun's Zfs has made its first appearance on the Mac in Leopard and, once up to production quality, will be eagerly adopted by those with loads of servers and physical drives.

But it is also the perfect answer for those with a collection of commodity drives, wishing to use Time Machine to its best. Over the next year, Zfs should help many to do away with the narrow tyranny of physical volumes. All it needs now are tools to support accessible administration.

▲ WaterRoof's many configuration windows give a superb insight into the sophistication of ipfw.

▲ Once up to production quality, Zfs will be a boon to those with numerous servers and physical drives.

20 TOP BUSINESS TOOLS

Macs have seen a big growth in use in the business world, and now there is an abundance of dedicated applications from which you can choose. To help you with your dilemma, we've selected 20 of the best.

Macs are for graphics, while PCs are for business. It's a statement that has gained credibility through repetition. But however convenient a generalisation, if it was ever valid, it's only half true now.

Macs have come a long way in the past five years. They haven't yet been ushered into many of the UK's corporate boardrooms, but for small businesses or freelancers who need a tool to manage their work life, Macs are often a better choice than Windows PCs.

There are two reasons for this. First, the growing appeal of Mac OS X has encouraged a new breed of business programs and a new audience outside the Mac's traditional core market. Second, the growth in the number of platform-agnostic online applications has been of greater relative benefit to the Mac than the PC, which already had a wide choice of business software.

The result is that there are some great Mac-compatible applications on which to build your business, and here we're listing the best. We've excluded favourites that you will be familiar with, such as Microsoft Office, MYOB Accounting and FileMaker. What we're left with are the lesser-known gems: the online and desktop-based applications that make your Mac a first-class business tool. ●

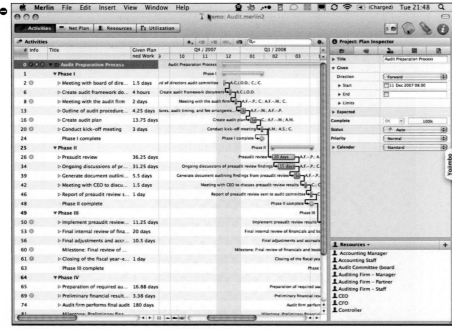

▲ The comprehensive Gantt chart in project manager Merlin 2 gives you a complete overview of your activities.

01 Merlin 2
URL *merlin2.net*
Price €145 (about £105)

Aside from Microsoft's limited Project Center, Macs were for a long time considered a poor second to Windows when it came to project management software. Well, that's no longer the case. As well as Omni Group's upcoming OmniPlan (*omnigroup.com*), Project Wizard's Merlin comfortably beats its nearest Windows counterpart, Microsoft Project, in both usability and functionality.

It's easy to set up a project – just enter its basic details and an available budget, or choose from an existing template. You then enter milestones and deadlines, and view a project's critical path and dependencies in the Gantt chart view in Merlin's Activities view, while the Netplan view more clearly displays the relationship between project components. You can also see just how effectively resources are being used in the Utilization view.

Refugees from Microsoft Project will be delighted by how seamlessly it imports native Project files, and Merlin also integrates with iCal and Address Book. Although collaborative networking isn't yet available, it's planned for an upcoming version of the software.

02 LogMeIn
URL *logmein.com*
Price free

You're on the road and you need to check some information on your office Mac. All would be well if you could contact it using Mac OS X Leopard's Back to My Mac

feature – but it's only designed for .Mac subscribers. That's where LogMeIn Free comes in. Install the 8MB file on your home Mac, leave it running and you can access your home machine through the LogMeIn website from any Mac or PC. This will come as a pleasant surprise to anyone – including Back to My Mac users – who has tried to punch holes in office firewalls to use remote access software.

When you connect, you can see and control your remote Mac Desktop in your browser. Usefully, you can trigger keyboard shortcuts to launch remote applications such as Spotlight. Even better, performance is decent over modest broadband connections.

LogMeIn doesn't charge for connecting to a single computer, but to transfer files between computers, print remote files locally, or control more than one machine, you'll need to upgrade to the Pro version, priced at about £35 a year.

03 Blinksale
URL *blinksale.com*
Price $12 (about £6) per month for up to 50 invoices

Is Word a good enough invoicing tool? Not when Blinksale is the alternative. At its most basic, this program's editing window lets you create multiline invoices that you can then email directly to clients. Neatly, if your client is another Blinksale subscriber, your invoices can be automatically added to their Blinksale account. But what's really impressive about this is the way it manages your invoices. When you've been paid, you can mark a stored invoice accordingly and

Blinksale tracks what's due. Its Dashboard view shows draft, open and closed invoices, as well as those that are past due, alongside their outstanding balances.

Invoices can be tagged with keywords for ease of organisation and when you select the program's Invoices tab, you can set which information you want displayed – invoices sent for the current financial year, for example. The amount that you've been paid and the invoice total are displayed below the list, so you can keep track of your earnings and any outstanding invoices.

If you're still not convinced, you can create three invoices each month for free.

04 Business Card Composer
URL *belightsoft.com*
Price $34.95 (about £18)

Because first impressions are important, business cards remain an essential business tool. If you don't have an ounce of design skill, then Belight Software's Business Card Composer is an outstanding way to quickly create the sort of cards that will impress potential clients.

Creating a card is a three-step process. First off is the design of the card. You can either select a basic design from more than 100 templates, corralled into a couple of dozen theme and subject categories, or create your own card from scratch. Business Card Composer includes a workable design whiteboard onto which you can add text, freehand design, images or a huge choice of bundled clip art.

▲ With LogMeIn, you can access and control your home machine from any Mac, or PC, from anywhere.

▲ In Blinksale, the total invoices and amount paid are totalled at the bottom of the list.

▲ With Business Card Composer, you can create business cards quickly that will impress your clients.

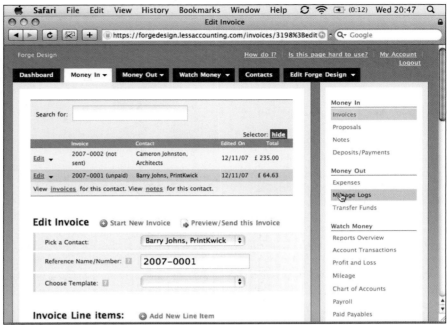

▲ Keep track of your income and expenses with the easy-to-use Web-based application, LessAccounting.

The second stage is to either manually enter data for the card or import information from your Mac's Address Book. This will replace the template's boilerplate text. The final step is to choose a print design. You can print onto a wide selection card stock from manufacturers such as Avery and Decadry, or even order your cards online – although as these come from the US, delivery could prove expensive.

05 Yojimbo 1.5
URL *barebones.com*
Price $39 (about £20)
Yojimbo could probably claim some of the credit for the Mac's growing popularity in the small business market. After all, there's no clear Windows alternative to this application, which stores and manages the disparate information you pick up during a business day – from text-based notes and useful web bookmarks to PDFs and images.

You can add items to the program by dragging them over the Yojimbo window or the tiny drop-dock palette that floats on the side of the screen. You can even do it through the clipboard – just press the F8 key and the current contents of the clipboard will be added to one of its collections.

Click on a collection and its contents are displayed. Yojimbo makes an impressive attempt at guessing the type of information that you've added and organising it accordingly – for example, drag a .Zip

archive over Yojimbo and it will be added to the Archives collection. This program soon becomes essential to anyone who's used it.

06 LessAccounting
URL *lessaccounting.com*
Price $19.95 per month (about £10 per month)
The problem with many accounting applications is that considering the simplicity of what they do – track income and expenses and tell you if you're making money – they are surprisingly complicated to use. The result? You stick with the back of an envelope.

Web-based LessAccounting could change all this. Like Blinksale, it lets you create invoices through a web interface, but you can also create proposals to send to customers, which can be converted to invoices when accepted.

LessAccounting also stores contacts – as you add them they are accessible from a menu on the invoice creation page. This online application does much more than

just creating invoices, though. It tracks suppliers and expenses, such as mileage, and from that information you can create reports, from outstanding creditors and debtors to a full profit and loss account. Any online accounting application means you don't have full control of your data, but at least reports can be exported to Excel-readable CSV format.

LessAccounting is pricey, but very flexible, although a free version lets you create five invoices, proposals or other data per month.

07 Writeboard
URL *writeboard.com*
Price free
Most business users will be aware of online alternatives to Microsoft Office such as Google Docs (*docs.google.com*) and Zoho (*zoho.com*). But if you're on the road and need quick access to a text editor, Writeboard is arguably the best option, because you don't need to login to use it. Just visit the site, enter a name for the document, a password and your email address, and you can start writing – Writeboard sends an email with a link to the document's URL so you can access it later.

Those who can't live without Word will find Writeboard's editing options spartan – there's no spell checker, word count feature or Edit window toolbar. Instead, Writeboard uses simple text formatting techniques to add styles, such as wrapping text in an underscore character to italicise it.

Writeboard is a great cross-platform collaborative tool, too. Saved writeboards ✛

▲ Yojimbo stores and manages all the information you pick up during the day and organises it for you.

▲ Writeboard is an online text editor that lets you share your work with other people anywhere in the world.

● can be shared, and when you or one of your collaborators edits a document, changes are stored as separate versions, which can be compared on the web page.

08 Anxiety
URL anxietyapp.com
Price free

Keeping yourself organised is the toughest part of business. Anxiety is a lightweight, Leopard-only to-do list manager that synchronises with Apple's Mail and iCal. When installed, Anxiety starts on login and floats above all running applications, displaying current tasks from your iCal calendar – different calendars are selectable from a drop-down menu.

While Anxiety's window acts as a handy reminder for upcoming tasks – even if it doesn't show their priority – you can also enter tasks directly into Anxiety by simply pressing the Return key. When the task is entered, it's automatically added to your iCal database. Double-click on a task and it opens directly in iCal or Mail for further editing. You can even create new iCal calendars just by clicking on the tick button in the top-right corner of the list window.

Anxiety uses Leopard's Calendar Store – Mac OS X 10.5's system-wide database that contains calendars, events and to-dos, which means it can't run on Mac OS X 10.4 or earlier.

09 Remember The Milk
URL rememberthemilk.com
Price free

An online to-do manager, Remember The Milk is a neat but powerful task manager for both home users and small businesses. When you sign up to the service, you're allocated your own remember the milk domain, which lists tasks that are due today and tomorrow. You enter tasks, organised by default under five lists, through a simple web-based form. You can assign them a due date or a priority, tag them for easier organisation and mark them as complete

▲ Anxiety is a lightweight Leopard-only to-do list that synchronises with Apple's Mail and iCal.

by pressing a button on the site's home page. Tasks can be shared with others through email or via SMS on your mobile.

Perhaps the tool's most essential feature is the fact that it integrates with iCal on your home Mac. As long as the list you create is public, you can copy its iCalendar URL from the list details box and in iCal, subscribe to it from the Calendar menu.

There's an optimised version of the site for iPod touch and iPhone users, but this is only available for paid subscribers.

10 Basecamp
URL basecamphq.com
Price free

Software developer 37 Signals has a knack of producing quality, easy-to-use web-based applications. Alongside BackPack, (an organisational tool) and HighRise (a shared contact manager) is Basecamp, a web application for managing projects.

Basecamp is a great tool for business collaboration with remote employees or offices. It lets you create team members, with set access rights. Each has their own Dashboard view of active clients and the projects they are involved with. These drill down to project windows that show late and upcoming project milestones, as well as list of completed tasks. If you need to change a milestone's due date, Basecamp can adjust the date of subsequent milestones to compensate. Milestones can also be linked with to-do lists, and as items on the list are

checked off, a record is kept of the date and the person who signed it off. Basecamp even includes the Writeboard document editing tool, so you can work on a project's documentation with others.

Basecamp works well with your desktop Mac too. Milestones can be shared with iCal and changes to a project can be highlighted through an RSS feed.

11 OmniGraffle Pro
URL omnigroup.com
Price $149.95 (about £75)

OmniGraffle may be used by many Mac owners as an illustration tool – a task at which it's more than adequate – but it's indispensable to business users who need to explain a process clearly, yet don't happen to have an artistic bone in their body.

It uses libraries of business-friendly object artwork to simplify the creation of common business illustrations, such as flow charts or organisational charts. But the way the program works also helps you adjust business charts with little fuss. For example, when you link objects with OmniGraffle's Link tool, they remain linked as you move the objects around the canvas. OmniGraffle also lets you quickly improve the look of an imported text-based document – it can import Microsoft Visio files, too – by applying a preset style to it as it is imported.

Another handy feature is the Outline view, which both lists the document structure hierarchically and a offers quick way to manage objects on the main canvas. Dragging them in the Outline view automatically rearranges them on the canvas.

12 Wesabe
URL wesabe.com
Price free

Wesabe is an online finance application with a difference. You upload your financial data in QIF or QFX format, or manually enter data and then Wesabe helps clean it up – for example, turning those lengthy transaction descriptions that no-one understands into a ●

▲ OmniGraffle Pro is ideal for those who want to create an illustration but don't have an artistic bone in their body.

▲ Remember The Milk is a neat and powerful task manager for both home users and small businesses.

▲ Basecamp provides simple tools to improve the communication between people working on a project.

▲ Wesabe is an online finance application that makes managing your finances easy.

▲ Pulse is a simple web application that keeps an eye on the amount of money you have in your bank account.

more understandable short name. Usefully, Wesabe automatically applies this to future statements as they are imported, and a benefit of a community site such as this is that if other members have edited a transaction the same way, Wesabe automatically suggests that shortcut for all of its members.

You organise your finances by tagging individual transactions with labels such as 'groceries' or 'going out' – you can even split tags to divide a transaction between labels. You can then use the site's spending summary to graphically illustrate where your money is going. The biggest advantage of tags is that Wesabe matches money saving tips – supplied by other members – according to your tags.

While Wesabe is US-based, UK banks are supported, and you can switch the default currency to Pounds Sterling using a drop-down menu.

13 iList Data 3.6
URL *lakewoodstudios.com*
Price $69.95 (about £35)
When it comes to databases on the Mac, conventional wisdom has it that FileMaker Pro is the only choice. Bento (*filemaker.com*) could change that, but until then, Lakewood Studio's iList Data 3.6 is a cheaper option for small businesses.

iList is an unusual mix of power and simplicity. Built on a robust SQL database, its clutch of startup templates is based on popular database tasks, such as image

catalogues or time-tracking. One useful business-oriented feature is the ability to create inline bar, dot or line graphs based on numerical data.

But its flexibility is its real plus point. You can use it to track any data type, including invoices, and records can be exported to Microsoft Word or Excel, while database images can be sent directly to iPhoto. You can get real value out of your data by building queries through either its Find tool or SQL commands. iList Data isn't as powerful as FileMaker Pro, but business geeks may love it.

14 Pulse
URL *pulseapp.com*
Price free
In a small business, profit and loss is a purely nominal figure. What really matters in the early years of a business is making sure that more money is coming into the company's coffers than is going out.

Pulse is a simple web application that keeps an eye on this critical area. Just enter the amount of money you have at present in your bank account, and as you receive income and spend money, you record it on the Pulse website. You can organise income and expenditure by allocating them either to user-specified categories or organise them by company or project – handily these details can be imported from 37 Signal's Basecamp application. You can also set up recurring transactions and allocate items to the future, assigning them an income

potential – essentially the likelihood of you actually receiving the income – which can be handy when budgeting cash flow. Cash flow is shown as a running total for the months ahead, so you can forecast easily if money is about to get tight.

15 Cha-Ching
URL *midnightapps.com*
Price $40 (about £20)
Not that the opposition is the stiffest, but Cha-Ching might qualify as the best-looking Mac or PC finance application ever made. However, its beautiful interface doesn't come wholly at the expense of functionality.

Cha-Ching is a finance manager that lets you track multiple business or personal bank accounts – it supports QIF and QFX imports, so you can download them from an online bank. What sets Cha-Ching apart is that as you add transactions, you can tag them with keywords, such as 'Salary' or 'Entertaining'. This not only lets you build 'smart folders' to display certain groups of transactions that match chosen criteria in the transactions window, but it can also be used when budgeting – you add the tags to include in a budget comparison – you can create as many comparisons as you want – and Cha-Ching will produce a chart graphically comparing those tagged income and expenses items.

16 Stikkit
URL *stikkit.com*
Price free
Not to be confused with the less useful Mac OS X Stickies, Stikkit is a free online application that can sort out your business by intelligently organising your bookmarks, calendar events, contacts and notes.

You enter text on a stikkit, a small yellow window. As you type, Stikkit analyses this text, looking for trigger words, such as 'at', 'on' or 'buy', to interpret them and organise the results automatically. As soon as you enter a simple Stikkit, such as 'Meet Mike tomorrow at 9', it interprets 'Mike' as a proper name, creates a contact for him

▲ Offering great flexibility when creating databases, iList is perfect for small businesses.

▲ With Cha-Ching, you can keep track of multiple business or personal bank accounts.

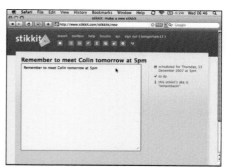

▲ Stikkit is a great way to quickly update your schedule if you're away from the Mac or even browsing the web.

and generates a new calendar event for the meeting. To prevent an item being interpreted, you just enter an exclamation mark at the start of a paragraph.

For Mac users, Stikkit is a great way to quickly update your schedule if you're away from the Mac or even browsing the web. Even better, like Remember the Milk, you can subscribe to Stikkit calendars in iCal.

17 Openomy
URL *openomy.com*
Price free

It's the freelancer's recurring nightmare – you're at a client's office and you realise that you don't have your most important files with you for your presentation. One way of protecting against this scenario is to store your most important files on Openomy, which is a website that lets you store your files online. These files, protected by password, are accessible from any computer with a web browser, so you can get access to them even when on-site with a Windows PC-toting client.

If you have a lot of files – up to 1GB – you can organise them on the site by assigning tags to them. And although files are private by default, you can mark them as public to give them a permanent web link and easy access from any web browser.

While Apple's .Mac web service boasts far greater capacity, it's hard to argue with Openomy's cost – it's absolutely free.

18 Contactizer Pro 3.5
URL *objective-decision.com*
Price €99 (about £72)

Objective Decision's Contactizer Pro 3.5 puts Mail, Address Book and iCal on steroids to organise your contact information, activities and communications.

Its Contact View shares the same underlying database as Address Book, so changes made in Contactizer are available

▲ By storing your files on Openomy, you can access them from any computer.

to other Mac OS X applications, but you can also tag contacts with colour-coded categories. You can import iCal details to use in calendar-based Event View, which shows upcoming meetings and tasks, while a Communication View is a hub for phone calls, emails, faxes and iChats, all of which can be linked to contacts. Handily, Contactizer also links to Apple Mail, so it has access to its message library database – and you can even send template-based personalised emails from Contactizer.

The newest addition to the program is a project manager that ignores fancy Gantt chart tools to list simple processes that must be followed to reach an objective. Although Contactizer manages huge amounts of information, you can manage it through smart filters, which can show today's communications at a glance or all tasks that need action.

19 Mozy
URL *mozy.com*
Price free for 2GB or £25 per year for the Mozy Unlimited option

Mac OS X Leopard's Time Machine may be a great backup tool, but as it doesn't backup off-site, you can't afford to trust your vital files to it. But Mozy, part small Mac backup application, part web-based recovery application, is a great tool to supplement local backups.

Mozy stores the files and folders you choose to backup online, and protects them with 448-bit encryption. It uses the same time-saving incremental backup technique as Time Machine, only copying files that have changed since the last backup. But it also supports versioning, tracking multiple iterations of changed

▲ Back up all your important files and folders online with Mozy – a great tool to supplement local on-site back-ups.

files. Mozy backups don't hog your Internet connection as you can set it to back up when your Mac has been idle for a set time.

The Mozy website shows backup details, but also lets you restore all or part of any version of your backed up data. You get 2GB of back-up free, but the unrestricted Mozy Unlimited option is a bargain for those who value peace of mind.

20 SpamSieve
URL *c-command.com/spamsieve*
Price $30 (about £15)

While Mac-based businesses remain resilient to almost all forms of viruses and trojans, one form of malware – spam – is still a blight on business life. While many email clients have some sort of built-in email filtering, we've never seen any application deal with email spam as effectively as SpamSieve.

SpamSieve works with Apple Mail, Entourage and a handful of other email clients. It uses highly tuned Bayesian spam filtering to learn what is spam and what isn't, alongside other tricks, such as checking your Mac OS X Address Book to ensure that messages from friends and colleagues are never marked as spam.

SpamSieve also keeps a customisable blocklist and whitelist to manage email from particular addresses. Don't expect wonders to start with: you'll need to train it with a few hundred spam and non-spam email messages. But after a while the spam that waits in your inbox every morning should start to dry up.

▲ Contactizer Pro 3.5 is an all-in-one solution for managing, sharing and organising your personal and business information.

▲ Using highly tuned Bayesian spam filtering, SpamSieve works with both Apple Mail and Microsoft Entourage.

Google
power user

Even now, a large element of what examinations are designed to test is our ability to recall information, but in this age of having the world of digital information at our finger-tips, this seems a little anachronistic. The best illustration of this is a corrupted quote of Samuel Johnson's, usually rendered: 'The next best thing to knowing something is knowing where to find it.'

The problem is that few people truly exploit the power of searching the Internet for information. At best, we punch a search term into Google and wade through the results, but there are dozens of tips, tricks and techniques that can help you get to the information you want, fast. Some of what we'll discuss, particularly early on in this feature, will apply as readily to any search engine, but we're going to focus heavily on Google. There are a couple of reasons for this: first, it's by far the most popular search engine and is integrated into Safari's search bar, and second, the richness and power of the features it boasts makes it ideal fodder for a feature such as this.

So, there are a few very basic concepts to get out of the way before we go on. Remember at all times that you're searching for terms that appear on results pages. Another way to think about this: search for the answer, not the question. Relatively few pages will have, say, 'how do I fit a SuperDrive in my eMac' compared to the number which will contain the phrase 'fitting a SuperDrive in an eMac'. This is a coarse example – Google would still bring up relevant results with the original term – but hopefully you get the idea.

Google is case-insensitive – entering 'MacUser' is no different to 'macuser' – and

Find the information you want on the Internet in a jiffy and avoid getting sidetracked by websites that promise the earth but deliver nothing with these handy hints at making searches a breeze.

it automatically assumes that you want all entered search terms to appear on the page. In the earlier days, you usually had to use + signs with multiple terms or the search engine in effect ran a standalone search for each one. Google also uses stemming, making intelligent guesses based on your search query to broaden it out and include related variations on your terms.

Most important, though, is that you realise you can combine these search techniques. Mix operators such as quote marks with prefixes such as cache: to bring up a set of super-relevant results; no longer will you wallow through multiple pages of results. We'll also highlight some of Google's market-specific tools and web-based applications that can help make your life easier. Google is running a closed beta of Google Apps for Your Domain, which lets you to run Gmail, Page Creator, Calendar and Talk on your own domain; you can apply to join the trials at *google.com/a*.

By the time we're through, you'll be searching like a pro and creating all sorts of compelling content online. Let the search begin. ✚

SEARCH TECHNIQUES

Quote marks

This is one of the most basic tricks, but few people seem to use it. Simply enter a search term or part of a search term wrapped in double quote marks, and Google treats it as a phrase, heavily weighting results to those pages that contain the words in quotes as a group and in the order entered. The search term *"mac mini" ram 2GB* will return hits about 2GB of Ram specifically for the Mac mini more reliably than if the model was entered just as two words, and you could use the technique to search for phrases from a quotation.

info:

The info prefix is a great way to get more information about a particular website. Enter it like this – *info:www.macuser.co.uk* – and you'll get the following options:

Show Google's cache of *www.macuser.co.uk*
Find web pages that are similar to *www.macuser.co.uk*
Find web pages that link to *www.macuser.co.uk*
Find web pages from the site *www.macuser.co.uk*
Find web pages that contain the term *"www.macuser.co.uk"*

The 'similar' link is identical to using related: as a search prefix, so if that's your reason for using info: you can save yourself a click.

URL

allintitle:

Searches for the specified terms in the title of pages. This search requires that all search terms entered be found in the page title. If you wanted to find stories about the iPhone and LG's Prada phone, you could search for *allintitle:iphone lg prada*, though this relies on the three search terms appearing in the page's title, not its content. You can also use intitle: if you don't want to force Google to include all entered search terms in the results.

cache:

As part of its indexing process, Google takes snapshots of websites. Searching these cached copies is a great way to go back and search older versions of a page that may have been edited, and you can easily tell Google to display results from its cache rather than from the live version of the site by prefixing your search query. Entering *cache:www.macuser.co.uk* iphone for example searches for the word iPhone in Google's cache of *MacUser*'s homepage and will highlight the word iPhone on the page.

allinurl:

Similar to allintitle:, but here we're looking for the specified search terms in the URL – web address – of a page. The operator inurl: is also possible.

+-

Put simply, a plus sign preceding a term means 'search for this', while a minus means 'omit this phrase from the results'. Let's say you wanted to search for the Virginia Tech supercomputer dubbed Big Mac. Ordinarily, the phrase 'big mac' would just return lots of pages about burgers, but entering *"big mac" -mcdonald's* means that the correct page is first in the list of results. You don't usually need to use + (see the introduction on page 136) but it's useful in some circumstances. Google, for example, usually omits common words such as 'the' and 'I' from searches, but there are occasions on which you might need to override this. *Star Wars Episode +I* for example, means that the 'I' will be heeded in the search term.

Advanced search

There are some more advanced tricks you can use. From any results page you can click the search types above the search box – Web, Images, Video, News and Maps – to switch to that type of search using your entered terms. At any point you can click the Advanced Search link to the right of the search box to bring up advanced options. These can be mixed and matched at will, and the result is nothing more than a specific search URL that's a combination of the prefixes and other techniques we've explored plus the few more below.

One trick that can't (currently) be replicated with a search box prefix is Advanced Search's Creative Commons option. This allows you to tell Google to search only for content licensed with so-called copyleft licences, available for reuse without getting specific permission from the author.

A number of the options available from the Advanced Search window, though, can be replicated with a few search prefixes. As with all prefixes, this matters as it makes it easy to enter these search terms straight into the search boxes in the toolbars of browsers such as Safari or Firefox, without first going to Google and clicking on the Advanced Search link.

site:

This limits results to those from the specified domain. The search *iphone site:www. macuser.co.uk* will return all of *MacUser*'s online coverage of the iPhone.

Personalised Search

Google's Personalised Search feature is still in beta, but the idea is to analyse the searches you perform in order to provide you with more relevant results as the system gets more used to the sorts of things you search for. Consistently clicking on links to pages about Steve Jobs rather than recruitment after doing a search for *jobs* will gradually mean that the recruitment pages will cease to appear in the results. This does mean that Google is 'listening in' to your search terms, but a robust privacy policy is in place, and you can suspend tracking of your search terms. You can't easily tie personalised search into terms entered into Safari's search toolbar module; instead go to *google.co.uk/psearch*.

date:

The basic use of date: is to restrict your searches to results from the last so many months. The term *iphone date:3* will return iPhone results from the last three months. You can also add in specific date ranges, but these have to be in Julian format, which look completely different to the Georgian dates we're used to. If you're sufficiently dedicated, once you've converted your dates to the correct format, use this syntax *daterange: startdate-enddate* but be aware that the date tagging won't be perfect.

Images

Google can also search for images, but since images are inherently more difficult to index than text, the results are rarely satisfactory. It's done from *images.google.co.uk*.

define:

Unsure of the meaning of a word? Prefix it with define: and you'll get a list of definitions drawn from all over the web. The system isn't free from error – using the Dictionary Widget if you're on Tiger can be more accurate – but it's an undeniably useful quick check.

Sets

What if you don't know exactly what you're searching for? You know it's the name of a film starring Jeff Bridges, say, but can't for the life of you remember what it was. Rather than digging through Wikipedia or IMDB, go to *labs.google.com/sets* and enter the names of a couple of films of his that you do know. Click 'large set' and you'll get a huge list of Bridges' work. It works remarkably well for many topics, and each result in the set is a clickable link taking you to a page of results using the link text as a search term.

Number range

To include a range of numbers in your search term; you use two full stops. If you wanted to know what Steve Jobs was up to when he wasn't at Apple, use *"Steve Jobs" 1985..1996*. It works for any number range including prices – such as £250..450 – but you'd be better using off product search (see page 141).

GOOGLE CALCULATOR

Put the Internet to work on more than just unearthing pages with the information you need; make it work things out for you as well. Thanks to its Calculator feature, Google can be as good at converting weights and measures as it is at finding web pages. You don't need to go to a special page as you do with the Google Images search; just phrase the query correctly to get it worked out for you. Try typing 'UK pints in a US pint' to see how much smaller an American pint is compared with an English one, or 289*0.175 to find the VAT part of a price (at 17.5%) on something offered at £289. You can do some of the same things with the OS X Calculator utility or Unit Convertor widget, but often it can be more convenient to use this feature directly from your browser.

Google's Calculator can perform basic and more complex maths, and deal with converting a broad range of units of measure and physical constants. Its scope is wider than any single person is ever likely to need, but as a worldwide service it aims to cater for just about every requirement. For example, you can convert octal (base-eight numbers) into Roman numerals, although we're not sure quite who would need to.

One particularly handy thing about using Google to perform these calculations is that if you get the phrasing of the calculation wrong Google will still attempt a regular Internet search with it. As a result, it will almost certainly show you a long list of sites that offer all the conversion information you need, even if it can't figure out how to perform the calculation. (If you'd like to try and force a calculation, try putting an equals symbol at the end. If it is mathematically resolvable in any way this should do the trick.)

The maths symbols, or operators, include plus, minus, multiply and divide, as you'd expect, and go on to cover exponent (raising a number to the power of something), modulo (giving the remainder of a division), root calculations, and, particularly usefully, a simple 'percentage of' calculation. For example, to find out what percent 12 is of 89, ask Google '12 % of 89'.

Going further, you can 'choose' (find the ways a given number of elements can be chosen from another number), find square roots, use trigonometric functions, logarithms in base e or base 10, and find the factor of a number. Use parentheses to evaluate certain parts of a mathematical expression before others, and, should you need to, use prefixes before numbers to define them as hexadecimal, octal or binary. This certainly goes much further than most people ever need, but it is all there should the occasion arise.

When it comes to units of measure, you can use both long and short names for most constants. This goes from the obvious – cm and km are synonyms for centimetre and kilometre – to the esoteric – c and g are the synonyms for 'the speed of light' and 'gravitational constant'. Others, such as 'the speed of sound', have no short name equivalent; just use the full term instead.

Examples

operator	function	example
+	add	121+157
-	subtract	212-34
*	multiply	21*6
/	divide	95/14
^	exponent (raise to the power of)	6^3
choose	number of ways a set can be chosen from another set	12 choose 3
'nth' root of	calculates the 'nth' root of a number	ninth root of 12
% of	find the percentage	20% of 128
sqrt	square root	sqrt(12)
sin, cos (etc)	trigonometric functions (degrees)	tan(45)
ln	logarithm base e	ln(12)
log	logarithm base 10	log(12)
!	factorial	6!

Note: while you can use these operators in the pure, classical sense, you can also do most of these calculations using much more sentence-like expressions. Rather than type the precise but cryptic-looking sqrt(12) you can ask for 'the square root of 12'. In this limited area, Google really does do an effective form of natural language comprehension.

DEDICATED SERVICES

Music:
The music prefix does a similar thing to movie. Enter it before an artist's name and you'll get a discography, reviews, links to official websites, image searches, news, discussions and direct deep-level links to major online music retailers such as the iTunes Store. You can also use it to look up specific albums. The level of detail is astonishing; although by no means complete, associated links to songs' cover versions and lyrics are amazing useful, and a very quick way to settle arguments. Google also maintains its own automatically-generated music charts at *google.co.uk/trends/music*. Data is gathered from opted-in Google Talk users, and all entries are hyperlinked to information pages identical to those generated with a music: prefix.

Blog searching
Google's blog search tool is a handy way of searching through what's being said on the millions of blogs that are updated every day. The dedicated service at *blogsearch.google.co.uk* offers basic searching of blogs as well as an advanced search option with some blog-specific terms. Let's say you remember reading a post on Boing Boing by Xeni Jardin around Christmas time. Simply perform an Advanced search, specify Boing Boing's url as the source, Xeni as the blog author, and the date range. Bingo. You can also use the inblogtitle: inposttitle: inpostauthor: and blogurl: prefixes but unfortunately only from *blogsearch.google.co.uk*, not from Safari's search box. Google allows you to create RSS feeds based on your search terms too. Let's say you particularly like the tips Gina Trapani puts up on Lifehacker; simply search **blogurl:www.lifehacker.com inpostauthor:gina** and you'll be provided with a dedicated link pulling her posts from the site. These search results can be added to your Google Homepage – see right – as well.

Movie:
This is a real beauty, and one that very few people know about. Simply prefix the name of a film with movie: and you'll be given local cinema listings with links to maps of their location, reviews, a link to the trailer, and a link to the film's page on IMDB. Click on the Show more movies link and you'll be taken to a page listing all locally-showing films; what's more, you have the option of sorting the list by the distance to the cinema, movie rating and popularity as well as title.

News
Google news serves as a digest of news coverage from many news outlets the world over. The main page at *news.google.co.uk* is spectacularly rich even by default, but by now you won't be surprised to learn that it's very customisable too. The page can be reordered with simple drag and drop, and you can filter the news to show only a particular channel, such as sports. The useful news visualisation tool Newsmap (*marumushi.com/apps/newsmap*) uses Google News as its data source.

Trends
Google Trends is utterly invaluable for anyone doing research. Found at *google.co.uk/trends* and technically still in beta, it's a great way to get a snapshot of the buzz around a particular thing. Enter in a search term and you'll get a graph showing Google's collated results for the buzz on the web. It's tied into Google News too, and important events connected with your search term are mapped onto the trend; it's usually easy to correlate news stories – Apple launching the iPhone, say – with spikes in interest. Better still, you can enter multiple terms, separated by commas, to compare trends. Results can be filtered by language, time and geographical location.

Books
Google Books – at *books.google.co.uk* – allows you to search through the contents of dead-tree publications. There's no denying that this is an astonishingly useful thing – imagine searching the entire works in the British Library from your laptop rather than trawling through the copies in the library itself – but there are limitations. Copyright and other intellectual property considerations – allied to a reluctance to embrace change – means that book publishers are nervous about allowing their works to be indexed. It's a search tool that will only improve, and as you'd expect, the advanced search options give you the ability to narrow the search by publication date, ISBN and publisher.

Scholar

The service at *scholar. google.com* allows researchers to track down peers' contributions. As with the blog search tool, there is a wide range of advanced options tailored specifically to academic research. You can restrict results by field and publication; Google's own advanced search help at *scholar.google.com/intl/en/ scholar/refinesearch.html* goes into these options in some detail.

Finance

Google's Finance pages – at *finance.google.com* – are another example of the deceptive simplicity of Google's interfaces. Load up the home page and you're presented with a simple text and graphics reporting of various markets. A market summary at the top left shows how the main stock exchanges are faring, and you're presented with a few business headlines.

Things get interesting when you look up a particular company. Enter its ticker symbol – AAPL for Apple, for example – or just start typing the company's name and Google will start autocompleting your entry. Here you're presented with a spectacular amount of very well-handled information. The most obvious element is the graph of stock price history. As with Trends, news stories are mapped to this so you can see what effect announcements and other news stories have on the stock price. The graph's date range can be expanded or contracted and other companies can be mapped onto the same graph for comparison.

The page shows a company summary, related companies, discussions, related blog postings, board biographies and details and much more than we can justify covering here. Explore; it's astonishing.

One other tip. You can use the stocks: prefix – such as **stocks:aapl** – to get a quick glimpse of a company's trading, and this page has links to the company's profile on Google finance and other providers.

Product Search

Here at *MacUser* we regularly use price comparison engines such as Pricerunner and Kelkoo to find the lowest price that a product's available for online. These two require online stores to supply their data in a specific format, however; Google's own price comparison engine – at *google.co.uk/products* – scours the web actively looking for and indexing shops. It doesn't reply on shops tying up deals such as with Pricerunner, and so its list of results is usually much longer, and it can often find cheaper outlets.

That said, you'll often find your results contaminated with irrelevant products, and the prices quoted are often misleading, either because Product Search picks up the wrong price from the page, or because it will list VAT inclusive or exclusive prices sporadically.

Specific areas

As well as dedicated search areas such as Scholar and Books, Google also makes available four flavours of its search designed specifically for four major operating systems. You'll find search engines for Mac, BSD Unix, Linux and Microsoft (yes, we know that this last option isn't OS-specific per se, but you get the idea) at *google.co.uk/mac*, */bsd*, */linux* and */microsoft* respectively.

Alerts

Google can set up alerts to help you track particular topics of interest; at *MacUser*, for example, we might set up a news alert flagging any story containing the term "Steve Jobs".

Go to *google.co.uk/alerts* to set one up. You have the option of searching news, blogs, the Internet, user groups or all four. Content that matches your search terms will be collated into an email that's delivered daily, weekly, or as soon as the term is matched. Annoyingly, at the time of writing, only email alerts are offered; there's no way to set up custom RSS feeds from the main alerts page. You can, as mentioned previously, set up a customised blog keyword RSS feed from *blogsearch.google.co.uk*, and do the same thing from News, so Google obviously has the technologies in place. We expect to see RSS feeds offered as an option from *google.co.uk/alerts* soon.

Homepage

By now, you're only human if you're beginning to feel a little overwhelmed. Never fear: there's a way to help bring all these disparate services together, and add a whole lot more. Google's personalised homepage allows you to drag in modules and reorganise them to suit.

Google itself supplies many – modules for Gmail, Google Maps, Groups, stocks and the like – but they're so easy to code that there are many hundreds covering almost every conceivable niche. Once you have the homepage set up as you like it, you can set it as your browser's default URL. You could also use a tool such as WebDesktop (*stevenf.com/software/webdesktop*) to display your personalised homepage on your Mac's desktop, setting it to refresh every so often.

APPLICATIONS AND MORE

Language tools

Google also has its own translation service – it's at *google.co.uk/language_tools* – and while no translation tools will give perfect results, it's good to have an option of using them. Like the venerable Babel Fish service at *babelfish.altavista.com*, Google offers you the ability to translate entire web pages in one go.

Analytics

Many website packages include basic web traffic statistics packages, but Google's own package, dubbed Analytics, and found at *google.co.uk/analytics*, is spectacular. The level of granular detail continues to astonish us, particularly given that it's free. If you have a website, you have nothing to lose by signing up for Analytics, and you'll almost certainly gain a much deeper understanding of how people are interacting with your site. There's also a very nice little Widget for viewing Analytics from Mac OS X's Dashboard layer; find it at *dashalytics.rovingrob.com*.

Reader

Google also has its own online RSS reader. Unlike the pairing of the desktop NetNewsWire application with an online service such as Newsgator – which allows you to sync from desktop to online and vice versa – Google Reader at *google.co.uk/reader* is an online-only system. This doesn't mean it's underpowered, though; indeed, it's more richly featured than some desktop clients we've used, and allows you to import and export lists of feeds from any serious RSS reader. You could use Reader to link together dynamic RSS feeds that you've created with, say, blog searches from Google's blog search page, and have access to them from any Internet-connected computer in the world.

Maps and Earth

Google Maps (*maps.google.co.uk*) have supplanted tools such as MapQuest and Streetmap for us. The service exemplifies Google's commitment to pared-down interfaces behind which immense power lies, and it's a great way to check where meetings are taking place or track down local amenities. Its API allows it to be integrated into your site with relative ease – take a look at *ononemap.com* for example – and again there's a lot of functionality tucked in behind the surface. The stand-alone application Google Earth (*earth.google.com*) performs some of the same functions, presented in a 3D environment, with emphasis on satellite imagery rather than schematic maps.

Docs and Spreadsheets

Writely, the online word processor that was one of the darlings of the early Web 2.0 movement, was acquired by Google in March 2006, and is now offered by it as part of its Docs & Spreadsheet bundle at *docs.google.com*. Though these don't have the same slick interface or user-friendliness offered by Zoho's suite, they're genuinely very powerful, and for anything up to and including middleweight uses, they compete on an equal footing with desktop applications such as those in Microsoft's Office suite. Both are collaborative, too, so you can easily invite others to contribute and publish the results. Being web-based, your documents are stored centrally – accessible from any Internet-connected computer on the planet – and you can upload documents in a range of formats, or email them directly to your Docs account.

Page Creator

Released to little fanfare a year ago, Google Page Creator (*pages.google.com*) gives you a basic set of tools with which you can build simple websites. They're hosted by Google – you get 100MB of free storage – though one criticism levelled at the system is that because the URL for your pages is based around your Gmail address, you could be opening yourself to spammers. Regardless, it's a handy way to throw up a few simple pages for a club or the like.

Widgets

From the page at *google.co.uk/macwidgets*, you can download Widgets for Tiger's Dashboard that give you access to posting to Blogger, Google's blogging platform, viewing your Gmail inbox, and showing your search history. You can also download a handy notifier that sits in your menu bar and alerts you to incoming Gmail email and upcoming Google Calendar events; it's at *google.co.uk/mac*.

Groups

Google groups (*groups.google.co.uk*) both offers you the ability to search through old Usenet archives, and to create groups of your own. These give you the ability to bring together groups of people for discussions – that can take place using email or through a web-based online system – create custom pages filled with rich text and graphics, and host shared files.

Gmail and Calendar

There remains little more to be said about Google's excellent email service that hasn't already been said. You get more than 2GB of storage space, a rich online email client, plus the ability to pull email securely down to your Pop3 desktop client. And that gets three cheers from us. Over at *calendar.google.com* you can access Google's online calendaring system, which allows you to subscribe to iCal-published calendars and vice versa.

TechTool Pro 5... coming soon!

Buy TechTool Pro 4 now...
...get a TechTool Pro 5 DVD upgrade FREE.*

*when it ships this summer. Does not apply to upgrade or update purchases.
Follow the instructions in the specially marked boxes.

TechTool Pro 4 – the complete Macintosh problem solving utility is now Leopard compatible.

Why throw away your money on a multitude of utilities that force you to learn different interfaces and deal with a variety of companies and/or different products? Micromat gives you everything you need in one box–for far less money. TechTool Pro is a complete Macintosh repair shop in a box. In fact, it's so good that Apple includes a copy of its sibling, TechTool Deluxe, in its AppleCare Protection Plan. If you experience freezes, kernel panics, or other problems, TechTool Pro can help you get your computer running smoothly again. Nothing else even comes close to TechTool Pro! Use TechTool Pro for:

Diagnostics and Repair
Ensure that your computer keeps running its best.

Optimization
Enhance the overall performance and simplify file layout of your hard drives.

Data Recovery
Recover important data from corrupted hard drives.

Safety
Protect your computer and hard drives automatically in the background.

eDrive
Create an emergency startup partition so TechTool Pro is always available.

TechTool Pro is a feature-packed release of the most comprehensive diagnostic, repair, and maintenance utility of all time! A must-have Macintosh application, this utility from Micromat is truly the one indispensable product you need to ensure your Mac is always trouble free.

Micromat, Inc., 5329 Skylane Blvd., Santa Rosa, CA 95403, USA
800-829-6227 707-566-3831 info@micromat.com www.micromat.com

Also From Micromat
DiskStudio &
TechToolProtege

WEBSITE
IN A WEEKEND

Could you build a dynamic website, complete with blogging and e-commerce tools, in 48 hours? We test nine CMS applications that can help you do just that.

Surely anyone can build a website in a weekend? Armed with a copy of iWeb, it's possible to create presentable pages in no time. But could you go a step further and build a dynamic website with easily updateable content in 48 hours?

Building dynamic websites isn't as difficult as you might think, thanks to the availability of content management systems (CMS). These work in a similar way to blogging applications: they separate content – a website's text and images – from its appearance and management, so it's easy for more than one person to edit. As the CMS resides on a web server, updating its contents is easy no matter where you are.

Most CMSes are modular, which makes it easy to add functionality, whether it's a shopping cart or an interactive forum. But perhaps the best thing about a CMS is that you don't need to be a coding expert to create a website. CMSs ship with ready-made themes that define a website's look. In most cases changing the site's appearance can be simply a matter of selecting a different theme and uploading it to your site.

In the past, the drawback of web-based CMSes was that they cost thousands of pounds, with hefty annual support costs. That fact alone ruled them out for many individuals and small companies. Their features were limited, too, and adding content could be an arcane process.

Since then the situation has changed. CMSes are available for a fraction of the cost – many are even free – and the number and variety of features on offer has ballooned. We've looked at some of the most popular low-cost systems on the market to find out how well they are suited to personal sites and business websites. The CMSes range from free or open-source applications with the backing of a large developer, to fully supported commercial offerings.

Their system requirements are broadly similar: most are based on PHP, a scripting language that runs on your website's server. This means you'll need to check with your ISP that your site supports PHP. CMSes are also built around a database – most frequently a variation of the popular SQL database – so your website provider will need to offer that too.

WORDPRESS

Contact *wordpress.org*
Price *free*

There can be few content management systems that are easier to manage than WordPress. Even its installation process – frequently a showstopper with such systems – is a cinch. Once you've downloaded the program folder from the WordPress website, you simply enter the MySQL database details supplied by your ISP into a configuration file, upload it with the rest of your WordPress files to your server's web space and step through the browser-based setup script. Your site should be up and running in minutes.

Although WordPress has a reputation as a blogging tool, the program's open source status has encouraged a vibrant developer community to build powerful plug-ins that take the program into the realms of low-end content managers. It's not as if boosting WordPress's power is difficult, either: you simply download the well-documented plug-ins from the WordPress site, upload them to your WordPress plug-ins directory and activate them inside WordPress.

This may satisfy business users who would otherwise find WordPress lacking some high-end options. For example, there are no built-in e-commerce functions, but you can download a free module (*instinct.co.nz/e-commerce*) that does the job very well. Similarly, those who want to display an online portfolio might be initially disappointed that there is no image gallery, but there's plenty of choice when it comes to plug-ins, including the excellent YAPB (*johannes. jarolim.com/blog/wordpress/yet-another-photoblog*).

WordPress's Dashboard administration section, an area hidden from site visitors where you manage blog content and layout, is well organised. Under the Write tab you can generate either blog-style posts or create pages for static content that's unlikely to change frequently. This provides a lot of flexibility, even allowing you to add custom fields or metadata to a post. WordPress offers good access management, so you can determine who can post or edit entries, upload images or authorise user comments. RSS support is top-notch too. WordPress not only lets you generate RSS feeds for recently changed content, but also lets users subscribe to comments made to blog posts – handy if you want to keep up to date with what's being said about your site.

The application comes with only a couple of built-in themes, but the WordPress website includes an extensive library of user-contributed themes, helpfully divided into categories. To use these themes you simply upload them to the themes directory on your website.

WordPress also makes it easy to import content from other blogs or CMS engines. Scripts are available for converting content from two dozen rival applications. Even neater is the ability to import data using the syndicated RSS feed from any website. Just save the feed locally, navigate to it in WordPress and click the Import button.

Unlike most other CMSes, updating your WordPress installation is as easy as setting it up in the first place. Simply delete your old WordPress files, keeping those you've modified, and upload the new ones.

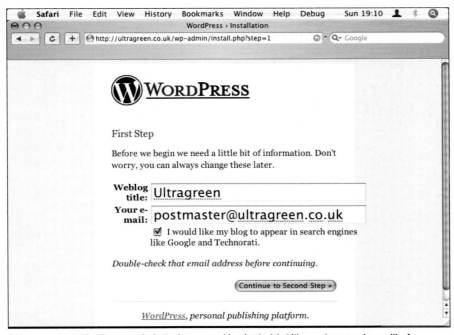

▲ The open-source WordPress may be better known as a blogging tool, but it's easy to use, and a wealth of sophisticated CMS features are available through plug-ins, thanks to its thriving community of developers.

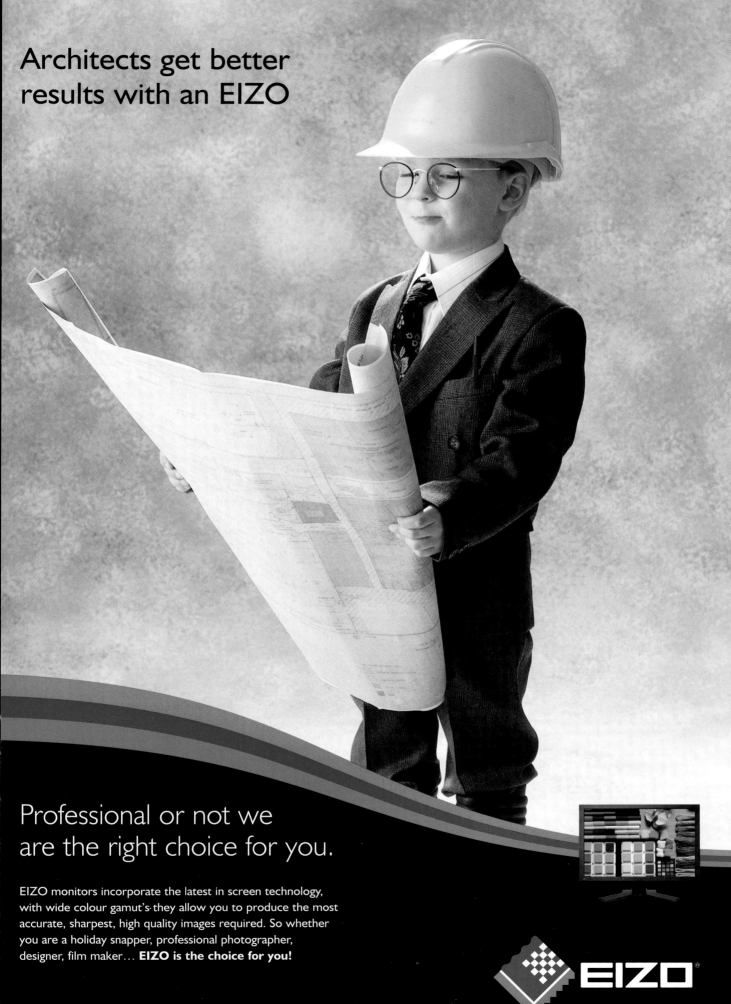

Architects get better
results with an EIZO

Professional or not we
are the right choice for you.

EIZO monitors incorporate the latest in screen technology,
with wide colour gamut's· they allow you to produce the most
accurate, sharpest, high quality images required. So whether
you are a holiday snapper, professional photographer,
designer, film maker… **EIZO is the choice for you!**

EIZO®

CMS MADE SIMPLE

Contact cmsmadesimple.org
Price free

As its name suggests, the open-source CMS Made Simple 1.1 is another web application that can help you build dynamic websites quickly. Installation is straightforward and – although it won't win any prizes for its looks – the Admin Panel is just as easy to understand as WordPress's. CMS Made Simple also provides excellent, well-written documentation in the form of a 'wiki'.

As with most other content management applications, CMS Made Simple separates content from style. The Admin Panel includes the JavaScript-based TinyMCE Wysiwyg text editor, which enables users who have little or no coding experience to style text and other content to make it visually appealing.

CMS Made Simple works along familiar principles. Web pages are based on templates that include variable 'tags'. These take information from the underlying database that defines how a page appears to a user. The templates can be fully

▲ A free version of Quick.Cms is available, but it's worth paying €21 (about £15) for the superior standard version, which adds photo gallery and news modules as well as the ability to create RSS feeds.

customised and the library of tags, while limited compared with some alternatives, is at least easy to understand.

Cascading style sheets (CSS) define the way templates look. Each default template has five general stylesheets already applied to it and one template-specific stylesheet attached. You can edit the style sheets by opening an 'edit stylesheet' form and pasting in fresh CSS code: there are no fancy extras such as versioning available. It's certainly a bare-bones approach, but it works well.

CMS Made Easy is a promising tool for managing web content. It doesn't yet have anything like the same extensive user community that surrounds the likes of WordPress, Drupal or Joomla, which inevitably means you have less choice when it comes to add-on modules. While modules are available that extend CMS Made Simple into a full e-commerce application and enable you to host an image gallery, in general they are not up to the same polished standard as those in other CMS applications. If your needs are simple, though, or you just want to dip a toe into CMS modules, CMS Made Simple provides much of what you need.

QUICK.CMS

Contact opensolution.org
Price free

The tiny Quick.Cms application is an ideal introduction to content management, as it's a doddle to set up and use. Its other principal advantage is that, unlike almost every other comparable tool, it doesn't rely on an SQL database to run. Instead, it does everything through PHP scripting – so your web server will have to be PHP compatible. The absence of a central database may not be too much of a drawback, because the small site we set up in Quick.Cms felt nippy, although we imagine data-heavy sites would struggle to cope under the strain.

As you'd expect, Quick.Cms separates content from style. By default, a single CSS file governs the site's appearance, although you can add further CSS files to the templates directory and apply them through the configuration menu.

Content creation is rudimentary. You create pages, which can be sub-pages or master pages and are categorised so that

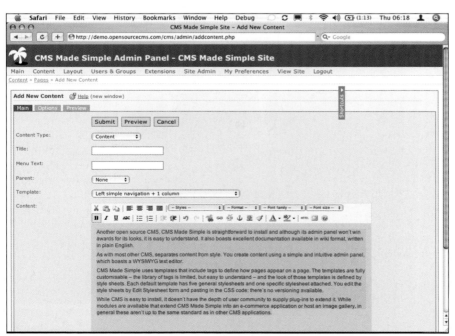

▲ It's not exactly beautiful, but CMS Made Simple's Admin Panel is easy to use and offers useful features such as the JavaScript-based TinyMCE Wysiwyg text editor, which lets users style text visually without the need for any coding.

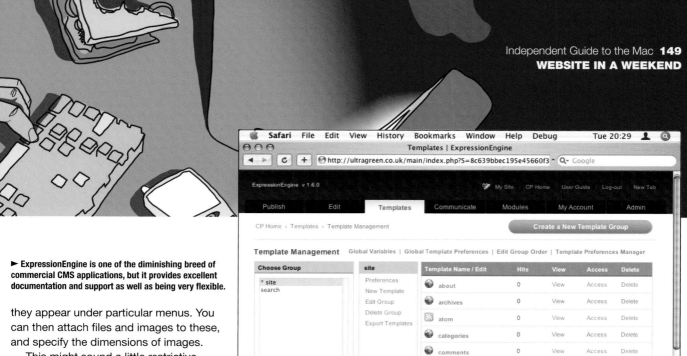

▶ ExpressionEngine is one of the diminishing breed of commercial CMS applications, but it provides excellent documentation and support as well as being very flexible.

they appear under particular menus. You can then attach files and images to these, and specify the dimensions of images.

This might sound a little restrictive, and there's little doubt that while setting up simple content management is easy, taking it much further is difficult without extra work. Quick.Cms has no concept of themes, for example, so if you want to modify the templates underlying your web pages, you'll need to master HTML or PHP coding.

A free version of the program is available, but the best value lies in the €21 (about £15) standard version, which includes a snappy, if unsophisticated, photo gallery, a dedicated news module and the ability to create RSS feeds. There's also a €59 (about £40) extended version, which adds features such as site maps, contact forms and newsletters. Although they're not bundled with Quick.Cms, the developer also offers a freeware shopping cart and forum module on its website.

EXPRESSION ENGINE
Contact *expressionengine.com*
Price from £50

EllisLab's ExpressionEngine is one of an increasingly rare breed of proprietary CMS, although at about £50 for a personal licence and £125 for the full commercial version, it still qualifies as affordable for personal or business use. There is also a free version, ExpressionEngine Core, for personal or non-profit use, which lacks a couple of the full version's features.

ExpressionEngine's installation is straightforward – you simply adjust a few permissions when you upload the ExpressionEngine directory to your website – and most of the installation is scripted through a browser.

The principles used to set up a website with ExpressionEngine can take some getting used to, but the application is backed by thorough documentation and

– as you would expect from a commercial program – good support. There are also excellent tutorial videos that explain the basics of the program.

An ExpressionEngine site can contain any number of 'weblogs'. These are not blogs in their traditional sense, but simple data containers that can hold information in discrete blocks on a page. Unusually, you can add custom fields easily to weblogs – anything from text to images or drop-down menus. Even more unusually, you can have as many weblogs as you want on your site.

ExpressionEngine relies on editable templates that are converted into HTML pages only when a user visits the site. This allows information to be presented dynamically through tags that pull content from the underlying database. These features give ExpressionEngine almost limitless flexibility.

Templates are edited either through ExpressionEngine's well-designed and attractive administration panel or – if you're wedded to desktop applications – through a standard FTP connection, which enables you to use third-party authoring applications such as Dreamweaver or BBEdit. Editing in the administration panel offers the advantage of 'versioning', where ExpressionEngine stores previous versions of templates enabling you to return to them at any point.

ExpressionEngine has some unique features. One that's particularly useful to designers is the built-in Image Gallery module. This isn't a half-baked plug-in: it supports image watermarking, cropping,

resizing, rotation and thumbnailing. ExpressionEngine also ships with a Simple Commerce module that lets you sell items through PayPal – something that most of the systems we looked at lack, although you can easily add shopping carts to Drupal and Joomla through plug-ins.

A powerful built-in forum module shares login information with other areas of the site, which is useful. It also uses the same database as the rest of ExpressionEngine, so you don't need an additional SQL database to run it. The downside is that it costs an additional $100 (about £50) – on top of the standard commercial licence. Another add-on is the multiple site manager, which allows you to create and manage multiple websites from a single ExpressionEngine installation. This costs £200 on top of the price of the main program.

Another plus for this program is its apparent security. In the past it has suffered less from security breaches than most systems, and it provides built-in spam-blocking tools, such as Captchas, which ask users to verify that they are a person rather than a web bot by entering text hidden in an image before they can enter comments and registration forms.

ExpressionEngine's disadvantage, apart from the fact that you have to fork out money for it, is that as it is a commercial application it has a smaller user community than most other systems. That means there are fewer third-party modules on offer. It's just as well that those available are so good.

audio-technica
always listening

Music to our ears

"Audio Technica's ATH-ANC7 is the best-sounding set we've heard, and includes active noise cancelling to reduce background noise."
Computer Shopper – July 2007

"Their isolation is excellent, and there's great timing and dynamic, detailed delivery... decent cans with excellent noise cancelling ability."
What HiFi? – June 2007

"Which of these models should you choose? ... when you throw price into the mix with comfort, noise reduction, and sound quality, my pick is Audio-Technica's ATH-ANC7."
Playlistmag.com – August 2007

"Not only do these little wonders provide superior sound quality but they also kicked some Bose butt in the noise cancellation category."
Gadling.com - September 2007

"...another winner... comfy, solidly built, absolutely great-sounding headphones. The circuitry cuts out a huge swath of engine, road or train noise, and the music is crystal clear."
The Ledger – June 2007

"...the Audio-Technica ATH-ANC7 is a serious piece of work at a seriously good price."
Sound & Vision Magazine – May 2007

"Amazing sound, balanced and sweet, from Segovia to Snoop Dogg. Lightweight and comfortable."
Wired Magazine – May 2007

ANC7

Available on the Apple Store online at **www.apple.com/ukstore** and priced at just £129.95

▲ Despite a fearsome reputation, Drupal offers a powerful modular approach to dynamic website creation for those willing to put the effort into learning how it works.

DRUPAL

Contact *drupal.org*
Price free

The open-source Drupal has a reputation for being one of the most powerful modular tools for managing content. Despite this, it's a fairly small application. The core version takes up only a couple of megabytes of space on a web server.

Drupal is also known for being difficult to use. That was certainly true of earlier versions, where even the installation routine could put off prospective users. Version 5 comes with an install script, which makes installation much simpler.

That said, Drupal and its terminology still demand a lot of the newcomer. For a start, its content is housed in individual 'nodes', which can comprise anything from stories – generally news-type entries that have an expiry date – or blog entries to pages or even part of a forum. This can be a difficult concept to grasp.

Drupal uses a simple HTML-like template language, and templates are modified through the admin panel, where you can also create menus and sidebars as well as add blocks of HTML for site navigation.

Once you understand how Drupal works, you'll have little doubt as to its power. A single installation can host several Drupal-powered sites in a single directory, each with its own configuration settings. You can add modules or themes to individual sites by creating new modules or themes folders in that site's subfolder.

► Joomla is a fairly large download, but it's packed with useful features, such as installation scripts, that make life easier.

Drupal offers excellent RSS support. By default you can create an RSS feed of your site's frontpage items, and there's an RSS feed aggregator that can import RSS feeds and present them as a set of HTML pages.

Another impressive feature is the Book, which groups sets of pages together. This makes Drupal good for teaching or collaborative work. A basic forum module is included, and you can turn it on simply by activating a checkbox.

Tweaking sites in Drupal isn't as easy as it could be, but there are six themes that you can switch between easily. These can also be configured quickly through a checkbox list to show important page elements, such as logos and site names.

Adding modules to the program isn't difficult – usually it's enough just to copy the module into the Drupal modules folder.

JOOMLA

Contact *joomla.org*
Price free

Joomla is a relatively recent arrival but, like Drupal, it's an open-source CMS

application that runs on the combination of PHP and MySQL, and can trace its heritage back to the highly popular Mambo CMS from which it developed.

Joomla runs on a MySQL database. A hefty 11MB installation, it isn't exactly svelte, but the extra time it takes to download pays immediate dividends. Most other CMSes require you to adjust file permissions manually to make sure that the correct folders and files are writable. That almost inevitably means a trip to an FTP application. But Joomla offers helpful installation scripts that flag potential permissions problems before the installation takes place, letting you know which you can safely ignore.

Joomla's Control Panel could lay claim to being the best-looking on the market, and offers management tools that allow you to limit authoring, editing or admin access. You can enter text content through a Wysiwyg editor.

As with other content management systems, Joomla uses templates to control the appearance of your website, and these are maintained separately from website content. Modules, such as menus or polls, add functionality to the templates.

Joomla also has an extensive pool of additional, user-created modules. Although the application doesn't come with a built-in forum module, for example, an integrated and sophisticated forum, Fireboard, can be installed in a few clicks.

Joomla doesn't offer the same multiple site management features as Drupal, but few users will stretch its capabilities. ⊕

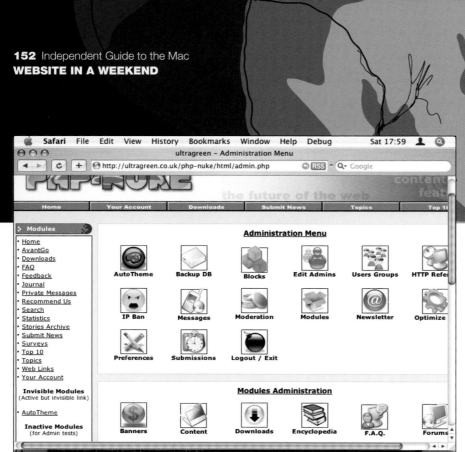

▲ PHP-Nuke's origins as a news publishing system can still be seen in its administration screen, which has modules for news and advertising. This CMS is one of the oldest and has 175,000 registered users, but its popularity is falling.

E107

Contact *e107.org*
Price free

Like most other CMSs, e107 uses the standard MySQL/PHP combination. Tailored as a general CMS, it's suitable for the beginner who's starting their first dynamic website. While it lacks thorough documentation, its well-written wiki compensates and it features useful 'how to' guides that cover topics such as how to add JavaScript to your site, or speed up page loading.

The administration panel lacks the sort of polish found in some other CMSes, but while e107 has far fewer plug-in modules available than WordPress or Drupal, there are powerful modules available, particularly for handling community forums. There are even bridges to popular forums such as phpBB, that can share user registration information with the main site.

If you're thinking of professional uses for your site, e107 offers a basic e-commerce module and comes with built-in features including banner management. Configuring your own standalone pages can be tricky though – and a fair understanding of PHP code is recommended.

▶ e107's interface lacks polish, but it offers basic e-commerce tools and includes 'how to' guides for beginners.

PHP-NUKE

Contact *phpnuke.org*
Price $12 (about £6)

Released nearly a decade ago, PHP-Nuke is one of the oldest content management systems, with 175,000 registered users. It was originally free software, but downloading the latest version costs $12.

PHP-Nuke works with SQL databases and requires PHP to be installed on the web server. It started life as a news publishing system, and although it has broadened its horizons into full-scale content management since then, it's much better at building news-led websites than online communities.

This bias is evident from the modules in the cluttered administration screen. The News module is for uploading news, while an Advertising module helps you set up banner ads and a download module is available for website visitors. PHP-Nuke's strong points include an easy-to-use newsletter generator, a poll module that lets you host surveys and a 'top 10' module that automates the creation of links to your most popular pages. There are also a few elements missing, most notably image gallery and shopping cart modules, and while the existing modules are useful, tweaking them is awkward.

Other drawbacks include the lack of a true built-in Wysiwyg editor, and the most difficult-to-read documentation we've ever seen in a CMS module.

More seriously, the program has been criticised in the past for its security leaks, and recent versions don't appear to have addressed this. Perhaps as a result of this – and because it's difficult to download a recent version – it has lost popularity to rivals, although it still offers a wide range of user-contributed modules.

MOVABLE TYPE

Contact *movabletype.org*
Price personal version free

Movable Type is certainly one of the most flexible CMSes around in terms of the range of databases that it can communicate with. As well as the popular MySQL, Movable Type works with several other database flavours; the Enterprise version of the software can be installed on Oracle databases, which makes it ideal for some corporate environments.

Movable Type is a hefty 4MB download, and despite a fresh installation wizard in the new version, it's still not quite as easy to get up and running as WordPress. But its administration panel is impeccably user friendly, dividing functions logically into Create, Manage, Design and Preferences sections.

However, while WordPress is written in PHP and is easy for anyone with basic web skills to implement and tweak, Movable Type is written in Perl. This is arguably more powerful and opens up new channels onto the server, which means it must sometimes be installed in a specific directory where its permissions can be controlled. As such, novices may do better using its hosted *typepad.com* service.

When editing entries, you have access to a full Wysiwyg editor, and you can assign publication dates and choose whether each entry is trackable – this feature lets you see which other websites are linking to your post – or accept comments from browsers to your site.

Movable Type's most obvious highlights are its support for unlimited blogs and a neat asset and file manager. This allows the system to track every image or other asset uploaded to your blogs, which makes them easy to re-use.

The application is also highly customisable. Like other CMSes, it uses a number of user-definable templates to generate pages, while variable content is added through Movable Type's own HTML-like template tags. It doesn't offer the same powerful custom fields as some systems, but plug-ins that add this functionality are available from the Movable Type website, and are clearly documented. One caveat is that the recent upgrade to version 4 may have broken some modules, but upgrades are arriving quickly.

Although CMSes are ideal for creating dynamic websites, with content fed from an SQL database when it is needed, Movable Type 4 makes it easy to create static web pages too. There is logic behind this dual approach. In general, static web pages load much faster than dynamic ones, so if your site has a lot of content that doesn't change, such a feature could be an advantage.

Movable Type was the first popular blogging tool to introduce support for trackbacks, but its RSS support isn't quite as powerful as that offered by WordPress

– it would be handy, for example, if you could subscribe to comments made to blog posts.

Fortunately, Movable Type 4 has a few tricks of its own. It includes OpenID support for people who comment on Movable Type posts. Any user can sign in to a Movable Type site using their OpenID details and comment without having to supply a site-specific login or password.

Like ExpressionEngine, Movable Type lets you create your own fields in individual blogs, although only as a plug-in module.

CONCLUSION

It's impossible to measure the merits of CMSes precisely against each other. Many are built for different purposes – PHP-Nuke, for example, was built as an engine for a news-driven site, while WordPress has its origins in the blogging arena.

Even taking that into account, if one content management application lacks a feature compared with a rival, there will probably be a plug-in somewhere that fills the gap. And as most CMSes are based on the PHP scripting language, it's possible – if you're prepared to get your hands dirty with code – to tweak whatever CMS you choose to suit your particular needs.

That said, if you want a CMS up and running over a weekend for personal use, it's hard to see beyond WordPress. We don't know a CMS that is easier to set up. What really stands out in its favour is the

breadth of its development community. Rival applications such as Movable Type may look more polished and have more built-in functionality, but many of its features can be replicated in WordPress through user-contributed plug-ins.

The choice is even more difficult when it comes to recommending a CMS for commercial purposes. PHP-Nuke may be fine for a news-driven site, but it's not suited to more general sites, and its lack of documentation and security concerns stand against it. CMS Made Easy is simple to use, but isn't as extensible as others.

Out of the box, Drupal is the most powerful CMS we looked at, with the most extensible architecture, as well as a massive user community that regularly submits additional modules. But it is also arguably the most complicated to use, and would take a fair amount of learning to begin to get the most out of it. Joomla, while not as feature-laden, is easier to use. That's important in a commercial environment where the tasks of updating and editing the website may be shared between a number of people.

However, if we were to pick the ideal CMS application for commercial use, we'd have to plump for EllisLab's ExpressionEngine. It's not open source like Drupal or Joomla, but it has two critical advantages. First, it has excellent support, and second, its approach is so flexible that we could see it being equally at home handling a single designer's website or a corporate site with huge traffic. ⊗

▲ MovableType 4 comes in a range of versions, from the free personal version to a five-user one. The Enterprise version supports Oracle as well as PHP, which makes it suitable for corporate websites.

100

MAC TIPS

We have gathered together all the top tips
and tricks that you'll ever need to make
the most of your Mac.

For years, Apple has been encouraging us to 'Work Smarter', the
implication being that this will happen automatically as soon as you
buy a Mac. In truth it takes a bit more than that. Like any large and
complex system, your Mac is a rich environment that demands
exploration. Behind the obvious headline features lie many smaller
ones that simply make it easier to do things, or provide alternatives
that will let you do those things in your own preferred way. And
behind all of this there are numerous shortcuts and settings that
may go unnoticed or may even be undocumented.

Perhaps surprisingly, it's often the experienced user who misses
out. When you are used to how things work, it's easy to overlook
that new button in a rarely seen dialogue or the changed menu item
that offers new functionality. Even knowing that a particular feature
is there, it takes some effort to incorporate it into one's natural way
of working. After you've installed a new version of any software it's
always worth checking its Help file. Most Apple Help files now
provide a What's New section that covers the main changes.

Working smarter means more than just learning tips and
remembering techniques, however, and in this feature we'll
cover hints on how to optimise your Mac for performance and
how to deal with and prevent problems that could bring your
Mac grinding to a halt. It's the only tips feature you need, and
it starts just across the page.

Dashboard & Exposé

◄ ► | Show All | Q

Exposé allows you to temporarily see all your open windows at once, so you can easily click on any window to bring it to the front. You can set a Dashboard shortcut to show or hide the Dashboard.

Active Screen Corners

All Windows ⬍ — ⬍

Application Windows ⬍ — ⬍

Keyboard Shortcuts

All windows: F9 ⬍

Application windows: F10 ⬍

Desktop: F11 ⬍

Dashboard: F12 ⬍

For more shortcut choices, press the Shift, Control, Option, or Command keys. (?)

◄ GATHERING WINDOWS IN EXPOSÉ

Most Mac users are familiar with using F9 and F10 to toggle Exposé on and off, but did you know that you can also usefully combine the actions of these two keys? Normally, F9 shows reduced versions of all the currently open windows, while F10 reveals all the windows belonging to the currently active application. However, if you have several windows belonging to the same application, then pressing F9 and selecting one of those will bring only that one window to the front. This can be particularly frustrating if you want to switch to the Finder in order to move or copy some files, and only one Finder window comes to the front. Instead, you can press F9 to show all windows, hover the cursor over the one you want to be foremost, then press F10 twice. The first press will gather together the windows belonging to that application and put them all in front of windows from any other applications, the second will get you out of Exposé and back to the normal Finder view. If you prefer, you can change the default Exposé keys for something else.

Work Smarter

USING THE CALCULATOR

Macs have provided a Calculator application right from the beginning. Over that time, its capabilities have been steadily increasing, but with little fanfare, so you may not have noticed some of the many things that Calculator now offers. For example, use the Paper Tape option (View > Show Paper Tape) to create a printable tape that records a whole sequence of calculations step-by-step. If you prefer, you can type your calculation directly onto the tape and click Recalculate Totals to show the result. The Convert functions are also very handy, allowing you to convert between all sorts of everyday measurements as well as various technical and scientific units. Particularly useful is the currency conversion option, which covers most major currencies and lets you download the latest exchange rates for an up-to-date result. Finally, you can also swap the default simple calculator for a Scientific model with various mathematical functions or a Programmer's calculator which can handle geek arithmetic in hexadecimal, octal and binary. For an added display of calculating prowess, there's also an option to use Reverse Polish Notation (RPN) for your calculations (if you don't know what this is, you don't need it).

OPEN DOCUMENTS IN ANOTHER APPLICATION

It's very convenient that double-clicking a document will automatically launch its application if necessary. However, you don't always want to use the default application. To open a document in another application, but without changing the default, right-click the document and choose Open With from the contextual menu that pops up. This will display a list of applications that can open that type of file as well as an option to pick some other, non-standard application if need be.

CLIPPINGS

A quick way to save a copy of just about any picture that appears in a document is to drag it to the desktop. Your Mac will automatically save it as a Picture Clipping, retaining the original file format. Do the same with text, and you'll create a Text Clipping, but the process doesn't always work as smoothly. Some applications let you drag and drop the clipping with no problem, others assume that moving the cursor is a sign that you plan to alter the selection. In this case, it often works to press the mouse button and hold it for a second or two before you begin to drag. This gives the application time to work out your intentions, and a text clipping will be created on the desktop. Cluttering your screen desktop with file icons is generally not a good idea, but as a temporary measure it's an easy way to collect images and text snippets from all over before you file them away to somewhere more appropriate or drag them into another document or application.

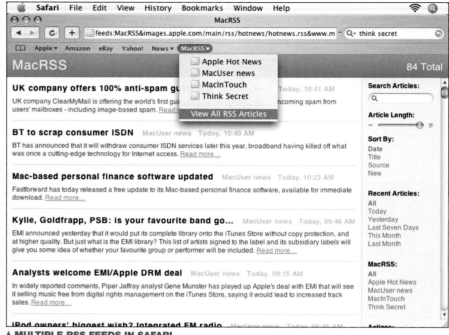

MULTIPLE RSS FEEDS IN SAFARI

Rather than show just one RSS feed at a time, Safari can aggregate feeds from multiple sites into a single window and display them all together. Start by creating a new Bookmarks folder (Bookmarks > Add Bookmark Folder), then place a bookmark in it for each feed that you want to include. To display the articles, click the Show All Bookmarks icon and then control-click the relevant folder. This will bring up a small contextual menu where you need to select the first item: View All RSS Articles. Alternatively, you could place the folder in your Bookmarks Bar, click on it to reveal its drop-down list and select View All RSS Articles from there. The articles from all the chosen feeds will now appear interleaved in time order with the source feed listed alongside each title. Look at the sidebar on the right of the window and you'll see that under the heading RSS Feeds you now have a list of all the sources as well as All. Clicking here lets you narrow down the view to any one feed or go back to showing them all. Additionally, if you change any of these parameters, the URL in the address bar changes too, allowing your filtered search to be itself bookmarked.

SEARCHING SAFARI HISTORY

So you've seen a useful web page earlier, but forgot to bookmark it, and now you need to find it. Rather than scroll through the thousands of items in your History folders, you can use Safari to search through the History entries. Click on Show All Bookmarks (the open book icon at the left of your Safari Bookmarks Bar), select History from the list of Collections in the left-hand sidebar. Go to the search field at the foot of the window, select In History from its pop-up and enter a search term into the field. Safari will search the URL and the page title, so it should be possible to find what you want or at least narrow the field.

EXTRA DOCK OPTIONS

As well as providing quick application switching, the Dock also gives you access to other controls. Rather than just click on an icon, press and hold the mouse button over it – after about a second, a pop-up menu will appear with various options. Some of these, such as Quit, Hide and Show in Finder, appear on all applications, but others are application-specific, which, for example, allows you to Get New Mail in Apple Mail or to change the Repeat and Shuffle settings in iTunes. When an application has more than one window open, its Dock pop-up lets you switch between them. You can access the pop-ups instantly by right-clicking any icon in the dock.

◄ SPOTLIGHT COMMENTS

There are so many items of metadata that can be attached to any file it's sometimes hard to know which ones to use. For example, you could group files that relate to the same project by placing them all in a common folder, by giving them a name that includes the project, by giving them a coloured label (select the file or files, click the action button in the Finder window's toolbar, and pick a colour), or by using Spotlight Comments (select the file, press Command-i and enter keywords or the project name into the Spotlight Comments field). Use whichever one of these feels right – but Comments are less immediately accessible, so they are good for data that won't change, while Label Colour is easy to change and to see, so it may be better suited to temporary use such as marking up files that need urgent attention. Of course, with media files, there is a vast list of additional metadata fields that can be employed.

▲ CREATING CUSTOM KEYBOARD SHORTCUTS

For anyone working in a primarily text-based environment, keyboard shortcuts are a great time-saver, allowing you to access most commands without having to fiddle with the mouse. Not all software is equally good at providing shortcuts though, so it's just as well you can create your own generic or application-specific shortcuts very easily. Begin by noting down exactly what the menu item is called – it's the name of the command itself that you need, not the name of the menu it appears in. Next, open the Keyboard & Mouse pane of System Preferences and click on the Keyboard Shortcuts tab. You'll see a list of all the System keyboard shortcuts that Apple provides. Click on the '+' button that's below this list. This will open a dialogue where you can select the application and enter the name of the menu command. Finally, click on the Keyboard Shortcut field and press the actual keys that you want to assign to this shortcut. Then click Add. You can also create a generic shortcut by selecting All Applications rather any specific one.

▼ SPOTLIGHT SYSTEM PREFERENCES

System Preferences are generally quite logical, but some topics inevitably span several panes. Mouse settings, for example, appear in Universal Access and Dashboard & Exposé, as well as the obvious Keyboard & Mouse. You can find all the panes that relate to a particular topic by typing it into the Spotlight field at the top of the System preferences window. A drop-down list of settings will appear and the appropriate Preferences pane for each one will be spot lit.

▲ iCAL CALENDAR GROUPS

iCal's ability to store multiple calendars is great for differentiating work and home commitments, or for keeping a whole family's diaries together in one place and yet separate. In the latest version of iCal, you can take this idea even further by making use of Calendar Groups. Choose File > New Calendar Group or just press Shift-Command-n to create a new group, which will appear in the Calendars list on the left of the window. It operates much like a folder so you can drag any calendar that's on the list into the group. The benefit is that you can now hide or reveal multiple calendars with just a single mouse click. Of course, you can still control each grouped calendar individually when you need to.

THE INSPECTOR

If you select a file and press Command-i, you'll open its Get Info window. But if you need to see Get Info for several files – perhaps to add a common Spotlight Comment to each one – then opening and closing Get Info every time will soon become very tedious. This is when you need to use The Inspector. Press Alt-Command-i and you'll open exactly the same Get Info window as before, the difference is that this window will remain open and display the data of any file you select in the Finder window. When you've finished, close the Inspector window.

SWITCH FINDER WINDOW VIEWS

To switch quickly between the different views available in a Finder window, you can press Command-1 for Icon view, Command-2 for List view and Command-3 for the Columns view.

MOVE UP THE HIERARCHY

One useful Windows feature that the Mac lacks is a button to take you up one level in the folder hierarchy to the folder or volume that contains the currently displayed level. However, you can achieve this easily by pressing Command-up arrow.

MIGHTY MOUSE BUTTONS

If you're using Apple's Mighty Mouse, make sure you're getting the full benefit of its four buttons. Most people won't want to change the behaviour of the main left-click and right-click buttons, but the scrollball and side buttons are up for grabs and they can usefully be programmed to do various tasks or to open any application. Choose Apple Menu > System Preferences > Keyboard & Mouse and click on the Mouse tab to change your mouse button settings.

SHIFT TO REVERSE

The Shift key is often used as a modifier to reverse the direction of a default action. For example in the Application Switcher, pressing Command-Tab moves you to the next application on the right, while Shift-Command-Tab moves you one application to the left. Similarly, in Safari, pressing the space bar scrolls a web page down by one screen, and pressing Shift-Space bar scrolls up by one screen.

OPENING DOCUMENTS FROM GET INFO

If you've opened a document's Get Info window to check details of the file or to see a preview of its contents, you can open the document directly without having to close Get Info and go back to the Finder window. Just double-click the preview panel.

► PRINTING ENVELOPES IN ADDRESS BOOK

The Address Book in Mac OS X Tiger onwards allows you to print envelopes directly from the application without having to copy the address label and paste it into a word processor. However, the technique is rather quirky. If you have a simple card for an individual or a business, there's no problem. Choose File > Print to open the Print dialogue and select Envelopes from the Styles field. Next, click on the Layout tab to choose an envelope size. By default, Address Book puts your return address in the top-left corner of the envelope, if you don't want to include it you'll need to click the Labels tab and de-select it. The process gets more complicated if you've entered a name into any of the family member fields, such as Spouse, Parent, Child and so on. Inexplicably, Address Book will include them all on the envelope. Thankfully, Apple hasn't extended this to include fields such as Friend or Manager, but it needs to be sorted out. Until then, you may want to put details of family members into the Notes field. Of course, there will be times when you want to write jointly to a couple, in which case you could create a duplicate card with the Spouse field filled in, but make sure you include both the first name and surname in the Spouse field.

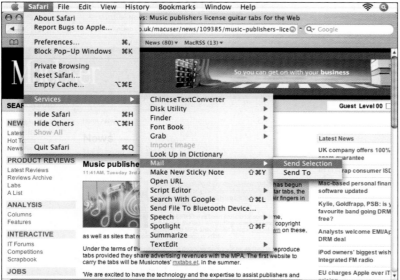

◄ SERVICES

Most applications include an item called Services in their application menu. This provides access to a strange ragbag of functions ranging from the obviously useful to the bizarrely esoteric. For example, how often do you need to calculate an Image Checksum or convert between Simplified and Traditional Chinese text? Making sense of Services isn't made easier by the fact that different items appear in the Services sub-menu according to which application you're in and, just because a command is there, doesn't always mean that it will work. Even so, it's worth looking at Services especially if you use a few applications regularly and so can become familiar with the particular facilities they offer. In many cases, you need to select something – often a piece of text – before you can apply a Services command to it. For example, one useful command creates an email with the currently selected text in the body of the message. Many applications will let you send the current document as an email attachment, but if you just want to send an extract, this is the easier option. Other useful commands will run a Google search on the selected text, create a Sticky Note from it or do a Spotlight search on it. In each case saving you from having to copy, switch application and then paste.

BE ORGANISED

According to the hype, you need never worry about where to save documents – just put them anywhere and let Spotlight find them when they're needed. It's true that Spotlight can track down anything anywhere, but that doesn't make reliance on Spotlight a smart strategy. Creating at least some basic folder structure gives you a better overview of what files you have relating to a particular subject, and is especially useful if you're working on a collaborative project. Also remember that when Spotlight returns a long list of matches, your ability to find the file you need often depends on knowing what it's called. A cryptically named file will be easier to find if it's in a sensible place than if it's floating in a free-form soup of files.

UNSAVED CHANGES

A quick visual check to show whether your document contains unsaved changes is to look at the Close button in the top-left corner of the window. If there are unsaved changes, this button will have a dark dot in the centre. Otherwise, its centre will be clear.

◄ TAB TO FIELDS OR TO ALL CONTROLS

Within any window or dialog box, pressing Tab will normally move focus to the next field or list, but you can extend this idea to allow buttons and other controls to be included in the tabbed sequence. To toggle between these two settings, just press Crtl-F7. Alternatively, you can make either behaviour the default. Just click Keyboard & Mouse in System Preferences and you'll find buttons to select the desired behaviour under the Keyboard Shortcuts tab. If you choose to allow tabbing to all controls, you'll be able to operate them from the keyboard, but you'll need to work out what keys to use. It's mostly fairly obvious – for example, in a vertical group of radio buttons you'd use the Up and Down Arrows to switch between them. In a pop-up list, those same keys will move through the list and Enter will confirm your choice. However, if you know what the list items are, you can often select one directly just by typing its initial letter. The situation with single buttons is less obvious, you'll need to press the space bar in order to toggle the button on or off. In an unfamiliar window all this can be confusing, but it's handy if you use an application regularly and know your way around it.

▲ SECURE YOUR FILES

Mac OS X doesn't allow individual folders or documents to be encrypted in situ, but it will let you create encrypted disk images that can contain any mix of applications, folders and documents. These encrypted images are protected by the AES-128 algorithm, which has never been broken and is approved by the US National Security Agency for secret documents. The slow way to create an encrypted disk image is to open the Disk Utility application and work through the process. A faster way is simply to drag the folder that you want to encrypt onto the Disk Image icon. This will launch Disk Utility and open a dialog box called New Image From Folder where you can name the disk image and specify a location where it will be saved. Unless this image is just for archiving, select Read/Write from the Image Format pop-up so that you can add, modify and delete the contents in future. Make sure you also select the encryption option (it's off by default), and then click Save. You'll be asked to enter and re-enter a password which can optionally be saved to your keychain. If you decide not to add it to your keychain, don't forget your password, as you won't be able to open the image again without it.

When the image has been created, you must delete the original folder and, preferably, use Finder > Secure Empty Trash to make sure that no easily recoverable traces remain of it. To access the contents of your secure disk image, just double-click it. Once you've supplied your password, this will mount the image which you can then open to show the contents. Provided you selected the Read/Write option, you'll be able to work with the files that are in the image and add new ones in the usual way. When you close and un-mount the image, everything inside it will once again be fully encrypted against the most prying of eyes.

▼ USING THE GRAPHER

Apple's free Grapher application, which lives in the Utilities folder inside your Applications folder, can do more useful things than might at first be obvious. Its main role is to plot 2D or 3D graphs of mathematical equations. You pick the style of plot you want (linear, logarithmic, polar, and the like), type in the equation and the graph appears. Rather less obviously, Grapher is an excellent way to produce your own blank graph paper. If you print the graph without first entering an equation, you'll get a blank sheet of graph paper that can be filled in by hand, which is useful if you just need an occasional sheet, and it could be handy in education too. Obviously, this works best on a laser printer rather than an inkjet. Another way to use Grapher is as an equation editor. Some applications, such as Microsoft Word, come with their own equation editor. Others, such as Apple Pages, don't. If you type the equation in Grapher, using its Symbol Palette for any special characters, it will be laid out in correct mathematical form. You can then copy this and paste it into another application.

▲ FINDER TOOLBAR AND SIDEBAR

The Dock isn't the only place where you can put commonly used files. Any application, folder or document can be dragged into the Finder sidebar and will then appear there in all Finder windows. You can also do this by selecting the item you want to put in the sidebar and pressing Command-t. Another even more prominent place for regularly used items is the toolbar that appears at the top of each Finder window. To move something into the toolbar, drag its icon there and hold it until a green '+' appears at the cursor. When you release the mouse button, the icon will be added to the toolbar in all Finder windows. To remove an icon from either place, right-click it and choose Remove From Sidebar or Remove Item.

▲ SAVED SEARCHES

There are lots of ways to make use of Saved Searches and it's worth doing so because they can really boost your efficiency whenever you need to perform a similar search more or less regularly. A Saved Search could be as simple as finding every Excel document on your hard disk or as complex as you want it to be. With metadata becoming more common and detailed in media files, the options for searching are expanding rapidly. To create a Saved Search you need to begin with the Finder's Find command and not with Spotlight. Choose File > Find or press Command-f to open the Find window. Using the pop-ups, select the attribute you want to match and what value it should have. You can add or delete criteria by clicking the '+' or '-' buttons at the end of each line. The button bar above lets you confine the search to a specific folder, disk or server. To see the full range of attributes or values that can be searched, choose Other from any of the pop-ups and you'll get a long list of possible options including such detailed attributes as the focal length of lens used to take a photo or the language of a text-based file. In order to save the search, click on the Save button and specify a name and location. Because you're saving the search criteria rather than just the result of the search, you'll get up to date hits every time you run it.

SCROLLBALL ZOOM

Pressing the Ctrl key while rolling the scrollball on a mouse that has one lets you zoom-in to an enlarged image of everything that is on screen. This is an OS-level action that works in all applications and the Finder, but some applications also support useful actions when you Alt-scroll. For example, in Adobe Reader this will zoom the PDF within the window without altering the overall screen display. In iCal, Alt-scroll lets you increase or decrease the hours visible in either Day or Week view.

DROP ICONS – AND WINDOWS
Mac OS X uses a small amount of its memory to display every icon on your desktop. That means a performance hit for those with cluttered desktops.

And while the arrival of Exposé has meant its much easier to manage multiple open windows, your Mac is still using processor cycles to redraw each one. Try to only keep those windows that you need open.

RUN MAINTENANCE SCRIPTS
Mac OS X runs regular maintenance scripts to clear system logs and temporary files. Under Mac OS X versions prior to 10.4, these were scheduled to run in the small hours of the morning. If your Mac was turned off or asleep, the scripts didn't run. If you use pre-Tiger operating systems run a utility such as Cocktail (*macosxcocktail.com*), which runs these tasks at the click of a button.

Apple has changed the way maintenance scripts are run under Mac OS X 10.4 Tiger, so scripts should now run even if your Mac is switched off overnight. Reports suggest, however, that the new system is buggy so manual maintenance is still worthwhile.

MAKE FREE SPACE
There may be no better way of improving your Mac's performance than by increasing its Ram or investing in a faster hard drive. But you can still accelerate it without investing in hardware.

Removing unwanted files and folders is one of most effective – and, strangely, the most therapeutic – ways of keeping your Mac fast and trouble free.

The fewer files on your Mac, the quicker you can search it and the faster backups can be.

But free space is most critical in terms of raw performance. You should aim to keep at least 15 per cent – but preferably more – of your hard disk free to allow sufficient room for Mac OS X's virtual memory. Any less and Ram-hungry applications can slow to a crawl.

TRASH
The quickest way to grab disk space is to empty the Trash, but don't forget the Finder isn't the only place to delete files. Many applications have their own Trash, including iPhoto, iDVD and iMovie. You need to delete their trash from within the application.

DELETE APPLICATIONS
All those applications you're never likely to use can take up surprising amounts of disk space. Dragging the applications themselves to the Trash may the quickest way to get rid of them, but it's often their associated files that annex most space. Between them, the Garageband and iDVD support files in the Library/Application Support/directory on your Mac's hard disk use about 4GB. To delete files, it's best to use the applications original installer – it often has an uninstall option – or use the free AppDelete (*reggie.ashworth.googlepages.com/appdelete*).

DELETE UNWANTED PREFERENCES
Check your User's Library/Preferences folder for old, orphaned preferences files. They may not take up much space, but a corrupt preferences files can affect performance.

REMOVE CLASSIC
When was the last time you used Mac OS X's Classic Environment? To delete it – and save disk space – open the Mac OS 9 System Folder on your hard disk, drag its contents to the trash and empty it. Now log out and back in again and drag the folder itself to the trash and delete the Mac OS 9 applications folder.

LIMIT YOUR APPS
Mac OS X's excellent multitasking abilities have spoilt Mac users in recent years, allowing us to keep plenty of applications open at once. But it's common sense that you should run only the applications you need. The more applications you have running, the less Ram they can grab for themselves.

TAME SPOTLIGHT
Spotlight's content indexing marginally detracts from performance while it's taking place, so it's a good idea to prevent it indexing unnecessarily. Add volumes such as a scratch disks or backup volumes to Spotlight's privacy list in the Spotlight System Preferences pane. This ensures that only those volumes and folders you need indexed are included.

USE A SECOND DRIVE
To optimise the performance of demanding applications, such as audio and video programs or Photoshop, use a speedy second hard disk as a project or scratch disk and make sure it has plenty of free space. Don't allow Spotlight to index it.

CLEAN CACHES
Application caches hold frequently-used data to allow quicker access time. Ironically, some application caches can become bloated over time and detract from performance. Commonly affected applications include Dashboard widgets (delete the Dashboard cache from the DashboardClient folder in your user's Library/Caches directory) and Safari. You can delete Safari's cache from inside the application: just select Safari > Empty cache.

SLICK SAFARI
Other drags on Safari's performance include a bloated history list (to correct this, select History > Clear History). If you really want to start from scratch you can reset Safari (Safari > Reset Safari). Not only does it delete your cache and scrub your History list, but it also clears the Downloads window, removes cookies, saved AutoFill data and Google search entries.

LOG OUT OTHERS
Mac OS X's Fast User switching looks so impressive because it maintains other users' system resources while you're logged in. To get the most speed out of your Mac, though, make sure you're the only user connected.

▲ RE-INSTALL MAC OS X
The most drastic, but effective, way to optimise your Mac's performance is to re-install it over a clean disk. Mac OS X 10.4 users can do this without losing any of your important data if you first copy your existing Mac OS X installation to an external FireWire drive using a utility such as SuperDuper! (*shirt-pocket.com*).

Now reinstall Mac OS X from the install CD using the Erase and Install option. When you perform the installation, make sure you perform a Custom Install, so you can elect not to install printer drivers or languages that you don't need.

You can then use Apple's Migration Assistant tool to copy your most important settings from your backed-up system.

▼ CHECK ACTIVITY MONITOR
Regularly keep an eye on what's taxing your processor with Activity Monitor, a utility in your Applications/Utilities folder. Select All processes from Activity Monitor's toolbar drop-down menu, and click the %CPU heading to sort the processes by descending order of CPU usage. You don't even need to open the Activity monitor window to check processor and memory usage, or disk or network activity – just right-click on Activity Monitor's Dock icon to view those details from the Dock.

◄ FIND FREE SPACE
How do you find those applications and files that are eating up your free disk space? In the Finder choose File, Find and in New Search window, select Size and choose greater than 100MB – or whatever.

To find invisible files, under the Kind pull-down menu, select Other and choose Visibility from the list. Choose Visible or Invisible items.

▲ OPTIMISED EMAIL

Improve email performance by archiving old messages to a backup disk and starting afresh. It's easy to do: copy your Library/Mail folder to an external drive – if you want to do this with an Imap mail server's contents, temporarily choose 'Keep copies of messages for offline viewing' in Mail's Preferences Accounts pane, under the Advanced tab. You don't have to remove your entire message base. In Mail, create a new folder and drag older emails to it. Drag this to the desktop and archive to a CD or DVD. You can now move your originals to the Trash. The simplest way to boost your speed is to rebuild Mail's database index, shrinking it and in most cases making it much faster. Quit Mail, drag the Envelope Index out of your user's Library/Mail folder, and relaunch the program. Mail automatically re-imports messages.

▲ LIMIT YOUR FONTS

Application launch times and font menu performance can both be affected by too many fonts – especially if there's a corrupt font. Just about every Mac user has dozen or more fonts they're never likely to use. Remove unwanted ones using Apple's Font Book application, but first make sure that Apple's core list of necessary fonts isn't affected – check Apple's list at *docs.info.apple.com/article. html?artnum=25710*. It's wise – as with any optimisation tip – to make a backup before deleting anything. Font Book also instantly shows you duplicate fonts – a bullet (•) appears before the names of duplicates in the Font list. These can be safely removed. You can check individual fonts for corruption using File > Validate fonts.

▲ NO WIDGETS

Active widgets eat an extraordinary amount of Ram – sometimes up to 10MB each – considering the simple tasks they perform. While you can't turn off the Dashboard entirely, the golden rule with widgets is to treat them like applications, only opening them when you need them. To close a widget with Dashboard active, hold the alt key down and click the close button at the top left of the widget.

◄ DON'T SAVE ENERGY

Allowing your hard drive to be put to sleep is a great way to save battery life on laptops, but for the best performance, make sure the Energy Saver settings in your System Preferences Energy Saver pane are speed optimised. Deselect the option to have your hard disk to sleep when possible to prevent slowdowns caused by your hard disk spinning back up from sleep.

► DELOCALISE

Another way to save space is by removing unwanted language localisations, which will have been installed if you chose the Easy Install option when you installed Mac OS X. While you can remove extra languages manually, the freeware Monolingual (*monolingual.sourceforge.net*) makes the process simple.

◄ UPDATE YOUR SOFTWARE

Most software can check for updated versions of itself. Turn this option on wherever possible as the performance and reliability improvements offered by upgrades can be significant, and it's far easier to have the application check these things for you than have to do the checking yourself. Updating software is particularly important if you're running an Intel Mac. Now that CS3 is here, just about every major application has a Universal Binary version, so make sure the latest version of your favourite software takes advantage of the speed boost that native Intel support brings.

► CLEAN OUT LOGIN ITEMS

Every program or process that automatically launches when you login to your Mac increases login time and increases Ram demands. Keep an eye on them in the Accounts System Preferences pane under the Login Items tab – it's odds on that you'll find a couple in there you never knew you had installed.

◄ REDUCE EYE CANDY

In the Dock preferences pane of System Preferences, select Scale Effect in the Minimize Using field and uncheck the Animate opening applications option. This saves a few processor cycles.

► TURN OFF FILE SHARING

Improve performance by turning off unwanted networking options. For example, if you don't need to share files on your Mac, Mac OS X's file sharing feature is a clear waste of processor cycles. Turn it off in the Sharing pane of System Preferences. You can also disable Bluetooth in the Bluetooth pane if you don't need it.

Take kernel panics seriously, if your Mac suffers from them. Their most common cause is a problem with hardware, particularly failed or failing memory modules. If you suffer a kernel panic, check all your installed memory using Rember (free from *kelleycomputing.net*), running a long test that is more thorough than quick tests provided by other tools. Also remove all non-essential peripherals, whether connected via USB or FireWire, suspect PCI cards, and so on. Prevent memory problems by purchasing Ram specified for your particular model. When buying for a Mac Pro, watch for the adequacy of the heat sink; if in doubt, buy from Apple.

◄ MAKE A BOOTABLE COPY

Once you are happy that a system update is problem-free, make a bootable mirror copy, for example using SuperDuper! ($27.95 from *shirt-pocket.com/SuperDuper/SuperDuper Description.html*) on an external FireWire or USB hard disk, and keep that as a recovery and emergency disk. If you have time when doing this, clone your startup disk to the external drive, then clone it back to your startup disk, to completely defragment and clean up your startup drive.

▼ CHECK YOUR LOGS

If your Mac is sluggish, is rattling away accessing a hard disk for no apparent reason, suffers from crashes (not kernel panics), or has missing services or strange errors, check your logs using Console, or similar. You may see Spotlight's indexing engine, listed as mdutil in Activity Monitor, choking over one file, for instance. If so, remove the troublesome file, or rename the folder containing it with the .noindex suffix to exclude indexing. Indexing should then complete normally and performance will be restored. If another service seems to be cyclically crashing and restarting, find out why, and deal with that issue.

◄ DO NOT DISTURB

Keep your core operating system and applications intact and undisturbed to avoid update issues. Try and do manual installations of system updates. Back up at least your key files before updating. If you have slimmed applications down by stripping foreign language localisations, restore the original version. If you have relocated Apple applications, put them back into their correct places and install the update. If your Mac suffers blue screen or other problems when restarting, wait: don't rush to do anything. If it's definitely frozen, force your Mac to shut down by pressing and holding the power button, start it up with your latest install CD/DVD or in single-user mode and repair the disk, and restart again.

▲ RESCUE DVD

Startup or restart problems strike when you are least prepared. Make yourself a rescue DVD and keep it to hand for those dreaded occasions. One way of doing this is to create a new 4.7GB DVD disk image in Disk Utility, install Mac OS X into that from your most recent system DVD, then apply the latest Combo updater. You should be able to burn this disk image to DVD using Disk Utility. Keep the disk image updated with the latest release of Mac OS X and its tools. To ensure you can cope with most emergencies, include Disk Utility, Network Utility, your backup and restore tools, and third party essentials such as Disk Warrior and TechTool Pro.

▲ SPARE ACCOUNTS

If you are trying to solve a setting or related problem, have a spare 'clean' admin user account available, and try logging into that. Preference and other setting files can become blocked, but should remain clear for this 'clean' user, so you can use the account to locate the problem. Ensure that it has a strong password, or it could prove vulnerable, for instance if you have SSH remote access enabled. For an ultra-clean environment, restart into that clean account with the Shift key held down to disable third party extensions. If you think that a preference file is causing a problem but are not sure exactly which one, set a Finder window to list the contents of the suspect Library/Preferences folder by Date Modified. Open the pane or application and change its preference settings. The file containing those settings should then be updated and appear at the top of the list, with the current modification time.

WRITE IT DOWN

Keep a written record, supported by screenshots, of all your key settings, especially those for your network and broadband modem-router. With it, record all key usernames and passwords. Lock this record away if necessary, but keep it accessible in case you need to check or reset any of those key items.

Let your Mac store usernames and passwords in its keychain. If you then want to access one of those protected services, but cannot recall the username or password correctly, use your Keychain Access utility to look up the stored username and password.

◄ RESTORING TRASHED OR MISSING COMPONENTS

Restore trashed or missing components from Mac OS X and its updates using Pacifist ($20 from *charlessoft.com/*). Open the latest Combo or other updater first and look for the items you need. You can also use this to revert individual components such as system libraries if a Mac OS X update breaks hardware or software you need to use, although using older software components can cause severe system instability.

▲ PESKY PERIPHERALS

When peripherals are playing up, shut everything down and check cables and connections. Swap components around to try to isolate the defect. With a monitor or graphics card problem, test your monitor on a different Mac, use a different cable, and so on, applying logic to deduce which of the host Mac, graphics card, cable, and monitor elements is at fault.

▼ BE WARY OF UPDATES WITH USB MODEMS

If your broadband connection relies on a USB modem, be wary of Mac OS X system updates. Check before installing an update that it will be compatible with the modem's driver. Otherwise you may lose your Internet connection if the driver is broken by the system update, and you might find it very messy to restore. When you can, switch to a networked modem-router that does not suffer this problem.

▲ TESTING, TESTING...

With network or Internet problems, use Network Utility first to 'ping' a known IP address, either on your network or a remote site such as Apple's (17.112.152.32). If that works well, try a domain name such as *www. apple.com*, which tests name resolution (DNS). If pinging IP addresses fails, you are no longer connected to that network. If your broadband connection is down, try restarting your modem via its web interface.

DON'T JUST REINSTALL

If you are trying to fix a problem, don't keep re-installing applications or Mac OS X itself: this is not Windows or Mac OS 9, where re-installing can be a panacea. Archiving and re-installing can recover Macs after they have suffered damage to their system files, though. This might be a valuable last-ditch measure if you have inadvertently been using your Mac when it 'optimised' your system during a Mac OS X update, and has led to file loss, but it often just creates a lot of work and adds to confusion. Instead of using sledgehammer solutions, try to identify where the problem lies and tackle the problem methodically.

Trouble-shooting

Energy Saver

◄ ► Show All

Sleep | Options

Put the computer to sleep when it is inactive for:

1 min — 15 min — 1 hr — 3 hrs — Never

Put the display to sleep when the computer is inactive for:

1 min — 15 min — 1 hr — 3 hrs — Never

☐ Put the hard disk(s) to sleep when possible

Restore Defaults   Schedule...

🔓 Click the lock to prevent further changes.

◄ BE WARY OF SLEEP

Some Macs don't like waking up from sleep and may freeze, requiring a forced restart. This can be the result of third party software or hardware, and is less likely when using the latest release of Mac OS X and any third-party software. Although important for laptops to conserve battery power, sleeping is of little benefit to desktop systems, and you should consider just sleeping the display, set in the Energy Saver pane. Putting hard disks to sleep can shorten their lives unless they are designed to withstand it, as those in laptops are. Routine housekeeping will only occur normally if your display is sleeping, but it won't take place if your whole Mac is asleep.

KEEP A WIRED SPARE

Wireless keyboards and mice are a boon, but you should always keep an emergency wired keyboard and mouse to hand. If the wireless ones fail, or you have to start your Mac up without Bluetooth software support, you can then connect the wired devices and work normally.

UPDATING THE UPDATES

Software Update will normally keep offering you an update that you think you have already installed, if that update has not been applied fully. For example, an update that replaces iChat will not take if you have tampered with your old iChat application, and you will continue to be offered that same update. If this happens, identify the file(s) that have not been updated, and use Pacifist or something similar to update them by hand, if necessary, then re-apply the update. Software Update should recognise that the update is complete, and leave you alone.

KEEP RECEIPTS

Disk Utility complains about losing communication when you try to check or repair permissions with a damaged bundle in your /Library/Receipts folder. If affected, remove those receipts one by one to identify which is to blame, and you will eventually be able to repair permissions again. Never trash those receipts, as that will stop Disk Utility from working properly until you have restored the receipts from backup.

ALWAYS DOUBLE CHECK

Test your backups and archives periodically. The best time to perform a test of full restoration is just before a major Mac OS update, such as installing Leopard, but you must have an additional reliable clone of the disk to be restored as well, in case restoration fails. In addition, every so often identify a document or application that should be stored in your backup set or archive, find it in the set, and restore it to a test folder.

KNOW YOUR BATTERIES

Know what PRam backup battery your Mac uses, and keep a spare to hand so that you can replace it as soon as required. Recent models either take the traditional half-AA 3.6 V lithium unit, or CR-2032 'coin' cells. iMacs that do not take the former seem to use CR-2032, although you can pay much more for branded replacements.

DOUBLE MAC SOLUTION

If you have more than one Mac, FireWire Target Disk mode can be an excellent way of dealing with serious glitches such as freezing during startup. Connect the problem Mac to your host Mac using a FireWire cable, and start up the problem Mac with the T key held down until the FireWire icon appears on its screen. You should then be able to access its startup disk as an external FireWire drive connected to the host. Also use this to recover key documents from a Mac that has suffered hardware failure, and to back up your disk before sending a broken Mac away for repair. Desktop systems with two ATA drives as Master and Slave will not mount both drives as FireWire targets: to access the second (Slave), shut down and swap Master and Slave settings, normally using jumpers on the hard disks. When you have finished accessing a drive in Target mode, remember to eject it from the host Mac before shutting the problem Mac down by pressing and holding its power button.

► CHECK YOUR BACKUP

Having made a recent full backup, test your UPS automatic shutdown software. Close all applications, and turn the mains power supply off at the wall socket. Time how long it takes your Mac to shut down, and when you have restored the mains and started up again, adjust or fix the UPS settings in your Energy Saver pane (or third-party tool such as PowerChute) so that it works properly. Also keep an eye on the battery in your UPS recharging, using that pane.

► KEEP IT SLIM

The commonest cause of bizarre behaviour in a mail client, such as missing emails, is letting its mailbox(es) grow too large. Although most recent releases of Mail, Microsoft Entourage and others can cope with mailboxes over 1GB, keep yours down to 100MB or less to ensure best performance. Periodically archive out messages that you need to keep but do not need to refer to daily, to keep your main mailbox or database down in size.

APC PowerChute Personal Edition

◄ ► Show All

APC www.apc.com

During an extended power problem:

⦿ Preserve battery power...

...by shutting down my computer when it has been on battery power for at least:

2 min — 4 — 6 — 8 — 10

○ Keep my computer on as long as possible...

...by shutting down when the remaining battery runtime is less than :

4 min — 6 — 8 — 10

🔒 Click the lock to prevent further changes.   About...

Database Utility

Select the database you want to maintain.

Identity	Date Last Modified
Main Identity	Today 13:13

Select the maintenance activity to perform.

⦿ **Verify database integrity**
Check database for corruption. If problems are found, you can choose to rebuild your database. If your database is working properly, no changes will be made.

○ **Compact database**
Compact and back up the current database files.

○ **Rebuild database**
Perform repairs, compact database files, and back up current database. If you have Hotmail, MSN, IMAP or Exchange accounts, you must download the folder lists and messages from the server again. If Sync Services are enabled, they will be disabled during the rebuild and must be re-enabled.

○ **Set database preferences**
Changes database maintenance preferences.

Quit   Continue

ON BOOT

alt	Allows you to chose which volume to boot from on modern Macs
shift	Starts up in Safe Boot mode
command-alt-P-R	Zap PRam; keep keys held down at least until second chime
command-alt-O-F	Boot into Open Firmware (PowerPC Macs only)
command-V	Boot in verbose mode
command-S	Boot into single user mode
C	Boot from CD
T	Put FireWire machine into FireWire Target Disk mode
X	If Mac OS X and Mac OS 9 are on the same boot partition, this will force the Mac to start up from OS X
left mouse button	Eject removable media

AS FINDER STARTS

shift	Disables the launch of login items specified in the Accounts preference pane

IN FINDER

tab	Select next icon alphabetically
shift-tab	Select previous item alphabetically
command-delete	Move selected item to Trash
space	When using Spring-loaded folders, immediately opens a folder you're hovering over
command-1	Switch to icon view
command-2	Switch to list view
command-3	Switch to column view
command-alt-W	Close all open Finder windows (except popup windows)
command-shift-alt-W	Close all open Finder windows (including pop-up windows)
command-right arrow	Open folder in list view
command-alt-right arrow	Recursively open folder and nested folders in list view
command-left arrow	Close folder in list view
command-alt-left arrow	Recursively close folder and nested folders in list view
command-up arrow	Open parent folder; opens user's home folder in OS X if no other windows are open
command-alt-up arrow	Open parent folder, closing current folder
command-down arrow	Open selected item; opens user's home folder in OS X if no other windows are open
command-alt-down arrow	Open selected item, closing current folder

APPLICATION SWITCHER

command-tab	Bring up application switcher, then…
tab	Move to the next application in the switcher
shift-tab or `	Move to the previous application in the switcher
q	Quit the highlighted application
h	Hide the highlighted application

CLICKS

alt-click in second application	Switch to second application and hide the first application
command-drag (window)	Drag window without bringing it to front
command-click (window title)	Displays pop-up menu showing path to current document or folder

ITEMS IN DOCK

command-click	Reveal Dock item in Finder
command-alt-click	Activate application and hide other applications
command-drag into Dock	Freezes Dock items so you can drop dragged item into folders
command-alt-drag into Dock	Force the target application to attempt to open item

POWER MANAGEMENT
On Macs with a power key

power	Bring up dialog for shutdown, sleep or restart
command-control-power	Unconditionally reboot; use as a last resort
control-command-alt-power	Fast shutdown

On Macs without power key

control-eject	Bring up dialog for shutdown, sleep or restart
command-control-eject	Unconditionally reboot; use as a last resort
control-command-alt-eject	Fast shutdown

IN POWER DIALOGUE

S	Sleep
R	Restart
esc	Cancel
return or enter	Shut down

Make RSS work for you

From getting a job to following a news story to making sure your MP is earning their keep, RSS is the way to go. Here, we dish up 10 ways to get the most from feeds.

It's no wonder that RSS is still really only used by alpha geeks; it's just another TLA (three-letter acronym) for folks to get their heads around. And that's a real shame, as RSS – 'feeds', 'live bookmarks' or whatever else you call them – can be spectacularly powerful.

Here, we're going to show you 10 innovative ways you can put RSS to work. What we're not going to do is plod through the basics of subscribing to normal RSS feeds. We're going to assume you might already have added, say, a magazine like *MacUser* to an RSS reader such as Safari, NetNewsWire or NewsFire. We're looking at novel ways of leveraging the power of RSS to help you find a job, track down the perfect item on eBay, create a personalised podcast, and much more.

We'll also be highlighting some of the features of Safari's RSS reading capabilities that few people still know about, showing you how to create your own RSS screensaver, convert RSS feeds to speech

to allow you to listen to news and more on your morning commute through your iPod, and much more.

And it's important that you bear in mind that we're only scraping the surface. Even within the examples that we quote, there are many options to explore to get the right results for you. The easy way to learn new ways of expanding the abilities of RSS is to watch out for your browser alerting you to RSS feeds for the pages you're on. One of the uses we'll demonstrate, for example, involves targeted feeds created from news search engines such as Yahoo! or Google, and we only noticed that such a thing was possible because the telltale blue RSS icon appeared in Safari's address bar once we'd landed on a page of results; other browsers have their equivalents, and keeping an eye out for feed alerts, particularly when you've done something such as search by tags to drill down into the results, can result in a leaner, cleaner and more personalised browsing experience.

RSS SCREENSAVER

You probably know you can set any RSS feed as a screensaver in Mac OS X, but you may not know that you can create your own customised RSS feeds using Quartz Composer. This tool is part of the developer tools that can be found on and installed from your original system discs, which came with your Mac, and allows you to conjure up personalised RSS feed screensavers.

DISCOVER RELEVANT PHOTOS

As well as generating RSS feeds for users and groups, Flickr does the same for any tag on the system. Just click on a tag (or navigate to *http://flickr.com/photos/tags/yourtag*, replacing yourtag with the relevant tag) and you'll get an RSS feed of images for that tag. Try it with tags for your place of birth, current home, interests and the like, and you can get nice little sporadic surprises in your reader.

GET A JOB

Think the grass might be greener on the other side of the fence? Use *The Guardian*'s job search pages to find something better. Best of all, because we'll generate a tailored RSS feed, you'll only be alerted to jobs you want, and seeing new listings quietly populate your feed reader is a great way to get in early with job applications. Go to *guardian.co.uk/jobs* and use the filters to narrow down your field of expertise, location and salary. Subscribe to the RSS feed generated at the results page.

FIND WHAT YOU ALWAYS WANTED ON EBAY

Go to *ebay.co.uk* and click on Advanced Search in the upper-right corner. Enter your search terms, then click Search. You might need to go back and further refine it – say, by specifying a minimum price of £200 on MacBooks to weed out cases and Ram – but once you're happy that the results are appropriate, subscribe to the RSS feed that you get on the results page. You'll now be alerted whenever new items are listed; great for tracking rare items or bargains.

READ EVERYTHING BY A PARTICULAR WRITER

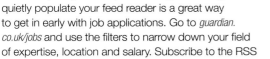

Point your browser at *news.yahoo.com* and click Advanced next to the Search field. Here, we're going to create a news feed that picks up everything Polly Toynbee writes in *The Guardian,* so enter her name in the 'the exact phrase' field, and 'Guardian' in the Source field. On the results page, you'll get an RSS feed to which you can subscribe. This particular example isn't perfect – you'll get stories that mention Polly Toynbee as well as those written by her – but there are tricks you could use to refine your search. Consider, for example, searching not for a writer but for the name of his or her column, or looking to see if bylines are prefixed by, say, 'author' or 'by'. Many news outlets already offer writer-specific feeds, so poke around the site first.

KEEP TABS ON A PARTICULAR STORY

You can track a particular news story through your RSS reader by using a service such as Google News. The most efficient way to do this is to take advantage of Google's own news grouping technology to track a current story. Go to *news.google.co.uk* and you'll get a list of headlines. Under each is a link that reads 'all 3462 news articles' or similar. Click this to show all coverage of that story, and subscribe to the RSS feed on this page. Any new coverage will pop into your reader.

SAFARI RSS

Safari has RSS abilities that put many third-party options to shame. Chief among these is the ability to create metafeeds based on individual feeds. Let's say you were only interested in news of the latest version of Mac OS X – Leopard. Create a folder full of links (anywhere in your Bookmarks menu) to Mac news sits' RSS feeds, and then select View All RSS Articles for that folder. In the search field – not the Google search field in Safari's title bar – type 'leopard' and, if you like, further define how you'd like to have the news presented by using the settings and sliders. Making any change to these alters the URL in the address bar, which can then be bookmarked. Drop it into your bookmarks bar and set Safari's preferences to auto-refresh RSS feeds, and whenever there are new stories about Leopard from the news sites you defined, you'll be alerted by a number appearing next to your bookmark.

OPML

Remember that most feed readers allow you to import and export feeds, so don't feel tied to any one piece of software. Most export feeds as an OPML file, although Safari is a notable exception. If you feel like getting your hands dirty, visit *tinyurl.com/ynwu9d* for a shell script and Automator action to make it easier to get feeds out of Safari.

TRACK A TOPIC

Similarly, you can perform searches from *news.google.co.uk* for topics, and subscribe to an RSS feed for that search term. In this way, you can keep track of, say, iPhone news without having to comb the web manually.

PERSONALISED PODCASTS

Del.icio.us is a social bookmarking site where, as far as anyone browsing the web is concerned, group wisdom narrows down the billions of web pages to a few good ones. At least, that's the theory. Visit *del.icio.us/tag* and you can click on tags in the cloud to generate RSS feeds for those tags. You can also enter your own tag text – such as 'steve jobs' – in the field at the top of the screen. Where it gets interesting, though, is that del.icio.us can track media types. Enter 'tutorial+system:media:audio' into the tags field and the system will create a page listing all audio files tagged with 'tutorial'; MP3s can be previewed inline. An RSS is also generated, so you've just rolled yourself your own podcast of tutorials from del.icio.us. Visit *del.icio.us/help/mediafiletypes* for details of tags for other filetypes.

CREATE A COMBINED FEED

Part of the joy of RSS is that you don't have to trawl through dozens of sites by hand, so it makes sense that instead of clicking through dozens of feeds, you combine them into one single megafeed.

There are a couple of ways to do this depending on what reader software you use. In Safari, you simply create a folder (Alt-Command-b to show bookmarks, and then Shift-Command-n to create a new folder) and add your

RSS TO iPOD

iSpeak It, $19.95 (about £10) from *zapptek.com*, uses your Mac's built-in text-to-speech capabilities to transcribe RSS feeds to audio tracks that can be synced to your iPod. Although the results aren't perfect, it is a good way to keep up-to-date with news stories, when paired, say, with our trick of creating a personalised Google news feed. You can correct the system's mispronunciation of words by applying manual overrides.

bookmarked RSS feeds to that folder. Now all you have to do is click that folder in the bookmarks bar and pick View All RSS Articles.

To make the process even faster, check the Auto-Click box next to this folder from the bookmarks view. This means you can simply click the folder rather than clicking, holding, and picking View All RSS Articles. Most RSS reader software has an equivalent, so check your manual. If you find it doesn't, you could use Feedshake from *feedshake.com* to combine multiple feeds into one single feed.

TRACK CHANGES TO DOCUMENTS

Many online services, especially those that encourage collaboration, offer the ability to publish an RSS feed of revisions. Click on any Wikipedia page's History tab, for example, and you'll get a rich summary of each change in RSS format. It's great way to track what's being said about a particular topic, and is particularly useful if you're in any sort of role that puts you in charge of the project being written about. Google Docs and Spreadsheets does a similar thing, as does the excellent collaborative notepad service, Writeboard.

STALK YOUR MP (LEGALLY)

Democracy really only works if you're aware of being what's being done in your name. While it's easy to see what's happening at a national scale, keeping tabs of what's happening locally can be a much more problematic. There's an easy way to track what your MP is up to, though, and, yes, it's all thanks to RSS. Visit *theyworkforyou.com*, punch in your postcode, and subscribe to the RSS feed on the next page. You'll be told how your MP contributed to Commons debates and what written answers they gave.

PIPES

If you're really, really into RSS, you could use Yahoo Pipes. The technology at play at *pipes.yahoo.com* is undeniably powerful, and allows you to remix and reuse information from feeds in ways that few people could have imagined. Although it's touted as an accessible system, we still recommend patience, creativity and a mind that works in gigahertz if you plan to create a pipe.

iPhone

iMac

iAccounting?

i don't know about you, but i'm sick and tired of people climbing on the iBandwagon. Take a woolly hat, add an iPod dock and call it an "iHat". How original.

Fortunately, some stuff really does add to the experience of owning a Mac. Like the new range of Mac accounting software from MYOB. It's been built from the ground up by their own dedicated Mac team, with stuff like iCal and .Mac integration and a proper Mac user interface.

it's enough to put an iSmile on anyone's face!

Try it **FREE** for 30 days. Visit **www.myob.co.uk/mac** or call **0845 260 0581**

Mind Your Own Business. Smarter.

Profit from Social Networking

Social networking isn't just about MySpace and having bands as 'friends'. With big players like BT getting in on the act, it's an important tool for businesses, too. Here's how you can use social network sites to build contacts and generate leads.

If you haven't heard someone in the past six months refer to 'my MySpace page', then you have probably been living under a rock. Social networks – websites designed to let you link together your friends and acquaintances in groups – have become the biggest thing to invade the Internet since, well, the last biggest thing to invade the Internet.

But can social networks be more than just fun? Can they also be serious tools for doing business? After all, business is all about making, tracking and keeping contacts, as reflected in the old saying that it's not what you know, it's who you know.

In this feature, we'll be looking at social networks from this perspective to see if you can use them as more than just fun pastimes. If you want to make new business contacts, which are the best social networks to join, and what kinds of things should you be putting in your profile if you want to be found by the right kind of business partners? We'll also look at some of the common mistakes people make when creating their profiles; things that do more to damage your professional image than add to it.

⦿ HOW SOCIAL NETWORKS WORK

The basic template for social networks was set back in 1997, with the launch of a site that proved to be well ahead of its time, Six Degrees.com. Six Degrees followed a simple model generally called the 'web of contacts'. In this kind of social networking, you list your friends and have some kind of access to friends of friends – for example, sending messages to anyone within a few circles of you, as well as seeing if there was any kind of relationship between you and any other user on the site via friends, friends of friends, and so on.

Despite becoming the hippest site around for a short period of time, Six Degrees wasn't a success, and it was bought out in 2000 for $125 million, with the site itself effectively closing in 2001. However, the core idea of listing friends and using them as a method to connect to other people was picked up by several other sites, with varying degrees of success.

Social networks really began to take hold of the public imagination with the inexorable rise of MySpace, which, in the four years of its existence, has risen from nowhere to a £330m takeover by News Corporation, and hundreds of millions of users. MySpace took the basic 'friends and friends of friends' approach of Six Degrees and added to it the ability to highly customise the information you display on your page, effectively adding features that had been common in simple web creation sites such as Geocities.

Importantly, MySpace was targeted not at hip first-generation web users, but at the true 'net natives' – teenagers and young adults who'd grown up with the existence of the web, and who were hungry for a kind of site that allowed them to express themselves and link to their friends. With a huge audience of young people, it made sense for anyone wanting to communicate with young adults to start doing so via MySpace. For example, bands set up their own MySpace pages in order to directly reach their fans. Because MySpace lets you easily embed streamed songs, it makes it easy for bands to do this, and, because people tend to listen to things that their friends also like, the 'web of friends' approach makes it an ideal way to get new listeners directly, without having to rely on traditional promotional tools such as radio.

This combination of the web-of-friends approach and customisation was the killer feature for social networking websites, and a variety of others have popped up in the wake of MySpace, either with the aim of targeting specific communities, or with added features.

▲ MySpace is great for sharing your new tunes, which means you can reach a large audience very quickly.

MYSPACE

URL *myspace.com*

MySpace was by no means the first social networking site, but it was the first one to gain serious traction and publicity – so much so that News Corporation was prepared to pay around £330m to buy it in July 2005. The site still dominates the social networking market, with more than 100 million members.

MySpace follows the standard template for social network sites, enabling you to add friends, post pictures and customise your page to a reasonable degree. The customisation is a good thing, as the default templates for a MySpace page are pretty ugly. You can, of course, leave messages for friends, either public on their page or private, and there's a small, simple blogging engine if you're interested in posting regular updates.

The key advantage MySpace has over its rival is numbers, rather than technology or design. With so many members, if you're hoping to use your MySpace page as a public billboard, then you're going to have the maximum possible audience. This extends to groups, too: there are more than 21,000 groups devoted to different types of business, which means there's almost certainly a specific group for whatever you're interested in, whether that's email marketing or market gardening.

The problem, though, is with the interface: unless you're finding groups and so on through your contacts, it can be quite tough to sort the wheat from the chaff. Try doing a search on 'Marketing', for example, and you'll be given all 158,000 MySpace pages that mention the subject, in no coherent order. It makes MySpace daunting to get into, and a lot more difficult to use than it should be.

Overall, MySpace's main advantage is it's sheer size, but this is also its main disadvantage. No matter what your business, you probably ought to have a MySpace page, but making it the main centre of attention might not be the best use of your resources.

◀ Social networks such as MySpace are the ideal way to contact friends of friends of friends…

FACEBOOK

URL *facebook.com*

MySpace's main competitor, Facebook, was restricted to students until a few years ago. Since opening up to everyone, the site has started to gradually grow in popularity, and since the beginning of the year, its growth rate has surpassed that of virtually every other social networking site.

Like MySpace, Facebook uses the 'web of friends' approach, coupled with a highly customisable profile page that lets you list your contact details and add new content. The site's design is cleaner and more 'grown up' than MySpace, and includes modules for comments, photos, status updates and much more besides.

Recently, Facebook added more customisation options by announcing what it called 'Facebook/F8', a method of creating small web applications that can be displayed on profile pages. Although this approach is nothing new – MySpace has offered this level of customisation for some time – Facebook/F8 has seen a massive increase in interest as a platform for social networking.

What's more, Facebook has one crucial advantage over MySpace: it allows you to place adverts and sell services from your profile without it taking any kind of fee. In fact, the service already includes a method of selling goods and services with its Marketplace application, which allows you to list items for sale in specific areas.

▲ **Facebook allows you to place adverts and sell services from your profile, and it doesn't take any fee.**

This makes Facebook arguably a better option for businesses looking to do more than just promote themselves; in fact, some businesses are already using Marketplace to advertise their services.

Overall, of the general social networking services, Facebook looks a better option than MySpace if you're seeking to advertise and directly sell products or services.

▲ **You can upload galleries, which is a great way to show off your work or products.**

However, bear in mind that it also has fewer visitors at present than MySpace. As such, it might be worth making a profile on both simply to ensure that you have all the bases covered.

LINKEDIN

URL *linkedin.com*

Unlike both Facebook and MySpace, LinkedIn is focused firmly on social networking for business – in particular, on making and cultivating individual contacts in your business life. The principle is simple and similar to the original template created by Six Degrees: you connect to people

using their email addresses, and through them you can connect to others. Profile information is firmly oriented around business, and you won't find any favourite music options or the ability to embed songs.

LinkedIn includes a section for hiring, so you can post job adverts for a small fee and reply to them for free. For any job advert, you can see if you're connected via your web of friends to the person posting the job or replying to your advert, which makes it simple to recruit friends of friends if you want to. You can also find people providing services according to how many people have recommended them, narrowing it down to people recommended by your first-degree contacts if required.

◀ **LinkedIn is focused solely on networking for business, rather than for making new friends.**

Most services on LinkedIn are free, although some are limited. For example, you're only allowed to request five introductions to people not in your immediate circle of contacts before you run out and have to wait to get more. However, you can optionally upgrade to a Business Plus account, which gives you additional features such as the ability to directly contact friends of friends without going through the friend and getting an introduction first. You also get expanded search abilities, which let you find business contacts more easily.

Overall, LinkedIn combines a lot of very smart features for business networking, making it something worthwhile for any individual to sign up to. What it lacks on the business side is any company-level tools, which means it's much more suitable as a promotional tool for sole traders than small companies. Whether it's worth upgrading your account depends on how much use you're getting out of it, but it's certainly worth getting yourself a free account and making some new contacts.

⊖ XING

URL *xing.com*

Xing, which until last year was known as Open Business Club or OpenBC, is another service dedicated to business rather than appealing to the general public. The product is unique in that the majority of users are in Europe, rather than spread out around the world, with a large core of users in Germany and many languages supported.

The site offers the full plethora of social networking features, allowing you to link to users as trusted contacts, and offers event co-ordination and so on. Most services are free, but some – including detailed searches and messaging to people with whom you're not directly connected – are for premium members only.

Premium membership costs £4.11 a month, but includes a variety of benefits above and beyond the site itself, such as a 5% discount on Avis car rental and additional benefits with some hotel chains.

Like Facebook, Xing offers a marketplace that allows you to post offers for jobs and the like, and it's easy to search and find services – many of them in the high professional end of the market. The most popular

▶ **Just like LinkedIn, Xing is dedicated specifically to business and not to the general public.**

offers have had thousands of views. When you consider the business focus of Xing users, this is impressive and potentially extremely useful.

The main drawback with Xing at present is also its main strength: its European focus. This means it lacks a large number of contacts from the US. Of course, if you can get your contacts to sign up when you do, this makes no difference – but it's worth bearing in mind if you're looking to sign up to just a single social networking site. However, the flip side is that if you're looking for a social networking service that has a large core of users in Europe, particularly in Germany, then Xing should be your first port of call.

▲ **Xing is largely European focused, which means you may miss out on US contacts.**

BT TRADESPACE

URL *bttradespace.com*

BT might not be the most obvious company to introduce a social network, but its recently launched Tradespace site shows some promise. Like LinkedIn, Tradespace is directed firmly towards business, but it differs in its approach: rather than target individuals, it aims for small businesses, allowing them to create a simple web presence, belong to interest groups, and recommend other businesses that are also on Tradespace.

Like a clearer, more business-focused version of MySpace, Tradespace allows your business to have a small blog, promote events, and upload podcasts and images. You can put up a downloadable business card, and optionally include a 'Call Free' button, which will place a call directly between your listed phone number and a customer.

Unlike other social networking services, Tradespace also gives you a range of statistical reports – for example, enabling you to track the number of requests for your business card and downloads of any podcasts you've put up.

The worst thing about Tradespace is that it can be difficult to navigate at times:

WHAT NOT TO DO

Let's face it – if you've used a general social networking service such as MySpace or Facebook, then you've probably created some kind of profile for yourself. And, if it's like millions of other profiles out there, what you've posted may not be the most professional thing you've ever written. There may even be pictures of you attached that might not paint the most flattering portrait of your social life.

But why would this matter? After all, social networking services are just a bit of fun, aren't they? Unfortunately, they can also be a prime source of information about you for potential employers and business partners, which means that a MySpace profile that includes jokey references to skiving off work might not be the best thing if you want to attract employers. For example, one senior BBC executive suffered some minor embarrassment when he posted photos taken of him at a friend's stag night to social photo site Flickr and forgot to make them available to friends only. While it might not have done any long-term damage to his career, it's clear that there are potential problems here.

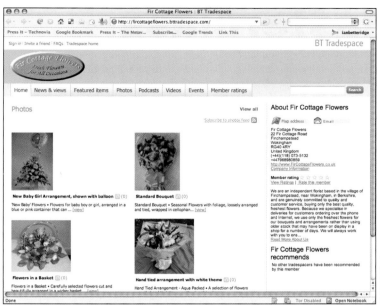

◄ **Tradespace is aimed directly at small business users who want a web presence.**

irritatingly, the front page doesn't allow you to log in, and you need to go to your own home page and sign in there in order to access your account details and change your page.

Overall, Tradespace is interesting, but feels a little '1.0' in nature at the moment. While almost everything on Tradespace is free, some features – most notably Call Free – are only available to subscribers who pay an optional fee of £15 a month, or £135 a year. However, if you simply opt for the free version, there's plenty you can do and it's certainly a service that's worth trying out. It will be interesting to follow the development of the service over the coming months.

And employers aren't stupid. They know that people use social networking sites, and that they're likely to reveal more about their personality, likes and dislikes there than in the 'personal' section of a CV. A few quick searches on Google, MySpace and Facebook might tell them more about a potential employee than an interview. And, importantly, it'll also tell them who their friends are, and if they have any contacts in common – a very important factor in business.

So bear in mind the prospect that an employer or business partner might be reading your profile. However, this doesn't have to mean stifling your personality and producing something bland and boring. Be yourself, but don't write anything that you wouldn't want a potential employer to read. Be open about who your friends are, but don't try to link to people as friends unless you really know them – if you're linked to someone that a potential employer knows, and it turns out that you're not really friends at all, then it won't do you any good and may even make you look silly.

However, don't be afraid to post things that reflect your real personality. Employers aren't stupid enough to think that people have no social lives, and the fact that you're

▲ **Try to avoid using drunken or embarrassing photos of yourself, you never know who is searching the web – some things just don't need to be shared.**

a sociable person is unlikely to do you much harm in all but the most prurient of businesses. That said, the higher the position you're looking for, the more cautious you should be. While pictures of you on a stag night might not be an issue if you're not managing people, it will be if you're a head of department – as our BBC executive found out.

Most important of all, monitor your web presence by doing some light 'ego surfing' – typing your own name into Google and checking to see where you turn up. It's great for your profile if you're on the first page of Google results, unless, of course, it's pointing to a MySpace page with photos of you passed out drunk on holiday.

MASTERCLASS

Masterclass

Welcome to *The Independent Guide to the Mac*'s comprehensive masterclasses. These easy-to-follow workshops will guide you through more than 20 key tasks, step-by-step, so that by the time you get to the end you'll know how to perform vital jobs using a wide range of applications.

We'll also show you how you can use your iPod as a tour guide, set up your printer, connect your camera to your Mac and get online. For anyone living in a home where other family members use Windows, or who is switching from a PC to a Mac, we'll also show you how to use Macs and PCs side by side. Finally, we'll reveal the remarkable history of the Mac and an extensive glossary to help you decode any Mac terminology that you might come across online, in print, or in discussions with your friends and colleagues.

MASTERCLASS
Getting online

Apple has built its range of Macs with a strong focus on the Internet, so getting online is a relatively simple task and going wireless altogether isn't much harder. Here's how.

Kit required Broadband connection + Wireless router
Time 15 to 30 minutes
Goal To get your Mac connected to the Internet and access your email accounts
Skill level Beginner

Getting online these days usually means signing up for a broadband account. Broadband prices have now dropped to the point where dial-up makes little sense economically, even for occasional Internet surfers. The exception, of course, is in those parts of the country that don't have access to a broadband connection. Those areas are few and far between, however, so we'll concentrate here on using a broadband connection to get online. We'll also cover setting up a wireless network so two or more Macs can share the same broadband connection wirelessly.

There are two types of broadband connection, cable and ADSL. From our perspective they offer exactly the same although technologically they are different. The only cable broadband supplier in the UK is Virgin Media and whether or not you can access its services will depend on the area in which you live. Check its website at *virginmedia.com* for more information. By contrast, there are dozens of ADSL broadband providers. We can't tell you which one to choose, so spend some time researching tariffs to find one that meets your needs.

If you opt for cable, you'll be supplied with a cable modem. You can connect this to your Mac or, if you want a wireless network, to a wireless router. Depending on your choice of ADSL supplier, you may be provided with a modem or an ADSL modem/router with a built-in wireless access point.

ROUTER SET-UP

The Basic Settings window shouldn't need any input. Just make sure that Get Dynamically from ISP is checked for IP Address and Get Automatically from ISP is checked for DNS.

The Wireless settings options allows you to name your wireless network and set-up authentication. You can also configure your router's firewall here if you need to change the default settings.

If you have cable broadband, it may have been set up to work only with the MAC address of the Mac which was connected to the modem. If so, you'll need to enter your Mac's MAC address, found in the Network System Preferences Pane by clicking Advanced and then Ethernet.

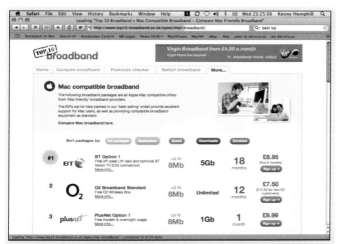

▲ **STEP 01 DECIDE WHAT YOU WANT FROM AN ISP** Before you can choose an ISP you need to decide exactly what you want. Is maximising connection speed important? For most of us 2-8Mbit/sec is fine. Will you be comfortable with a monthly bandwidth limit, or do you need unlimited downloads?

▲ **STEP 02 RESEARCH** Do a cost and feature comparison, using a site such as *moneysupermarket.com*, comparing providers and the services they offer, being careful to note limitations. If you want wifi, look for a provider that includes a wireless router. Are you cabled? If so, Virgin Media's cable service may suit better than ADSL.

▲ **STEP 03 LOOK OUT FOR SPECIAL OFFERS** Check sites like *moneysavingexpert.com* to see if your chosen provider is running any special offers. If so, read the terms and conditions carefully, particularly with regard to any minimum contract period. And before you place your order, check what their Mac support is like.

▲ **STEP 04 GET HOOKED** To enable you to use a telephone and modem on the same line, you need an ADSL filter. If one wasn't supplied with your modem or router, you'll need to buy one separately. Connect it to your telephone socket and plug your modem into the larger connector and telephone into the smaller one. You don't need a filter for cable.

▲ **STEP 05 CONNECT YOUR MAC** If you're connecting your Mac directly to an ADSL modem, all you need to do is power it up, plug it into your Mac's Ethernet port and open System Preferences. Click on the Ethernet heading in the sidebar of the Network pane, and configure using your ISPs instructions.

▲ **STEP 06 USING A WIRELESS ROUTER** The only difference here is that you enter the information from your ISP in the router's configuration web page, instead of System Preferences. The IP address of the configuration page is in your router's manual, along with instructions on how to set it up.

▲ **STEP 07** **SWITCH ON YOUR MAC'S FIREWALL** Now that your Mac is permanently connected to the Internet, it's at risk of being infected by a virus or other malicious software. To protect it, you should use the firewall built into Mac OS X. Open System Preferences then Security and click the Firewall tab.

▲ **STEP 08** **CONFIGURE FIREWALL** Click on the Advanced button and enable Stealth mode by checking the box. This prevents other computers on the Internet 'pinging' your Mac, a technique for checking whether your Mac is there before launching an attack. Click on OK and quit System Preferences.

▲ **STEP 09** **CONFIGURE YOU ROUTER'S FIREWALL** If you have a wireless router connected to your Mac, it too will have a firewall. Check the manual that came with it to find out how to configure it. Usually the default settings, as in the grab here, offer the most protection. Be very careful before making any changes.

▲ **STEP 10** **SETTING UP YOUR EMAIL CLIENT** If you want to send and receive email, you'll need an email application, such as Apple Mail, which is bundled with Mac OS X. To set it up, go to Applications and double-click Mail. Go to the Mail menu and select Preferences. Click on the Accounts tab in the toolbar.

▲ **STEP 11** **CREATING AN ACCOUNT** Click the '+' button on the bottom of the left-hand sidebar. Fill in your name, email address and password. The email address and password should have been provided for you when you opened your account with your ISP. Uncheck Automatically set up account, and click Create.

▲ **STEP 12** **ENTER YOUR ISP'S SETTINGS** Your ISP should have given you details of its servers in order that you can send and receive email. Your account will almost certainly be Pop 3, so choose that and fill in details of the Pop 3 server. On the next screen fill in details of your ISP's SMTP server.

▲ **STEP 13** **SETTING UP ANOTHER EMAIL ACCOUNT** If you have your own domain and an email address that goes with it, you should enter the details for that domain's email server in the incoming mail section. But in the outgoing mail page, you must still enter your ISP's details.

▲ **STEP 14** **IMAP MAIL** If you use .Mac mail, you should follow step 11, but check the Create account automatically box. If you have a Gmail account and want to use it with your iPhone, or another computer, follow Google's instructions for setting up an Imap account. You can find these by logging into your Gmail account in a web browser.

▲ **STEP 15** **SET YOUR PREFERENCES** Take some time to trawl through Mail's General preferences and set it up the way you want it to work. If you get lots of Mail, you may want it to automatically check every five or ten minutes, for example. Visit the Composing and Viewing tabs too, and configure those to suit your needs.

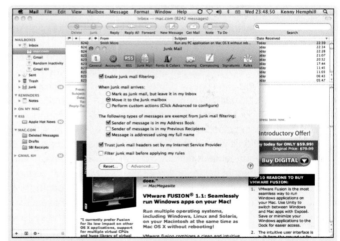

▲ **STEP 16** **JUNK MAIL FILTERING** Dealing with junk mail is a necessary evil, but luckily Mail has a decent junk mail filter. In Mail's Preferences, click on the Junk Mail tab. Tick the checkbox marked Enable junk mail filtering, and select the second of the next set of three options, Move it to the Junk mailbox.

▲ **STEP 17** **CONFIGURING JUNK MAIL FILTER** Now you have to decide which mail to 'whitelist'. As a minimum you should select Sender of message is in my Address Book. Check your Junk Mail folder regularly to make sure it's not catching legitimate messages. If it does, select Not Junk at the top of the message, to train Mail's junk filter.

▲ **STEP 18** **SETTING UP RSS** If you want to subscribe to RSS feeds but don't have a specialist reader, you can subscribe to and read feeds in Mail. In Mail's Preferences, click on the RSS tab and set your default RSS reader as Mail. Now whenever you click on one of those little orange icons, the feed will be added to Mail. ⊗

MASTERCLASS
Setting up a printer

Whether you use your Mac for work or for leisure, at some point you will probably want to print something. Here's how you can take the frustration out of setting up a printer.

Kit required Printer
Time 10 minutes
Goal Setting up a printer
Skill level Beginner

Printing is one of the most common tasks that any computer is asked to perform, yet setting up a printer and getting it to work flawlessly every time is still a frustrating business.

The easiest way to connect a printer and print to it with the minimum of fuss is to connect it to a USB port on your Mac. However, if you want to share the printer with other Macs or PCs on a network, it's not the best option. You can share a printer directly connected to a Mac with other machines, but it means that the host Mac has to be running and will consume processing resources on that Mac.

The best solution if you want to share a printer is to connect it to your network directly. You can either do this with an Ethernet cable, or wirelessly on a wifi network. You'll need to consider whether you want to connect the printer to a network before you buy it because this will govern the kind of printer you buy.

Something else you'll have to consider is the type of material you'll be printing. For example, if you're going to be churning out text documents in high quantities, a laser printer is the best option. If you

want a printer to render your digital photos on high-quality paper, you should choose an inkjet. And if you want a device capable of scanning, copying and faxing as well as printing, you'll need to buy a multi-function device.

You should also consider consumables such as ink and paper. Ink, in particular, is very expensive when you measure the cost per millilitre and it's tempting to consider buying generic ink cartridges rather than the manufacturer's own brand, or to have your existing cartridges refilled.

Although many generic inks are very good these days and produce decent prints, printers are complex beasts and the communication between printer and ink cartridge is essential to the smooth running of the printer. For this reason, ink cartridges on inkjet printers have a microchip fitted to them. Buying generic ink means swapping the chip on each tank, which is a fiddly and messy business. Remember too, when buying a laser printer to take into account the average cost per print and the lifespan of the drum. There is a surprising variation in both between manufacturers.

▲ **STEP 01 USB PRINTER: INSTALL THE INK CARTRIDGES** This process will vary depending on the printer you have, so be careful to read the Quick Start Guide. Plug the printer into the mains before you start so that the print head can be moved to the correct position. In most cases, the slots for the cartridges will be colour-coded, making it easy to see where each one goes.

▲ **STEP 02 USB PRINTER: CONNECT THE USB CABLE** With the printer switched off, connect one end of the USB cable (which you may have to buy yourself) to the printer and the other end to your Mac. Now switch the printer on and wait for it to run through its set-up routine. Once it's done, check whether Mac OS X already has drivers for it installed by opening System Preferences.

▲ **STEP 03** **INSTALLING DRIVERS** In System Preferences, click on Print and Fax. If your printer shows up in the list on the left of the window, you need do nothing more. If not, and it's a USB printer, you need to install the drivers. Quit System Preferences and insert the printer's CD into your Mac. Choose to do a Custom Install and deselect the applications you don't want.

▲ **STEP 04** **CONFIGURE USB PRINTER** Now go back to Print and Fax in System Preferences. You should now see your printer listed. As it's the only printer connected to your Mac, it will automatically be the default printer. Select the default paper size, this is the paper that will be printed to if you hit Print from an application and don't change any options.

▲ **STEP 05** **ADDING A NETWORK PRINTER** Network laser printer drivers tend to be more generic than USB printers so there's more chance that your Mac will have the right one installed. Connect the printer to your network router and go to System Preferences/Print and Fax again. Press the '+' button and wait for your Mac to discover the printer. When it does, select it and press Return.

▲ **STEP 06** **ADDING A WIRELESS PRINTER** Printing over a wifi network is still in its infancy and so manufacturers use different methods to install and set-up printers. Getting a wireless printer up and running can be a frustrating business, even for experienced users, so consider before you buy whether you really need wireless. And read the manual that came with your printer carefully.

▲ **STEP 07** **SHARING A PRINTER** To share a printer connected to a single Mac, go to System Preferences and click on the Sharing pane. Tick the box next to Printer Sharing and in the main window, tick the printer you want to share. To print from another Mac, add the printer by going to the Print and Fax pane and clicking on the '+' sign: the shared printer will be clearly identified.

▲ **STEP 08** **PAGE SETUP** Ensuring the printer is configured correctly before printing is essential. In any application, go to File then Page Setup… Choose your printer from the Format for menu and the paper to which you're printing from Paper Size. Now choose Landscape or Portrait from Orientation, and if you want to change the Scale do that too.

MASTERCLASS
Working with your camera

If you have a digital camera, the iPhoto application, which came already installed on your the Mac, is the ideal tool to store and organise your photos.

Kit required iPhoto
Time 30 minutes
Goal Connect your digital camera to your Mac, download your photos and organise your collection in iPhoto
Skill level Beginner

Whether you only ever take snaps with your mobile phone, carry a compact digital camera wherever you go, or have spent serious money on a digital SLR and extra lenses, there's no better platform than the Mac for making the most of them.

And the good news is that one of the best applications there is for organising and sharing your pictures, iPhoto, came pre-installed on your new Mac. Just plug in your camera to a USB port on your Mac, or slot its memory card into a reader, if you have one, and iPhoto will do the rest.

iPhoto imports your photos and organises them into rolls. It's smart enough to read the date each photo was taken and split them up into what it calls Events. So, for example, if you went to a wedding on Saturday and a 40th birthday party the following Friday, iPhoto will split the photos from each into separate Events.

Although iPhoto's editing features are fairly basic, it's fine for most needs, including removing red-eye, straightening, cropping and boosting contrast. And you can always export pictures to another application, such as Photoshop Elements, for more

refined editing. iPhoto's real strength however, is the way it allows you to share photos, either by publishing them on a website, emailing them, or printing them in a book. We covered that in the iLife section on page 48.

Here we'll take you on a whistlestop tour of iPhoto and show you how to use it to get the most from your pictures. We'll also explain how to export photos from iPhoto to your preferred image editor.

Keys to using iPhoto is to let it take the strain of organising your photos and make any adjustments to albums and events within the application.

Although it is possible to locate individual pictures in the Finder and manually move them around, copy them, or open them in other applications, you should avoid this at all costs. This is because iPhoto stores multiple copies of each image and maintains links between them.

Manually moving photos around will break those links and will cause untold mayhem within iPhoto. Much better to import, edit, organise, and export from within iPhoto. That way you don't have to worry about the directory structure at all.

▲ **STEP 01 CONNECT YOUR CAMERA** Either use the cable that came with your camera to plug it into a spare USB port on your Mac, or slot its memory card into a card reader. iPhoto will launch automatically and ask you if you want to download all or a selection of photos from the card. To import a selection, click on the first one, hold the Shift key and click on those that you want.

▲ **STEP 02 MANAGE EVENTS** Click on Events underneath the Library heading to see how iPhoto has split your photos. Events are created by date, but this doesn't always make sense, as events can last several days or fill only part of a day. From the Events menu, you can Auto Split Events, which separates them into morning and afternoon, merge Events or even create new Events.

▲ **STEP 03 REVIEW IMAGES IN EVENT** Place your mouse pointer over an Event and drag it from side to side. Its photos will be displayed sequentially. The speed at which you drag the mouse dictates how quickly you scroll through the pictures. When you find one you like, stop scrolling and either click the right mouse button or hold down the Control key and click to reveal a contextual menu.

▲ **STEP 04 SET THE DISPLAY IMAGE** With the mouse button held down, move the pointer down to Make Key Photo, to use the current photo as the display picture for the Event. To view all the photos in an event right-click or Control-click on the Event again and choose Open Event in a Separate Window. In this window you can control the size of the images using the slider.

▲ **STEP 05 EDIT IMAGES** You can't edit pictures in this window. So, click on Photos in the Library and scroll down to the picture you want to edit. You can click the Edit button in the toolbar to edit the picture, but the full-screen display is much more satisfying. Right-click on the image and select Edit using Full screen. Drag your mouse to the bottom of the screen to access the controls.

▲ **STEP 06 ADD EFFECTS** iPhoto's editing controls are pretty sophisticated. You can use automatic tools such as Red-eye removal and Enhance to get instant results or play around with the other controls to see how they affect your photo. This is also the place to crop or straighten your picture and, using the Effects button, to convert it to black and white or sepia.

▲ **STEP 07 MAKE ADJUSTMENTS** To gain more control over adjustments, click on Adjust. Here you can alter the contrast, change the exposure, sharpen, and add a tint to your picture. Pay attention to the histogram and avoid clipping the edges of the graph, but don't be afraid to experiment. Hitting reset is all it takes to get back to where you started. When you're finished, click the cross.

▲ **STEP 08 EDIT IN ANOTHER APPLICATION** Editing pictures in iPhoto is fine for most purposes, but if you want to get really creative with your photos, you'll need a dedicated image editing application. Photoshop Elements is ideal, if you have it. Right-click on the image you want to edit and this time select Edit in External Editor. Choose the application you want to use. ✪

MASTERCLASS
Using Macs and PCs together

Macs and PCs needn't be strangers and connecting them to share files has never been easier. You can even run Windows applications on your Mac.

Kit required Mac OS X 10.5 + PC with Windows XP or Vista
Time 15 to 30 minutes
Goal To connect your Mac to a PC; run Windows applications on your Mac
Skill level Beginner/intermediate

Using Macs and PCs together has never been easier, which is partly the reason for the rise in popularity of the Mac in homes and offices around the world. Apple realised several years ago that if the Mac was going to break out of its tiny niche it had to be able to communicate easily with Windows PCs.

So, now when you connect a Mac running Mac OS X Leopard to a network containing Windows PCs and workgroups, they automatically show up in the Finder's sidebar. Connecting to one of them and sharing files is no more complicated than double-clicking on it and entering a username and password.

You don't, however, need separate computers to use a Mac and a PC together. In Leopard there are

two ways of running Mac OS X and Windows on the same Mac and sharing files, Internet access, and peripherals. One method is Boot Camp, which comes with Mac OS X Leopard and allows you to install Windows XP or Vista on a partition on your hard drive and boot into Windows instead of Mac OS X when you start up your Mac.

The other method is known as virtualisation and allows you to run Windows applications alongside Mac applications without having to restart your Mac, or even work with Windows Explorer, you just use the applications you need. Two companies, VMWare and Parallels Inc currently produce virtualisation applications for the Mac.

INTERFACE

The Advanced button in Network Preferences displays a list of all the ways in which you can connect to a network or another machine.

The NetBios name is the name used to identify a Mac or PC on a network. It is resolved to an IP address on TCP/IP networks in the same way that a web address is resolved to an IP address on the Internet.

The Workgroup menu lists all the PCs and workgroups your Mac can see on the network. If a machine doesn't appear automatically in the Finder's sidebar, you can select it here.

▲ **STEP 01 CONNECT TO A PC** To connect to a PC and share files in Leopard, double-click on it's name in the Finder's sidebar (you might have to click on More at the bottom of the list, and enter a username and password to authenticate yourself. You will then have access to the files and folders enabled by the administrator.

▲ **STEP 02 IF THAT DOESN'T WORK** If the PC to which you want to connect doesn't appear in the Finder's sidebar, go to System Preferences and click on the Network tab. Click on the method you used to join the network and click on Advanced. Now click on WINS, which stands for Windows Internet Name Server.

▲ **STEP 03 SELECT THE PC YOU WANT TO CONNECT TO** The window that opens displays the NetBios name of your Mac and has a drop-down menu which displays the names of the other workgroups on the network. From this menu, select the group or PC to which you want to connect and click on OK. Now click on Apply in the Network pane.

▲ **STEP 04 SHARE FILES AND FOLDERS** To access your Mac from a PC, or another Mac, open System Preferences and click on Sharing. Tick the File Sharing checkbox. By default the Public folders for each user account are shared. You can add other folders by clicking on the '+' button.

▲ **STEP 05 SET PRIVILEGES** The box labelled Users lists groups of users that are able to access each shared folder and their access privileges. To change this or modify other users' privileges, click on the drop-down menu and select Read Only, Write Only or Read & Write.

▲ **STEP 06 CHECK IT WORKS** From another Mac on the network, open a Finder window. You should see the Mac you want to connect to in the sidebar under Shared. Double-click on it and when prompted, enter a username and password. You should now have full access to the folders for which you set appropriate privileges in Step 5.

▲ **STEP 07 CHECK OTHER ACCOUNTS** Disconnect from the shared Mac and repeat Step 6, but this time log in as a regular user and then as a guest. Check that you have only the privileges set in System Preferences on the shared Mac. So if you set guest access as being able to read but not write, for example, that's what you should be able to do.

▲ **STEP 08 ENABLE SMB SHARING** Next click on Options in the File Sharing section of the Sharing pane in System Preferences and check the box labelled Share files using SMB and check the names of the users whose files you want to share. You'll have to enter the password for each account you want to share. Now click on Done.

▲ **STEP 09 SET-UP YOUR MAC FOR PC NETWORKING** If you want to change the Computer Name of your Mac, do it here. Now, make a note of the name or IP address of your Mac, shown in the middle line of the Sharing window after afp://. You can connect to this Mac using either it's name or IP address.

▲ **STEP 10 CONNECT TO YOUR MAC FROM A PC** In Windows XP open My Network Places, or in Windows Vista select Network from the Start menu. Double-click on the name of your Mac and in the username box enter the name or IP address you noted in Step 9, then backslash, then an account username. In the box below, enter the appropriate password and click OK.

▲ **STEP 11 GET READY FOR BOOTCAMP** The easiest way to run Windows on your Mac is to use the Bootcamp feature of Mac OS X Leopard. This creates a partition on your hard drive onto which you can install WIndows and start-up your Mac as a Windows PC, then restart in Mac OS X when you want to go back to working in Mac OS X.

▲ **STEP 12 PARTITION HARD DRIVE FOR BOOTCAMP** Go to Applications/Utilities and launch the Boot Camp Set-Up Assistant. This guides you through the process of installing Boot Camp and a copy of Windows on your Mac. The first stage is to specify the Boot Camp partition size. Select either Divide Equally, Use 32GB, or use the slider to specify a partition size.

▲ **STEP 13** **CONFIGURE STARTUP DISK** With Boot Camp and a copy of Windows successfully installed, you can now boot your Mac into either Mac OS X or Windows. You can specify which to use in System Preferences/Startup Disk or by holding down the Alt key when you start your Mac and choosing when prompted.

▲ **STEP 14** **CHANGING BACK AGAIN** If you decided to startup in Mac OS X and want to change to Windows, you just repeat Step 13. But going the other way round is different. In Windows, open the Boot Camp control panel by clicking on its icon in the System Tray on the bottom right of the Windows desktop. Now select Mac OS X as the startup disk.

▲ **STEP 15** **REMOVING WINDOWS** If you no longer need Windows, you can remove it easily. Copy any files you need to a separate disk, and with your Mac started in OS X, no applications running, and you the only user logged in, go to Applications, then Utilities. Open the Boot Camp Assistant and click Restore the startup disk to a single volume then Continue.

▲ **STEP 16** **INSTALL A VIRTUAL MACHINE** As an alternative to running Boot Camp in order to run Windows on your Mac, you can install a virtual machine. This allows you to run a PC or multiple PCs on your Mac and access the applications on them without having to reboot, or even work in the Windows environment.

▲ **STEP 17** **PARALLELS OR FUSION?** There are two options if you decide that you want to install Windows as a virtual machine on your Mac, Parallels desktop and VMWare. They both do exactly the same thing, but in different ways. A less-polished, but free option for running Windows in a Virtual Machine is the Open Source Virtual Box (*virtualbox.org*)

▲ **STEP 18** **SECURITY** If you plan on running a PC on your Mac, either through Boot Camp or a virtual machine, you should take specific precautions to protect you Mac from malicious attacks. Running Windows makes you more vulnerable, and you're not protected by Mac OS X's firewall. Install security software such as Intego's Dual Protection range. See *intego.com* for details. ✪

MASTERCLASS
Using your iPod as an interactive tour guide

If you need to create a compelling tour guide or interactive learning aid, you can use your iPod's Notes capability for surprisingly effective results.

Kit required An iPod with Dock Connector
Time Depends on complexity of the presentation
Goal To create an interactive guide for use on an iPod
Skill level Intermediate

The iPod is primarily a portable music device, but this doesn't mean you should confine its use to such a one-dimensional pursuit. The increased size and quality of the iPod screen has enabled a number of new and interesting ways to use the device.

The Notes capability of the iPod has been available for a long time now, but it's hardly a feature that will get regular use. With a little work, however, the Notes option can put an iPod to work in a very effective way. If you've ever been to an historic monument or museum, it's likely that you'll have been offered an audio guide to help you navigate your way around. You can use an iPod to create a similar but much more interactive presentation that would really

impress. You don't have to limit yourself to interactive audio guides, either: the Notes section can also help make lessons more interesting and, best of all, it doesn't require all that much work.

All you need is an iPod with a Dock Connector, but you'll get more use and interactivity from more recent iPods with colour screens and video capabilities. If you want to create truly professional interactive documents, you can use applications such as GarageBand to create podcasts or vodcasts to extend the Notes feature's usability. Pictures, text, music and video can all be put to good use with an iPod guide – and, best of all, it's really simple to do.

INTERFACE

The iPod is more than just a music player. With a little work it can be made into an interactive tour or lesson guide.

You can insert video, audio and images to your guide. Creating it is simply a case of getting to grips with your content and iPod tags.

▲ **STEP 01 GETTING STARTED WITH NOTES** In order to use Notes, your iPod has to be set up for use as a storage disk as well as a music player. Connect your iPod to your Mac, and click on the devices and then on the Summary tab. Go to the Options area and click the Enable disk use checkbox.

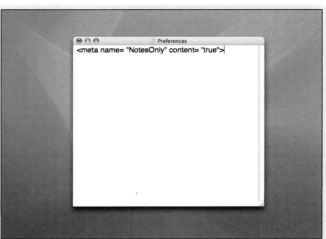

▲ **STEP 02 DISPLAY ONLY NOTES** It's a simple process to lock the iPod so users can't navigate away and use the other features. Create a new file in TextEdit, make sure it's a plain text document and then save it as Preferences. Type *<meta name="NotesOnly" content="true">* in the body of this document. Copy this document to the Notes folder on the iPod.

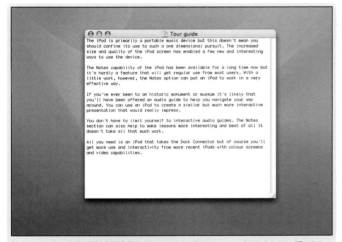

▲ **STEP 03 RESTRICTIONS** It's obvious that too much text on an iPod screen will be a bit overwhelming for most users, so it's best to keep your text down to shortish chunks. Another reason to limit text is that text files are limited to 4KB. This equates to about 1000 words. As we'll show later, you can link together a number of text files to create longer presentations.

▲ **STEP 04 ORGANISING THE NOTES FOLDER** To keep things in order, it's best to think about how your notes will be organised. Give your tour an appropriate folder name and store all your notes there. If you have multiple languages or versions, store them appropriately, too.

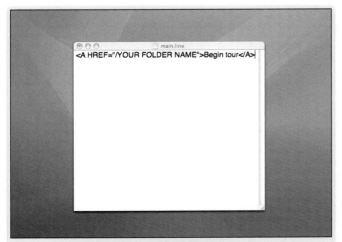

▲ **STEP 05 CONTROLLING THE NOTES INTERFACE** The Notes folder will contain any images you need as well as the main folders. To hide these and provide only a link to your tour folder, you need to create a .linx file. Open a new Text Edit document , type *<A HREF="/YOUR FOLDER NAME">Begin tour</A>* save this as *main.linx* and put it in the Notes folder.

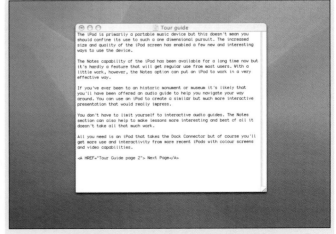

▲ **STEP 06 LINK TO NOTES** If you've created a long document, you'll need to split it into smaller documents so it doesn't go above the 4KB limit. You link these together by placing the following text at the bottom of each document: *<A HREF="NAME OF NOTE TO LINK TO"> Next Page </A>* Now when the user reaches the end of the text file, they simply click on the link to move on.

▲ **STEP 07** **LINK TO PICTURES** Each text note can link to any Jpeg image. This is great if you want to put an image of what you're describing at the foot of the note and not affect the 4KB limit. You need to copy the images you want to use to the top level of the notes folder. Next, type *<A HREF="/image name">Link title</A>* into the note from which you want the image to link.

▲ **STEP 08** **LINK TO AUDIO** One of the most compelling features here is the ability to link to audio stored on the iPod. This time, you don't have to copy the audio to the Notes folder. Type *<A HREF="song=TRACK NAME">LinktoTRACK NAME</A>* into your note. Make sure the TRACK NAME is replaced with the name as it appears in iTunes.

▲ **STEP 09** **LINK TO VIDEO** If you want to go one better than plain old audio and text, you can link to videos stored in iTunes. Again, it's simply a case of putting a link in the note where you want it to appear: *<A HREF="video=VIDEO TITLE"> Link to VIDEO TITLE Music Video</A>* When the video finishes, you'll be returned to the note.

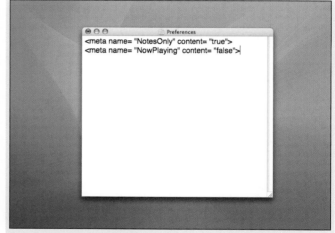

▲ **STEP 10** **CONTINUE SHOWING NOTE** If you've included a link to an audio file, it will play in the normal manner, showing the album art and title. If you'd rather it continue to show the note, you need to add a new meta tag to the Preferences file from step 2. Type *<meta name="NowPlaying" content="false">* and save the file. Now audio will play without displaying album artwork.

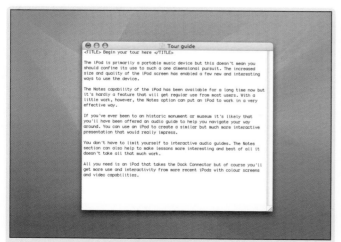

▲ **STEP 11** **NOTE TITLE** By default, the iPod will display the filename of each text document. If you wish to give a note a different display name than the document title, all you have to do is type a title tag into the note. For example, type *<TITLE>NEW NAME</TITLE>*, save it and the iPod will display this name rather than the document's actual title.

▲ **STEP 12** **PODCAST ALTERNATIVE** If the idea of typing guides and linking them all together is a bit much for you, you can use GarageBand to offer an audio alternative. All you have to do then is create an audio link as described in step 8.

MASTERCLASS
Graphics in Word 2004

It's easy to add graphics to your Word documents, but there are multiple ways to manage them when they're on the page. Here we show you how to get the most out of each.

Kit required Microsoft Office 2004
Time 30 minutes
Goal Positioning graphics in Word
Skill level Intermediate

Take a Word 2004 file to a print bureau and they'll either slam the door in your face, laugh up their sleeves and charge you double, or try to persuade you to do it in InDesign instead. Word itself isn't a problem, it's Word documents with graphics that cause the trouble. Pictures appear to reflow from one page to the next without reason or warning, move around of their own volition even when they're 'floating' (that is not inline graphics), and even if you 'disconnect' them from the text, using the Advanced Layout dialog, they carry on doing it anyway.

Things improved markedly in Word 2008, but if you have yet to upgrade then you may need to apply a few workarounds.

A document that's fine on one machine can come out differently on another, depending on the margins, the font metrics, the wrap preferences – who knows? Word appears to have all the capabilities of a conventional DTP program, but it's an illusion. DTP programs let you assign fixed, immovable positions to objects on the page, but Word will never quite let go of the idea that pictures 'belong' to bits of text.

You can't stop it doing this either. But once you understand what Word is doing it is possible to work around it. This will make it easier to add and control graphics in your own documents. For good measure, it will also help you troubleshoot documents that you've been sent by other people.

INTERFACE

Market Share Survey Q1

SALES PERFORMANCE, PROFIT LOSS FIGURES AND FINANCIAL FORECASTS FOR 2008 IN ALL EU TERRITORIES

Executive summary

Duis autem vel eum iriure dolor in hendrerit in vulputate velit esse molestie consequat, vel illum dolore eu feugiat nulla facilisis at vero eros et accumsan et iusto odio dignissim qui blandit praesent luptatum zzril delenit augue duis dolore te feugait nulla facilisi. Nam liber tempor cum soluta nobis eleifend option congue nihil imperdiet doming id quod mazim placerat facer possim assum.

Lorem ipsum dolor sit amet, consectetuer adipiscing elit, sed diam nonummy nibh euismod tincidunt ut laoreet dolore magna aliquam erat volutpat. Ut wisi enim ad minim veniam, quis nostrud exerci tation ullamcorper suscipit lobortis nisl ut aliquip ex ea commodo consequat.

Duis autem vel eum iriure dolor in hendrerit in vulputate velit esse molestie consequat, vel illum dolore eu feugiat nulla facilisis at vero eros et accumsan et iusto odio dignissim qui blandit praesent luptatum zzril delenit augue duis dolore te feugait nulla facilisi. Nam liber tempor cum soluta nobis eleifend option congue nihil imperdiet doming id quod mazim placerat facer possim assum. Lorem ipsum dolor sit amet, consectetuer adipiscing elit, sed diam nonummy nibh euismod tincidunt ut laoreet dolore magna aliquam erat volutpat. Ut wisi enim ad minim veniam, quis nostrud exerci tation ullamcorper suscipit lobortis nisl ut aliquip ex ea commodo consequat.

Circulation restricted

Consultation process

Duis autem vel eum iriure dolor in hendrerit in vulputate velit esse molestie consequat, vel illum dolore eu feugiat nulla facilisis at vero eros et accumsan et iusto odio dignissim qui blandit praesent luptatum zzril delenit augue duis dolore te feugait nulla facilisi. Nam liber tempor cum soluta nobis eleifend option congue nihil imperdiet doming id quod mazim placerat facer possim assum.

Inline graphics act like text characters, flowing with the text automatically. This one's been set up as a drop cap.

Floating graphics can be given regular or irregular text wraps, and they can be anchored to move with the text they're associated with.

It's possible to fix the position of graphics on the page, but (annoyingly) they may still change position if the text moves.

▲ **STEP 01 SWITCH TO PAGE LAYOUT MODE** Whenever you're working with graphics in Word it's important to switch to Page Layout mode. There are two reasons for this. The first is that in other modes (Outline mode, specifically) not all graphics formatting options are available. The second is that you need to see exactly how the text and graphics flow on the page.

▲ **STEP 02 INSERTING INLINE GRAPHICS** We'll start by inserting a piece of clip-art, though this works just the same if you select an external file. First, place the insertion point where you want the picture to go, then insert it. It's added as an inline graphic embedded in the text at the insertion point. If the text reflows, the graphic goes with it.

▲ **STEP 03 INLINE GRAPHIC PROPERTIES** To resize an inline graphic, just drag a corner handle. When you click on a graphic, the Picture toolbar appears. You can click the right-facing arrow at the side to show the wrap properties. As you can see, ours is an inline graphic. You can turn these into floating graphics just by choosing one of the other wrap options.

▲ **STEP 04 GRAPHICS AS DROP CAPS** That's not what we're going to do here, though. Instead, we'll demonstrate a neat little Word trick for insetting the graphic in the paragraph. To do this, use the Format > Drop Cap command and choose the number of lines for the drop. Then just add a small Distance value so that the text doesn't go right up to the edge of the graphic.

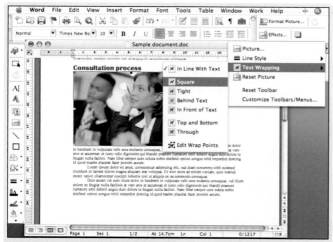

▲ **STEP 05 FLOATING GRAPHICS** Now we're adding another graphic – and again we have to choose an insertion point (all graphics are imported as inline). To float the image, select it and then choose one of the wrap options, using the Picture toolbar. Go for Square or Tight – Behind or In Front puts the image on a separate layer and the text no longer wraps around it.

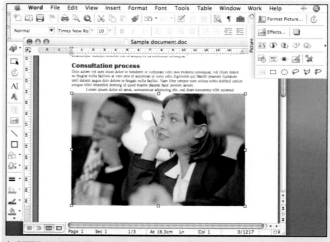

▲ **STEP 06 RESIZING AND REPOSITIONING** Now that the graphic is floating it's easy to move it to a new position by dragging it from the centre, and to resize it by dragging the corner handles. But although the picture now appears to be independent of the text, its position will change if the text reflows after any editing changes.

▲ **STEP 07 STOPPING GRAPHICS MOVING** This is the Word behaviour that causes all the problems. Its designers obviously felt that everyone would want pictures to stay alongside specific text. First, use the Format > Picture command and select the Layout tab. Now click on the Advanced button and the Picture Position tab, and deselect the Move object with text checkbox.

▲ **STEP 08 PAGE REFLOW PROBLEMS** But Word's not done yet. If we test these settings by typing in a few blank carriage returns above our 'Consultation process' heading, sure enough the picture stays where we put it. But if we type a few more, the picture disappears off the page. What's going on? This is not a bug. Word is doing exactly what its designers intended...

▲ **STEP 09 SHOW NON-PRINTING CHARACTERS...** To see what's happening you need to use the Show/Hide button on the toolbar to display non-printing characters. If you now click on a graphic, you'll see an anchor symbol located next to a nearby piece of text. The graphic is still anchored to a specific piece of text.

▲ **STEP 10 MOVING ANCHORS** The graphic will indeed stay where you put it unless the text it's anchored to gets shunted to a different page. Word will not tolerate this – it will move the graphic to the new page too. The only way to fix this is to reposition the graphic's anchor – here, you can see it's been moved from the second paragraph under the heading to the heading itself.

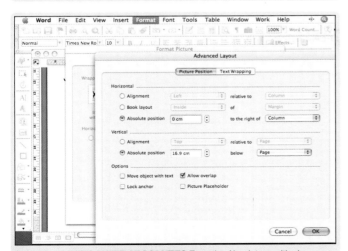

▲ **STEP 11 NOT QUITE ABSOLUTE?** Even the Absolute positioning in Word's Advanced Layout dialog isn't absolute. Look at the positioning pop-ups to the right of the Horizontal and Vertical settings. The picture's absolute position will in fact be relative to a number of choices, including the page, current page margins, current column and specific lines or characters.

▲ **STEP 12 IRREGULAR WRAPS** When you understand Word's graphic anchors, everything starts to make sense. It's then easier to add other graphic items such as this red 'Circulation restricted' bullet and have it behave in a predictable manner. It's been set up as a floating object with an irregular text wrap, but the anchor symbol shows it's locked to the 'Executive summary'.

MASTERCLASS
Tables of Contents in Word

The longer your documents, the more your readers will demand some kind of breakdown of what's in them, and where to find it…

Kit required Microsoft Office
Time 30 minutes
Goal Create a Table of Contents in Word
Skill level Intermediate

You could write a book about Word if you were so inclined, but you could also write a book in it. Long text-based documents require some kind of navigational help so that readers can steer straight to the bits they need. That's where you need a Table of Contents (TOC).

In its simplest form, a TOC tells you what the chapters are and what page they start on. But they can be a lot more complicated than that, adding extra 'levels' for headings and sub-headings within these chapters. What you don't want to do, of course, is plod through the whole document jotting down headings and page numbers and then typing them in manually yourself. But with some forward planning and some consistent text styling, you don't have to. Word generates its TOCs by finding every instance of specific text styles and putting them in a list – simple as that.

Word's TOCs can accommodate up to nine heading levels, but you need a bit of common sense, or the TOC will end up longer than the publication it describes. What Word generates is a 'field' object. If you click on a TOC it's highlighted in grey to show this. You don't edit the text within a TOC directly; instead you simply edit the TOC's overall properties (including its text styles). Our 'Digital imaging dictionary' example demonstrates how TOCs are defined, styled and formatted. Follow this simple guide to make your documents easier to navigate.

INTERFACE

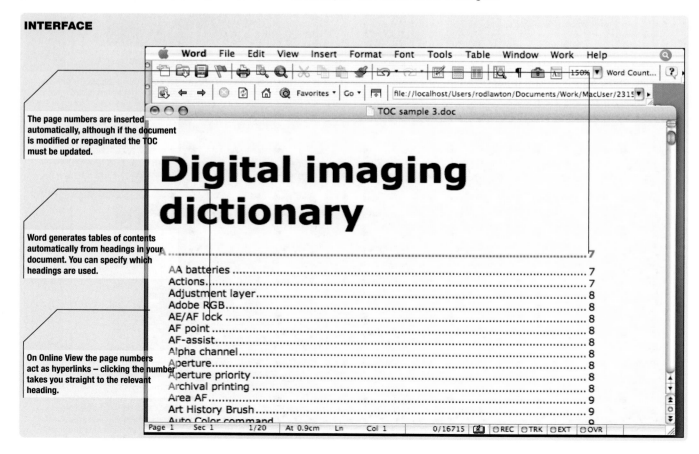

The page numbers are inserted automatically, although if the document is modified or repaginated the TOC must be updated.

Word generates tables of contents automatically from headings in your document. You can specify which headings are used.

On Online View the page numbers act as hyperlinks – clicking the number takes you straight to the relevant heading.

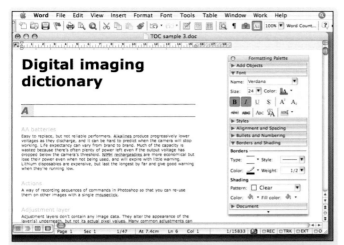

▲ **STEP 01 DEFINING TEXT STYLES 1** You can use Word's default text styles for the headings in your document, but it may prove less confusing to define your own because these will be easier to identify later. The first step is to choose the text properties – here we're using 24pt Verdana bold italic with upper and lower borders (see the settings in the Formatting Palette).

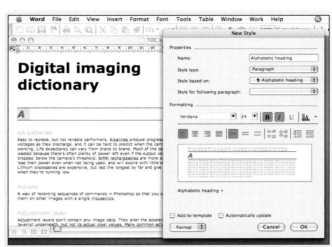

▲ **STEP 02 DEFINE TEXT STYLES 2** Once text has been styled up manually, it can easily be turned into a Style. With the modified text still selected, extend the Styles section of the Formatting Palette and then click the New Style button. The New Style dialog will display the text formatting you've just applied, so all you have to do is type in a Name that you'll remember later.

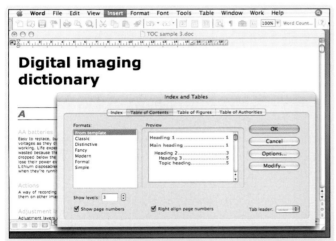

▲ **STEP 03 TABLE OF CONTENTS DIALOG** We've set up one more text style for the topic headings in our document, and now we can create a TOC using the Insert > Index and Tables command. Now click the Table of Contents tab. The Preview panel, centre, shows what the TOC will look like with the current settings, and you'll almost certainly need to change the defaults.

▲ **STEP 04 ALLOCATING STYLES TO TOC HEADINGS** The Options dialog lists all the Styles in use in your document. To the right of each is a TOC level box. If you don't want a Style to appear in the TOC, leave the box empty. Find the Style which represents your primary TOC heading and type a '1' in the box. Lower down in the list we've typed '2' next to the 'Topic heading' style.

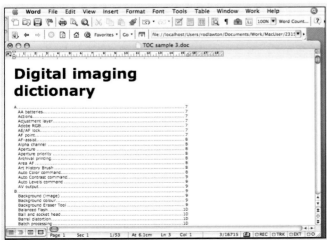

▲ **STEP 05 THE TOC INSERTED** Now we can go ahead and insert the TOC. These are placed at the insertion point. We've put ours directly below the document's main title. We can see now that all the instances of our 'Alphabetic heading' style are the main TOC headings (Level 1), and the 'Topic heading' items are secondary (Level 2) items. That was easy, wasn't it?

▲ **STEP 06 MODIFYING THE TOC STYLES 1** The text formatting in our TOC looks a little bland. To change this you use the Insert > Index and Tables command again – there's no way of directly modifying existing tables. This time, click the Modify button. This displays the TOC styles. These go all the way down to a Level 9, although we've only used two levels in our example.

▲ **STEP 07 MODIFYING THE TOC STYLES 2** We want to change the Level 1 style so that it stands out a bit more. To do this, we select it in the list and then press the Modify button to get the Modify Style dialog. We've set the text to bold, chosen the same brown colour used for the alphabetical headings in the document and increased the paragraph spacing.

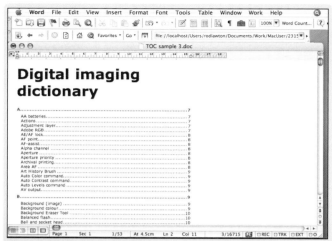

▲ **STEP 08 FINISHED TOC** Now when you've finished with the modifications you'll be asked whether you want to replace the existing TOC or not. The Level 1 TOC headings now stand out much better. They do take up quite a bit of space in the document, although there is a way of reducing this space without reducing the size of the text and making it hard to read.

▲ **STEP 09 INSERTING SECTION BREAKS** Instead of using a single column for the TOC we can run it across two columns. And we don't have to commit to a two-column layout for the whole document, either, because we can split it up into Sections. First, we need to put the insertion point directly before the TOC and choose Insert > Break > Section Break (Continuous).

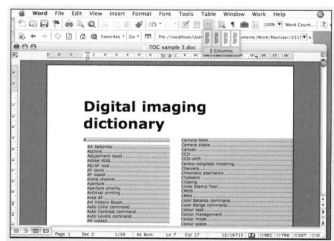

▲ **STEP 10 SWAPPING TO TWO COLUMNS** We also inserted another continuous section break after the TOC, effectively enclosing the TOC in a section all of its own. Now we click anywhere inside this section, click the Columns button on the toolbar and choose a two-column layout. However, this does affect the formatting in our example.

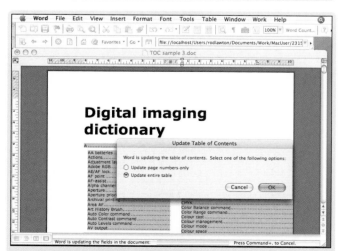

▲ **STEP 11 UPDATING THE TOC** This reflects the fact that TOCs don't contain 'live' data. Whenever you make a change to the documents' text or, in this case, changes to the formatting, the TOC must be updated. To do this, control-click on the TOC and choose Update Field. Update page numbers only is for minor repagination – we need the Update entire table button.

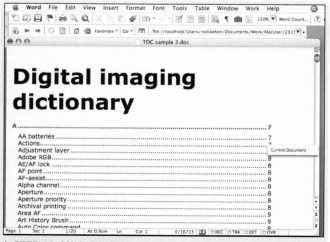

▲ **STEP 12 ONLINE VIEW** We're not quite done yet. Word's TOCs have an extra trick up their sleeve. If you switch to Online View, which is for documents designed to be read on screen rather than printed, you don't just get the chance to add a fancy background. You'll also discover that the page numbers are hyperlinked to the headings they refer to.

MASTERCLASS
Text Styles in Pages

Text Styles in Pages 08 will quickly make your documents look so much more professional – and it's well worth making the effort to master them.

Kit required iWork 08
Time 30 minutes
Goal Create quick and consistent text styling
Skill level Intermediate

There are three very good reasons for using Text Styles in Pages. The first is that they greatly speed up the job of formatting text in long documents and the second is that they bring consistency. In addition, Text Styles are an easy way to make global changes. Want to alter the body copy font or the heading style in your 60,000-word novel, for instance? It's about 15 seconds' work…

Pages has three types: Paragraph Styles, Character Styles and List Styles. Paragraph Styles are used for styling headings and larger bodies of text. You can't apply a Paragraph Style to single words, phrases or sentences unless they're on a line/paragraph of their own. For this, you need Character Styles, which

override Paragraph Styles, so that you can use the latter for basic text formatting throughout the document but apply a Character Style for words or phrases you want to emphasise in a particular font, colour or style. What's clever about Pages' Character Styles is that you can choose what Paragraph Style properties they override. You can opt to simply change the text colour, for example, or its font.

Paragraph and Character Styles are found in most word processing documents but Pages has a third – List Styles. These define the bullets for simple lists or the number/letter scheme but don't include font or formatting information. They work alongside existing Styles, so you don't get any style conflicts.

INTERFACE

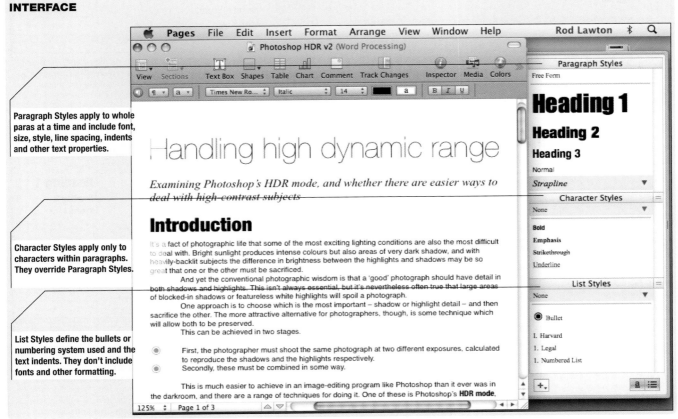

Paragraph Styles apply to whole paras at a time and include font, size, style, line spacing, indents and other text properties.

Character Styles apply only to characters within paragraphs. They override Paragraph Styles.

List Styles define the bullets or numbering system used and the text indents. They don't include fonts and other formatting.

▲ **STEP 01 PARAGRAPH STYLE** To apply a paragraph style to some text, select the text and then click on a Paragraph Style in the Styles Drawer. Here, we've applied the Heading 1 style to the text. You don't have to select the whole paragraph – just placing the insertion point somewhere in the paragraph is enough as Paragraph Styles always apply to whole paragraphs at a time.

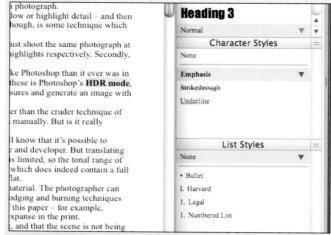

▲ **STEP 02 APPLYING A CHARACTER STYLE** Character styles are slightly different. You use these when you want to apply styles to text within a paragraph, not to the paragraph as a whole. We could just have put this HDR mode text in bold to emphasise it but using Emphasis Character Style gives us more flexibility later, including the ability to change this style globally.

▲ **STEP 03 MODIFYING AN EXISTING PARAGRAPH STYLE** The current Heading 1 style used for our heading was inherited from the original Microsoft Word document (Pages imports Word styles automatically). What about using a different font? First, select the text, then make any changes you want with the Formatting Bar. Here, we've swapped Impact for Helvetica Neue.

▲ **STEP 04 UPDATING THE STYLE** When you do this, you'll notice that the drop-down arrow to the right of the style name in the Styles Drawer turns from red to black. This indicates the style has been overridden by manual adjustments. Just click on the arrow to open the drop-down menu and choose Redefine Style from Selection to update the style.

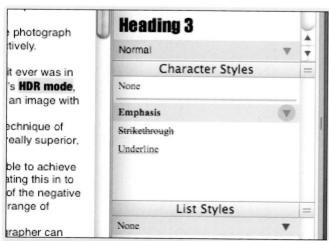

▲ **STEP 05 MODIFYING A CHARACTER STYLE** The procedure is the same for Character Styles. First, select a piece of text that uses the Character Style you want to modify and make your changes manually. You will see that the arrow to the right of the Character Style turns red, as here. Again, click on the arrow to open the pop-up menu and redefine the style as before.

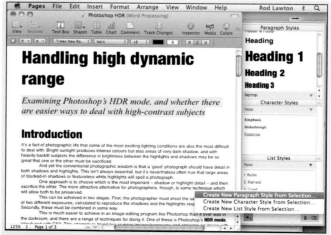

▲ **STEP 06 CREATING A NEW PARAGRAPH STYLE** Creating Paragraph Styles from scratch is as easy as modifying existing ones. First, style up the text manually – here we're using italicised 18pt Times Roman as a standfirst. Now, click and hold the '+' button in the bottom left-hand corner of the Styles Drawer and choose Create New Paragraph Style from Selection.

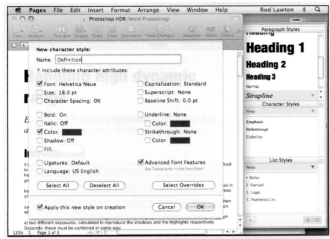

▲ **STEP 07 CREATING A NEW CHARACTER STYLE** You can create new Character Styles in the same way but there is a key difference. When you create either kind of style, a dialog prompts you for a name for the style. But the Character Style dialog has extended options. You can use these to control the degree to which the Character Style overrides the existing text attributes.

▲ **STEP 08 DELETING UNWANTED STYLES** Depending on the origins of your document there may be a large number of styles already which you're not using and just get in the way. You can delete them by clicking on the style's pop-up arrow in the Styles Draw and choosing Delete Style. If the style is in use, you'll be prompted to choose another style to apply to the affected text.

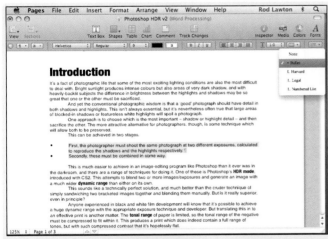

▲ **STEP 09 APPLYING A LIST STYLE** Finally, we'll take a look at List Styles. The simplest and most obvious use for these is when you have a series of bullet points in the text. You just select the text and choose the style you want from the List Styles pop-up on the Formatting Bar (you may need to increase the width of the document window for this to be visible).

▲ **STEP 10 CHANGING THE BULLET PROPERTIES** The default bullets are on the small side but this is easily fixed. Using the Text Inspector – click on the List tab to see the options available. Here we've chosen a larger bullet style from the pop-up on the left, then fine-tuned its vertical alignment, its size and the text indent, using the controls on the right.

▲ **STEP 11 MODIFYING A LIST STYLE** When you've made manual changes to a List Style you can redefine that style in the same way that you update Paragraph Styles and Character Styles. Click on its arrow in the Styles Drawer and choose Redefine Style from Selection. Alternatively you can create your own List Styles from scratch.

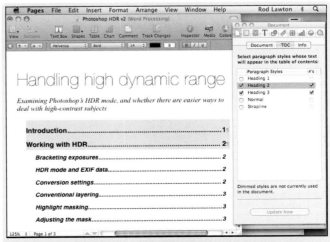

▲ **STEP 12 CREATING TOCS** Pages Styles don't just speed up your document formatting and make it more consistent. They enable you to generate Tables of Contents (TOCs) automatically from the Insert menu. This displays a dialog listing all the Paragraph Styles used in your document. Simply select those which you want to appear in the TOC.

MASTERCLASS
Handling photos in Pages

Sooner or later you'll want to illustrate a document with photos. It's a prospect you probably face with dread in Word, but in Pages it's simple.

Kit required iWork 08
Time 30 minutes
Goal Understand what you can do with photos in Pages
Skill level Intermediate

Pages is very good at handling photos. In principle it works in much the same way as Microsoft Word. In practice, it's a whole lot simpler and more predictable in the way it goes about it. Like Word, Pages offers either inline graphics or fixed graphics. Inline graphics are embedded in the text and move around with the text when you make changes. Fixed graphics stay in the same place on the page and the text flows around them. The problem with Word is that even if you think you've added a photo as a fixed graphic, it will still try to keep it with the text unless you disable this feature, which can be a real nuisance.

Pages offers some surprisingly sophisticated photo and layout tools. You can add rectangular masks to photos to crop unwanted areas, or you can make them with shapes. Masked photos can be given outlines and drop shadows, too, and you should try out the neat Reflection effect while you're at it. The text wrap options for fixed graphics are extensive and easy to use, even irregular wraps around cutouts.

Pages integrates with iPhoto and Aperture too, so that if you open the Media panel you can drag and drop photos directly from your albums. It's much faster and simpler than having to return to the Finder to retrieve media. It's even possible to make basic image adjustments within Pages using the same tools available in iPhoto. All this is explained in detail in our workthrough.

INTERFACE

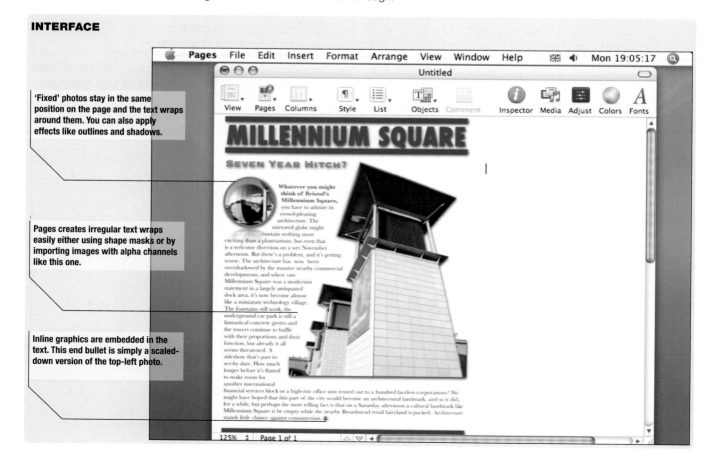

'Fixed' photos stay in the same position on the page and the text wraps around them. You can also apply effects like outlines and shadows.

Pages creates irregular text wraps easily either using shape masks or by importing images with alpha channels like this one.

Inline graphics are embedded in the text. This end bullet is simply a scaled-down version of the top-left photo.

▲ **STEP 01 PREPARING YOUR PHOTOS** You can start off by choosing the photos you want to use in your layout. Here we're creating an Album in iPhoto and adding the images we might want to use. The Media panel in Pages displays a cut-down version of the iPhoto interface, but you can still browse all your Albums and carry out text searches.

▲ **STEP 02 ADDING PHOTOS WITH DRAG AND DROP** You don't have to use the Media panel at all. You can drag and drop photos directly from iPhoto or from the Finder. Simply dragging an image across drops it on the page as a 'fixed' graphic. To add a photo as an inline graphic, hold down the Command key as you drag and move the mouse to position the insertion point.

▲ **STEP 03 CHECK THE WRAP OPTIONS** If you don't hold down the Command key, new images are added as fixed graphics – check the settings in the Wrap Inspector. At the top are radio buttons for fixed versus inline positioning, below this you choose the wrap style (one side, both sides, top and bottom) and the bottom section offers regular versus irregular wrapping.

▲ **STEP 04 RESIZING AND MOVING PHOTOS** To move a fixed graphic, just drag it. The text reflows in real time as you do it. To resize the photo, drag any corner or edge handle. Note that the image proportions are constrained automatically. Inline graphics work slightly differently in that only the bottom and right-hand drag handles are available.

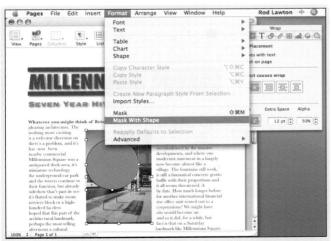

▲ **STEP 05 ADDING A SHAPE MASK** At the moment our imported photo is a regular rectangular shape, but we want to make it circular to echo the shape of the mirrored sphere. To create a shape mask, first create the shape and position it over the photo you want to mask and use the Format > Mask with Shape command. The shape's line and fill don't matter.

▲ **STEP 06 MANAGING MASKS** And here's the mask applied to the photo. At the moment, the mask is still visible and selected, and we can resize it and move it if we need to. Once you click away from the graphic, though, the photo is masked fully and the mask and photo move around as a single item. To edit them individually again you need to double-click.

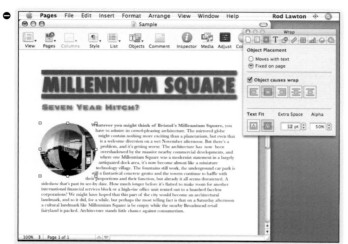

▲ **STEP 07 IRREGULAR WRAP SETTINGS** Now the masked photo's been moved into position at the start of the text block. The text wraps automatically around it. This is one of the beauties of Pages – it picks the right wrap settings by default, and these can be examined in the Wrap Inspector. If the wrapped text is too close or too far away, change the Extra Space value.

▲ **STEP 08 GRAPHIC EFFECTS** Pages looks simple, but it has unexpected depths. We can apply a Stroke to our masked photo and choose a thickness and a colour from the Graphic Inspector. A nice drop shadow is just a checkbox away and the finished layout in our main annotation on page 202 demonstrates the very attractive Reflection effect too.

▲ **STEP 09 IMAGES WITH ALPHA CHANNELS** For our main image we want to use a cut-out shot of some modernistic towers, and while we could try to create a custom shape mask in Pages, it would be laborious and crude. Instead, we need to do a bit of preparatory work in Photoshop. We've simply promoted the background image to a layer and then deleted the sky.

▲ **STEP 10 PLACING THE MAIN IMAGE** Pages can import Photoshop files directly, so there's nothing more that needs doing. You don't have to actually create an alpha channel in Photoshop – simply erasing the unwanted parts of the image layer is enough. The photo's been dragged into Pages from the Finder and the text wraps automatically – simple as that.

▲ **STEP 11 IMAGE ADJUSTMENTS** Not quite happy with the colours or the contrast or the sharpness? Clicking on the Adjust button opens up the familiar iPhoto Adjust palette. It's clever and surprising, and it might save you a bit of time and effort, but it's more likely you'll want to do all your editing separately, since the iPhoto adjustments are pretty crude and basic.

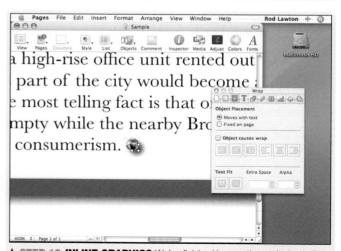

▲ **STEP 12 INLINE GRAPHICS** We've finished by creating a closing bullet from the circular photo used at the start by copying the image, placing the text insertion point at the end and pasting. The stroke was removed and the image resized to fit the line height. Be warned, though, that Pages doesn't resample photos when it resizes them, so file sizes can swell.

MASTERCLASS
Advanced charting in Excel

See the invisible and predict the future! And you thought Excel was just a spreadsheet? The right chart can reveal the meaning in your data…

Kit required Microsoft Office
Time 30 minutes
Goal Getting the best from Excel's charts
Skill level Advanced

Charts are a great way to prove a point. A graphical demonstration of a product's success or a department's contribution to company profits will always be instantly obvious in a chart, in a way that bare figures aren't.

But charts can do more than just convince other people of something you already know. Quite often, a chart can help you see something that would be impossible to grasp from simply looking at the numbers. Feeding a mass of seemingly random data to a scatter chart can show you quickly and visibly whether there's a correlation or not.

In our workthrough, we have created two sets of data. The first shows the monthly rental of a flat together with its distance from a mainline railway station. It's very hard to tell from simply looking at the figures whether there is a strong correlation or not but when the scatter chart is plotted, any correlation becomes very easy to see. This chart, therefore, can reveal invisible patterns in the data.

The second set of figures correlate the prices of petrol and biofuel over time. After plotting these lists of prices, we will use them to forecast what will happen to them using an Excel feature called Trendlines. These can take the existing data and extrapolate it into the future, using a variety of mathematical models to make the results much more than just guesswork.

INTERFACE

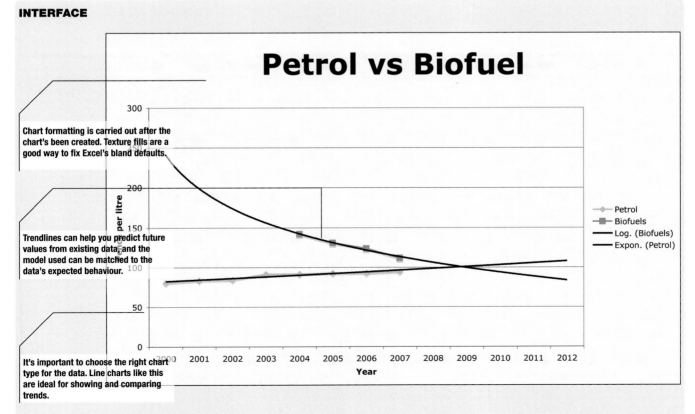

Chart formatting is carried out after the chart's been created. Texture fills are a good way to fix Excel's bland defaults.

Trendlines can help you predict future values from existing data, and the model used can be matched to the data's expected behaviour.

It's important to choose the right chart type for the data. Line charts like this are ideal for showing and comparing trends.

▲ **STEP 01 FORMATTING SCATTER CHART DATA** The secret to creating any chart is to arrange the data carefully before you start. You need contiguous data tables (no gaps) with labels at the top, at the sides, or both. Here, we've simply got two columns, one headed 'Price' and one headed 'Distance'. These cells and the data below have been selected.

▲ **STEP 02 CHOOSE THE CHART TYPE** Now we click on the Chart Wizard button on the toolbar. The first step is to choose the chart type. We've gone for the 'XY (Scatter)' type. Scatter charts plot data points from two coordinates on the x and y axes. In this example, each property we look at has a 'price' (rental per month) and a 'distance' (from the station) value.

▲ **STEP 03 TITLE AND AXIS LABELS** Excel is pretty good at identifying data series and axis labels automatically from the data, but you will need to specify a title for the chart and the x and y axis labels. This is done in step 3 of the Chart Wizard. Here, you're just creating the necessary chart objects. Any formatting comes later, when the chart's been made.

▲ **STEP 04 OBJECT OR SHEET?** The last step of the wizard asks whether you want the chart created as an object on the current sheet or on a separate worksheet of its own. The advantage of a new worksheet is that you can give it a descriptive name and go straight to your chart at any time in future just by clicking its worksheet tab at the bottom of the window.

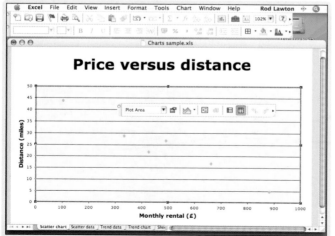

▲ **STEP 05 FORMATTING THE CHART** This is the finished chart with the scatter points plotted. We've made a couple of other formatting changes too, because Excel's chart defaults look pretty grim. To change an object like the chart title or the plot area, select it and then click the Format button on the Chart toolbar. Here, we've given the chart area a texture fill.

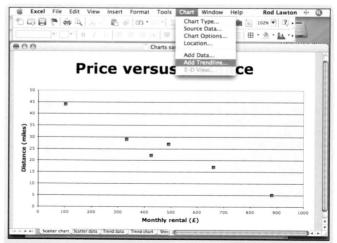

▲ **STEP 06 ADDING A TRENDLINE** Now it's clear just from looking at the scatter points that there is a pretty strong correlation. So can we use this data to predict prices for other distances (and vice versa)? Yes. We can get started by selecting the data series (just click on any of the points) and choosing Add Trendline from the Chart menu.

▲ **STEP 07 LINEAR TRENDLINES** Trendlines are a 'best-fit' line through the data, and they can be created with a variety of mathematical models. Our data is too limited in terms of the sample size to justify a complex trend analysis, though, so we're going for the Linear Trend/Regression type. This will just draw a straight line through the data points.

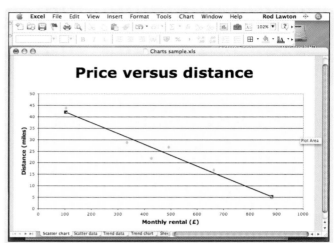

▲ **STEP 08 ASSESSING THE TREND** And the results actually look quite convincing. All of the data points are actually quite close to the line, so the correlation seems good. You could now use the Trendline to predict the cost of a flat at a given distance from the station, or set your maximum budget and see how close to the station you could afford to live.

▲ **STEP 09 WORKING WITH TWO DATA SERIES** Now we're going to try something more ambitious. This time we want to make predictions rather than simply establishing a pattern. We've got two sets of data here – the prices of petrol and biofuels plotted against the year. However, our data is incomplete. We've got data up to 2007, but we want to plan for 2012.

▲ **STEP 10 DUAL LINE CHARTS** We've used the Chart Wizard to produce a line chart from our two data series. Note, that although the bottom axis goes all the way to 2012, our data stops at 2007. We left the cells under the years 2008-2012 blank on purpose to make sure Excel produced a chart long enough to accommodate our predictions.

▲ **STEP 11 ADDING THE TRENDLINES** Here, simple Linear Trendlines seem just a bit too… well, simple. We expect the price of biofuels to start high, drop quickly and level out, and a Logarithmic Trendline will reflect this. Petrol prices, on the other hand, are likely to rise sharply as oil reserves fall and biofuels take over, and an Exponential Trendline will mirror this behaviour.

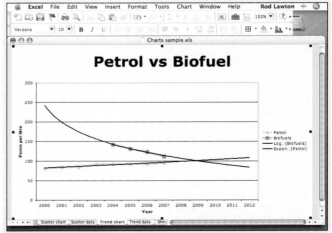

▲ **STEP 12 ANALYSING THE CHART** As you can see from the results, these Trendline types don't distort existing data into new shapes. Where the data points show a fairly linear progression, the Trendlines stick to it. But what our Trendlines can do is show us (a) when the petrol and biofuel costs are likely to be the same, and (b) a broad window of similar pricing.

MASTERCLASS
Filtering mail in Entourage

Every day we're bombarded by emails, the vast majority of which are time-wasting trash. If you've installed Entourage to bin the junk, here's how to ensure it does the job properly

Kit required Microsoft Office
Time 30 minutes
Goal Get your email sorted automatically
Skill level Intermediate

Entourage's junk filter does its best but it isn't really smart enough to figure out what we need to read and what we don't. Let's face it, any junk filter that fails to spot when our ISP's mail server inserts '*** SPAM ***' in the subject line can't be that bright. And there's always the worry that Entourage's junk filter' will chuck out messages it shouldn't – if you check the Junk folder now, you'll soon see that there's plenty to worry about.

In fact, it's easy to tell Entourage what isn't junk and stop it getting it wrong again. One option is to use mailing-list rules, which can automatically identify and file regular newsletters and bulletins – from there it's a short step to setting up your own custom rules that

are just more advanced versions of the same thing. Rules intercept incoming mail and carry out specific actions depending on whether it meets the criteria.

Let's say you've an interest in *Coronation Street* memorabilia and you subscribe to dozens of possibly relevant mailing lists. You could set up a rule which checks messages for any *Corrie* reference and have them automatically flagged and filed. But do check that your rules really do work before letting them loose on your mail. And don't get so carried away that you create dozens of super-complex rules that you can't understand six months later when you've forgotten what you did and why.

Clever is good, but useful is better.

INTERFACE

You might miss something important if messages are automatically diverted into folders. So set up rules which flag messages from specific senders.

Mailing list rules can automatically divert newsletters to specific folders and it takes only a minute or two to set them up.

Is your Inbox full of rubbish? Entourage's junk filter can clear some of it, while a few well-planned 'rules' can deal with the rest.

▲ **STEP 01 HOW THE JUNK FOLDER WORKS** Microsoft includes a
Junk filter (called SmartScreen) in Entourage which automatically diverts what it
thinks is junk to a special Junk folder. You're advised to check this folder now
and then to make sure there's no 'real' mail in there, and you'd be wise to do
so because the filter is far from perfect and often bins 'real' mail.

▲ **STEP 02 WHAT IF IT'S NOT JUNK?** If you find a message that isn't
junk in the Junk folder you can select it and press the Not Junk button to return
it to the Inbox. You'll also be asked if you want to prevent this happening again.
Adding the sender's name to your address book is one solution – but creating
a mailing list rule is a much better one…

▲ **STEP 03 MAILING LIST RULES** Mailing list rules are useful for regular
newsletters, and they're also a good introduction to user-defined rules, which
we'll come to shortly. You can also create a mailing list rule using the Tools >
Mailing List Manager option. This is the dialog you get but it must be filled in
carefully. Don't just accept the defaults.

▲ **STEP 04 GET THE LIST ADDRESS RIGHT** It's the List address box
you need to pay attention to. By default this will contain your own email
address – the one the list is sent to. If you leave this as it is, the mailing list rule
you create will apply to all your incoming mail. Instead make sure you insert the
email address of the sender – you can get this from the message header.

▲ **STEP 05 CHOOSING A FOLDER** The default action for mailing lists is
to route them to a particular folder which you choose, using the pop-up menu
under the List address box. This opens a dialog box where you can choose
an existing folder or create a new one. Here, we're setting up a mailing list rule
to divert a regular Colour Confidence newsletter to its own folder.

▲ **STEP 06 APPLYING RULES RETROSPECTIVELY** Any mailing list
rule you create will apply only to new mail. Mail already received stays exactly
where it is. But you can apply the rule to existing mail too. (It's probably best
to apply it to a single message first to make sure it's working properly.) Select
the message(s), Ctrl-click it and choose Apply Rule > All Rules.

▲ **STEP 07 CREATING A CUSTOM RULE** Entourage doesn't distinguish between mailing list rules – they all come under the general heading 'all rules'. They're also limited to storing messages in specific folders. However, you can create much more sophisticated rules of your own (Tools > Rules) based on complex message criteria and producing more than one action.

▲ **STEP 08 CHOOSE THE RULE CRITERIA** This is a two-step process. First, you choose the criteria for identifying messages. Our MotoGP rule looks for emails from a specific email address, though you can also check subject or message content. It's possible to have multiple criteria and make the rule check for all of them or any of them in incoming mail.

▲ **STEP 09 CHOOSING THE ACTION** Next, you decide what you want to happen when specific incoming messages have been identified. Just as you have multiple criteria for identifying messages, you can set up multiple actions which you then want applied to the mail. Our first action here is to move the message from the Inbox to a different folder…

▲ **STEP 10 ADDING MORE ACTIONS** Our second action is to flag these messages. Typically you'd flag messages that you need to act on in some way but you can also use flags to prioritise messages to ensure you read the most important first. You could also display an Entourage 'notification', play a sound, forward the mail to another address and more.

▲ **STEP 11 APPLYING RULES TO EXISTING MAIL** As with mailing list rules, you can apply these custom rules retrospectively, though do check them in individual messages before you apply them to the entire contents of your Inbox. This time when you open the Apply Rule menu, you'll see that any custom rules you've set up can be applied individually.

▲ **STEP 12 DOES IT WORK?** Our MotoGP rule has identified all existing mail from the Pramac D'Antin MotoGP press office, moved it to a folder of its own and flagged it. It'll now check incoming mail and do the same with any new messages. Just be careful when setting up rules that you don't make them so numerous and so complex that you forget what they do.

MASTERCLASS
Using signatures
in Entourage

How many hours of your life have you wasted in manually signing off emails with your name, your phone number and your address?

Kit required Microsoft Office
Time 15 minutes
Goal Setting up signatures in Entourage
Skill level Beginner

Setting up signatures seems such a piffling little job that many of us simply never get round to it. Each time you sign off it just appears so much easier to type out a couple of lines of text manually than to ferret around in Entourage's entrails, looking for a way to set up a signature.

Okay, so it doesn't take long to type out your name. But what about your phone number or your mobile, your office address? A signature won't just save you time but it will also prevent you from making silly typing mistakes. Signatures also add a little polish and consistency to your messages.

They're a great way to promote the company that you work for, creating a subtly more businesslike impression. Without a consistent signature, it looks as though you're making it all up as you go along and if you work for a company, you may or may not be communicating on their behalf.

In fact, it doesn't take long to set up a few handy signatures. You can have one for friends and family, another for business colleagues and another for customers. All of these signatures are freely interchangeable between your email accounts – you just choose the one you want to use from a list at the top of the message window. Or you can pick a specific signature as the default for any given email account. There's even a good case for using Entourage's Random signature feature… Honestly.

INTERFACE

To add logos and other graphics to signatures you first have to set the formatting of both the Signature and the message to HTML.

These two hyphens are a standardised 'signature delimiter' used by many email programs to remove signatures from replies.

URLs are automatically made clickable in plain text signatures but in HTML signatures, make sure that you add the 'http://' in front of the web address.

Engine test results — Inbox

Delete   Junk   Reply   Reply All Forward   Print

From: Mike Beeton
Subject: **Engine test results**
Date: 17 September 2007 14:34:25 BDT
To: Frank Osborne
▶ 1 Attachment, 63.4 KB (Save ▾) (Slideshow)

Hi Frank,

Have you had time to look at the engine data from Saturday's tests yet? I'm keen to compare the telemetry with January's prototype.

Crimson-Sports

http://www.crimson-sports.co.uk

▲ STEP 01 **WHERE SIGNATURES ARE STORED** You can set up as many signatures as you like, any of which can be added to an outgoing message. To see your signatures, edit them or add new ones, go to Tools > Signatures. Note the checkboxes to the left under the Random column. Random signatures aren't such a crazy idea as they might sound, as you'll see.

▲ STEP 02 **INSERTING A SIGNATURE** This is straightforward. Write your message as normal, then look for the Signature pop-up on the toolbar at the top of the Message window. This displays a list of all the available signatures – the same list that you see in the Signatures window. When you choose a signature, Entourage inserts it on a new line.

▲ STEP 03 **ADDING WEB ADDRESSES TO SIGNATURES** You can use your signature to add your name, your phone number or your address. You can also use it to add the URL of your website. There's no need to add any special formatting – just type it in as you would in the address bar of your web browser. Don't worry that it's not highlighted as a link.

▲ STEP 04 **WHAT THE RECIPIENT GETS** If you send someone a URL as part of your signature, it arrives as a 'hot' hyperlink. When they click the link, it opens the site in their default web browser. (If you want to double-check that your email is arriving with a clickable link, just type your own email address into the Cc: field when you send the message.)

▲ STEP 05 **HTML FORMATTING** But what if you want to use your company logo in your signature? By default, Entourage sends plain text messages that don't support graphics; this also applies to its signatures. So when you want to create a signature with graphics, you first have to select the HTML option from the Format menu.

▲ STEP 06 **INSERTING A LOGO** There are two ways to add graphics. You can either use the Message > Insert > Picture command or open a Finder window and simply drag the image across. Ensure that you resize the image first, though, choosing dimensions suitable for on-screen viewing, because there are no facilities for resizing, moving or cropping images in this window.

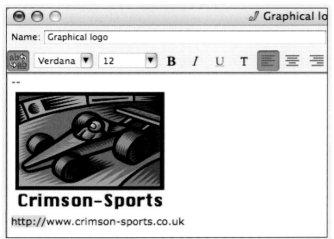

▲ **STEP 07 FIXING LINKS** There's one more thing you have to do. Bizarrely, Entourage will automatically make a URL 'hot' in a plain text signature but it won't do the same in an HTML signature, so that a link in this format won't work when it arrives with the recipient. What you have to do is insert 'http://' in front of it.

▲ **STEP 08 USING HTML SIGNATURES** Now here's another thing that can trip you up. You've created your HTML signature but when you try to add it to the end of a message, the graphics are missing. That's because the message itself is set to plain text format – here again you need to choose the Format > HTML option (or change the Entourage preferences).

▲ **STEP 09 WHAT THE RECIPIENT SEES** Assuming that your recipient has their email client set up to receive and display HTML-format messages, your signature should display correctly. This is how our message looks in Apple Mail. If some recipients complain it's not working, you'll have to design a plain text signature just for them.

▲ **STEP 10 SIGNATURES WITH BACKGROUNDS** You can even add a background image. Entourage will tile this image repeatedly to fill the size of the message window, so bear that in mind when choosing graphics. Here, we've chosen a simple texture. Note that the background image doesn't just sit behind the signature – it will fill the whole message window.

▲ **STEP 11 RANDOM SIGNATURES** Now what about these signatures? They might seem like a pointless novelty feature, but actually they can be useful. We've set up four signatures for our Crimson Sports company, each with a different slogan. If we insert a Random signature at the end of our messages, the recipients will get different slogans every time.

▲ **STEP 12 DEFAULT SIGNATURES** You don't have to choose signatures manually. Each of Entourage's accounts (Tools > Accounts) can be set up with a default signature – select the Options tab in the Edit Account window and choose a signature from the list. Now, whenever you create a message with that account, the signature is added automatically.

MASTERCLASS
PowerPoint's drawing tools

Given the state of most PowerPoint presentations, you might think its drawing tools date back to the Stone Age. We show you how to make a more modern show.

Kit required Microsoft Office
Time 30 minutes
Goal Get the most out of PowerPoint's drawing tools
Skill level Intermediate

It's PowerPoint's templates that are to blame. Whoever put them together didn't spend much time at design college and they certainly don't reflect the scope and the versatility of PowerPoint's drawing tools either. These are actually on a par with those from a half-decent vector-drawing program, and include fully-editable Bézier curves and transparency, together with extremely useful drafting tools, such as 'sticky' connector lines.

It's not really possible to demonstrate the full scope of PowerPoint's drawing tools in just 12 steps, but our workthrough does show a glimpse of their potential. We've based it on a typical business presentation – promoting a new product to the board

or to potential distributors. The 30 minutes a slide like this might take to put together is easily justified if it tips a sale one way or the other. The main thing is to forget about the templates supplied with the program and start from scratch. If you're not a professional designer, just take inspiration from magazines or ads. The pro secrets are consistency and simplicity. Keep the number of fonts to a minimum, use just two or three colours and keep all the line weights the same.

The example seen here is a static slide, but don't forget that PowerPoint's animation tools can be used to build a slide like this an item at a time, giving the presenter time to introduce each item to the audience and add to the interactive feel.

INTERFACE

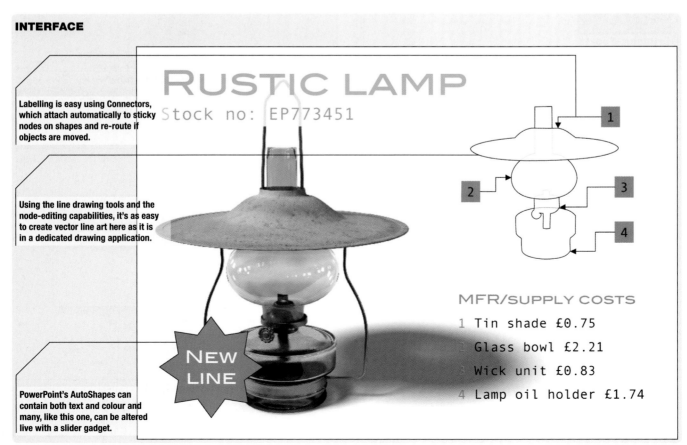

Labelling is easy using Connectors, which attach automatically to sticky nodes on shapes and re-route if objects are moved.

Using the line drawing tools and the node-editing capabilities, it's as easy to create vector line art here as it is in a dedicated drawing application.

PowerPoint's AutoShapes can contain both text and colour and many, like this one, can be altered live with a slider gadget.

▲ **STEP 01 IMPORTING PHOTOS** When you insert a photo, the Picture toolbar will display automatically. This includes a Crop button that we can use to trim the white space around this image. To resize a photo, drag a corner handle, to reposition a photo, drag from the centre. Any vector art you insert is handled as a picture initially, but it can be converted into an editable object.

▲ **STEP 02 ADDING A TITLE BOX** Now we've added a title box for the slide and chosen the fonts and colours. But we need some way to dim the image behind the box, otherwise the text becomes illegible. We can do this by making the box background partially transparent. First, the fill colour is set to white, then the Transparency slider is set to 50% in the Format Text Box dialog.

▲ **STEP 03 ADDING AN AUTOSHAPE** The next step is to add a flash advertising the fact that this is a new product. For this we can use one of PowerPoint's ready-made AutoShapes. This also demonstrates a neat bit of interface design – most of the pop-up palettes on the Drawing toolbar can be dragged off and floated on the screen, so they remain available all the time.

▲ **STEP 04 CHANGING AUTOSHAPE PROPERTIES** AutoShapes are more than static ready-made elements. Many of them can be modified quickly, like this eight-point star – look out for the yellow diamond-shaped gadgets. In this case, dragging the gadget changes the depth of the star's rays. The effect varies with the shape.

▲ **STEP 05 ADDING TEXT TO AUTOSHAPES** To add text to an AutoShape, control-click it and choose Add Text from the shortcut menu. Note that the AutoShape doesn't strictly act as a container for the text. If you make the AutoShape smaller, the text will simply overhang the edges. If you use the Format > Font command you can use a slider to adjust the font size live.

▲ **STEP 06 DRAWING LINES** The next job is to draw outlines for the main components of the lamp, and for this we need the Lines palette. Again, this can be torn off the Drawing toolbar and floated on the screen. The two most useful lines for this job are the Curve (bottom left) and Freeform (bottom centre) tools. One produces curved line segments, the other produces straight lines.

▲ **STEP 07 THE ROUGH VERSION** There's no need to be too accurate with this. It's easier to modify a small number of points carefully than it is to edit or delete a large number. To make the tracing job easier, the shape's fill has been set to white and the transparency to 50%. This means the photo shows through underneath, this makes it a lot easier to trace the outline.

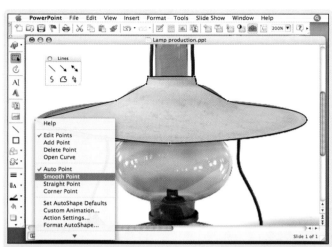

▲ **STEP 08 EDITING POINTS** To modify shapes, first control-click the shape and choose Edit Points from the shortcut menu. You can now move the points around individually. To change the point type, control-click the point and choose from Auto (the default – no handles), Smooth Point (a symmetrical Bézier node), Straight Point (asymmetrical Bézier node) and Corner Point.

▲ **STEP 09 ADJUSTING CONTROL HANDLES** These control points are very easy to modify. The points don't highlight when you select them, but the cursor changes when you're over them and in practice there's no problem selecting points or their handles. In just a couple of minutes it's possible to produce a pretty good approximation of the lampshade.

▲ **STEP 10 CHANGING THE STACKING ORDER** This is the result of tracing the other lamp components in the same way and then moving the shapes to the top right corner, where they're going to be used for labelled annotation. To give the required cutaway effect, each shape has a white fill set to 50% transparency. Then stacked in the right order with the Arrange pop-up.

▲ **STEP 11 NUMBERED LABELS** The numbered labels are easy enough to do – these are simply text boxes with a solid red fill. It's best to create and format one box first and then duplicate it for the rest, rather than reformatting each new box individually. We could also have used an AutoShape with text inside it – that would be better if you wanted a circular shape, for example.

▲ **STEP 12 CONNECTOR LINES** Finally, we can add the Connector lines linking the numbered labels with the shapes. These Connectors have their own tear-off palette on the AutoShapes flyout. To use them, position the mouse pointer over the first shape and sticky blue nodes will appear. Now drag the line from one of these to connect with a sticky node on the other shape.

MASTERCLASS
Advanced animation in PowerPoint

Too many PowerPoint presentations are just dull and static screens of data. But they don't have to be when the built-in animation tools are so straightforward to use.

Kit required Microsoft Office
Time About an hour or so
Goal Discover PowerPoint's animation tools
Skill level Intermediate

If you've spent any time at all with
PowerPoint you'll know that it comes with a wide range of slide transitions to liven up presentations. But there's a lot more you can do, and you may end up quite surprised by PowerPoint's capabilities.

Any object on a PowerPoint slide can be given an animation effect. The object starts off hidden, but then appears on the slide when the user clicks or when the previous animation effect has finished. This means that you can 'build' slides progressively, creating animated sequences that run on their own, or you can control this 'build' manually using the mouse.

Central to this is the Custom Animation dialogue, the hub of all PowerPoint's animation options. It looks complex, but it doesn't take long to get to grips with. PowerPoint on the Mac does have its limits (the Windows version, amazingly, even supports customisable motion paths), but there's still enough there to add some pizzazz.

We've only scratched the surface here, picking out just a couple of neat Entrance effects to work with. PowerPoint also offers Emphasis and Exit effects so that you can make an object appear and disappear too. Also, our workthrough only shows animation effects working one after the other, but they can also run simultaneously.

You can have a lot more fun with PowerPoint animations than you might have imagined.

INTERFACE

This whole top section of the slide 'assembles' itself automatically as the slide opens, complete with sound effects.

You can save time with preset animations. For example, this text can be made to appear one letter at a time to the sound of typewriter keys.

Text can also be made to appear one line at a time when you press the mouse button.

■ your security specialist
online vaults inc.

Five short questions

1. Is your data backed up?
2. Are your backups stored remotely?
3. Are they stored securely?
4. Who's responsible for their maintenance?
5. Does anyone in your company know?

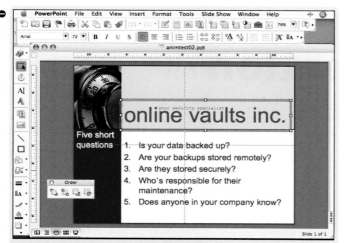

▲ **STEP 01 START AT THE END** It's tempting to try to assemble the finished slide one item at a time, animating as you go, but in fact it's much easier to start with the finished slide and work backwards. When all the objects are already in place, all that's left to do is work out how they get there and in what order.

▲ **STEP 02 ANIMATIONS AND ACTIONS** We'll start by selecting the first object we want to appear on the slide – the close-up of the combination lock. The animation options can all be found on the Slide Show menu. You can use Preset Animations (we'll use one shortly) but for the moment we're going with the Custom Animation option.

▲ **STEP 03 CHOOSE AN EFFECT** This opens the Custom Animation dialog. On the left is a list of the objects on the slide and below it is a small preview of the slide. Our photo (Picture Frame 4) is shown here as being selected. At the top right, we need to click the Add Effect button, then choose an Entrance effect from the list – we've gone for Fly In.

▲ **STEP 04 CHOOSE THE EFFECT SETTINGS** The animation effect is now added to the list on the right of the dialog, but we need to change its Start option. The default is On Click, but we want the animation to begin as soon as the slide is opened, so we change this to After Previous. We've also set the Fly In direction to From Top using the Property pop-up.

▲ **STEP 05 CHOOSE A SOUND EFFECT** The animation might look cool, but it's completely silent, which rather lessens the impact. You can add a sound to any animation by clicking the Effect Options button and choosing a sound from the pop-up. You'll need to try a few to find one that matches the duration of the animation – Camera works well here.

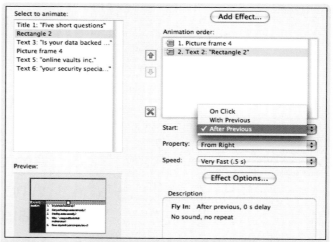

▲ **STEP 06 ANIMATING THE NEXT OBJECT** We want the blue-green box across the top of the slide to appear next, and it's the same procedure. Again, we've gone for the Fly In effect, and this time we've set the Property (direction) to From Right. We've also set the Start to After Previous so that it carries on automatically from the last animation.

▲ **STEP 07 FADING IN THE TEXT** Next, we want the company name, Online Vaults inc, to fade in gently. It's good to introduce a little variety into your animations, but do stick to just two or three different styles and sound effects. It's like mixing fonts and colours in a design: one's not enough, two's good, but more than three is playing with fire.

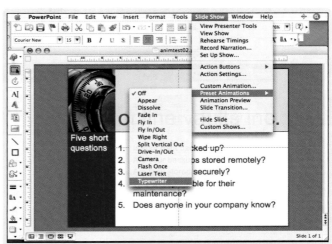

▲ **STEP 08 PRESET ANIMATIONS** Now we mentioned Preset Animations earlier, and here's a good opportunity to show them in action. Our company strapline is 'your security specialist', and we've used Courier, a 'typewriter' font, deliberately. PowerPoint's Typewriter preset makes the characters appear one by one to the sound of a typewriter.

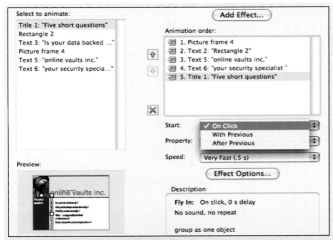

▲ **STEP 09 MANUAL CONTROL** That's the 'automatic' part of the slide taken care of. The elements assemble themselves neatly on the screen one after the other. Now, though, the presenter will want to control the pace of the presentation. The next item, the 'Five short questions' box, will Fly In from the bottom, but only On Click.

▲ **STEP 10 TEXT ANIMATION** Now for the box containing those questions. We want the questions to appear one at a time, so once we've chosen the animation effect (Fade) we need to click Effect Options and choose the Text Animation tab. What we don't want is for the text to appear a word or a letter at a time, so we set the Animate text pop-up to All at once.

▲ **STEP 11 TEXT GROUPING** The Group text pop-up, directly below, controls how much text appears with each mouse click. If you're using one of the outline-style text boxes in PowerPoint's standard slide layouts, you'll see a list of heading levels – usually you'll want 1st level. If you've created a text box manually, 1st level will be the only choice.

▲ **STEP 12 THE FINISHED ANIMATION** That's it, we're done. The animations effects are listed in the window in the order we created them, but we can change that order by selecting any effect and using the up/down buttons to the left. All of the animation effects can be re-edited if necessary – it may take a few 'rehearsals' to produce a polished result.

MASTERCLASS
Creating a navigation bar in PowerPoint

How do you transform a tedious linear slideshow into an interactive multimedia resource? Well, a good place to start is to add a navbar.

Kit required Microsoft Office
Time 30 minutes
Goal Make navigation simpler in slideshows
Skill level Intermediate

PowerPoint presentations are designed for use by public speakers who talk and swap slides while the audience listens. This is fine for 'linear' presentations and, if necessary, the speaker can use the on-screen controls to backtrack to previous slides to revisit a particular point. However, this approach isn't much use when you want a presentation that users can work for themselves, and where they'll want 'random access' rather than a strictly linear tutorial.

What's needed is a 'navbar', a gadget that shows every slide in the presentation and lets you click on a button, or a thumbnail, to go straight to that slide. It's really quite easy to do, thanks to two key PowerPoint features. The first is the fact that you can add objects to

every slide in the presentation by creating them on the Master slide. The second is that any object, even those on the Master, can be hyperlinked to a specific slide.

Our sample presentation offers tips on photographic composition, using six different photos, one for each slide. The navbar we create uses thumbnail versions of these photos, which we prepared in advance. And just to enhance it, we added a series of steps at the end that show how to animate slide objects so they appear one at a time rather than all at once. Although PowerPoint's pitched as a pretty dour business application, it's actually a half-decent multimedia authoring tool once you scratch beneath the surface.

INTERFACE

This navbar has been created on the slide Master so it appears automatically on every slide.

These thumbnails, like any slide object, can be assigned a hyperlink. In this case, they link to different slides in the presentation.

It's impossible to modify Master items on individual slides, but you can cover the thumbnail with another graphic to 'highlight' it and show your location.

Landscape photography tips
Lines lead the eye and give the image 'movement'

Balance
Viewpoint
Lines
Diagonals
Details
Filters

Converging lines give a strong sense of perspective, leading the eye into the picture.

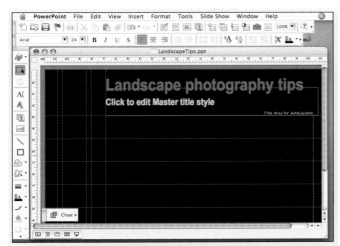

▲ **STEP 01** **USING GUIDES ON THE MASTER SLIDE** We're going to create our navbar on the Master so it appears on every slide in the presentation. The navbar will be made up of six different thumbnails and titles arranged vertically, and we want to make sure they all line up. PowerPoint offers guides to help us. To create more guides, Alt-drag an existing one.

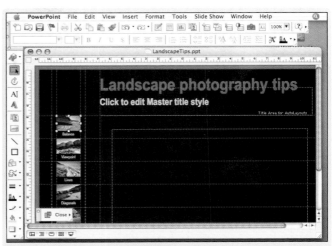

▲ **STEP 02** **INSERTING THUMBNAILS** With the guides in place, it takes just a few moments to add thumbnail images (Insert > Picture > From file). We created a single text frame, and sized and positioned it below the first thumbnail, then duplicated for the others. The AutoLayout text boxes have already been repositioned at the top of the Master slide and restyled with our chosen fonts.

▲ **STEP 03** **CLOSE THE MASTER** We can now Close the Master and start adding slides. This is easiest in Normal view, where we can click in the Outline pane, select anything already there and delete it. Next, in the Formatting palette, open the Add Objects section and click the Blank Slide icon. This adds a new, blank slide that shows only the items on the Master.

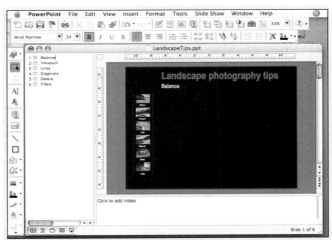

▲ **STEP 04** **ADD THE SLIDE TITLES** In the Outline pane, we can start adding our slide titles. The Slide pane to the right shows the current background and all the slide titles we plan on adding. Once you've typed a title, press return to create a new slide. Keep typing in the titles, followed by return, until you have a slide for each thumbnail in the navbar.

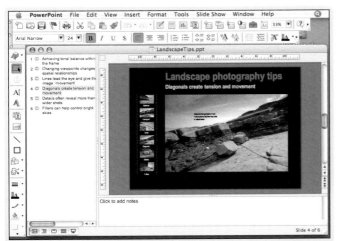

▲ **STEP 05** **ADDING THE CONTENT** That's the basic structure of the presentation done. Now you can start modifying the content for each slide. We've started by extending the slide titles and, since this is a presentation about photography tips, we've added explanatory boxes and arrows. These can be left as they are or animated to appear in sequence.

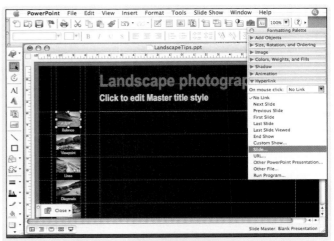

▲ **STEP 06** **RETURN TO THE MASTER SLIDE** Next, the whole point of a navbar, of course, is that it should provide push-button links to each slide. For this, we need to go back to the Master, where we can click on the first thumbnail, and then open the Hyperlink section of the Formatting palette, open the On mouse click pop-up menu and choose Slide.

▲ **STEP 07** **ADDING HYPERLINKS** The Hyperlink to Slide dialog shows not just the slide titles, but a thumbnail of each slide, making it easy to identify the right one. We simply go through each thumbnail in the navbar, linking it to the relevant slide. There's some redundancy, of course: if you click the thumbnail for a slide when you're already on that slide, it will simply re-open it.

▲ **STEP 08** **TESTING THE PLAYBACK** Now is a good time to run the Slide Show to check it's behaving correctly and that every thumbnail links to the slide it's supposed to. There's no reason why you shouldn't add transitions for a little extra gloss, although that will slow down the navigation slightly, of course. Without transitions, PowerPoint displays new slides instantly.

▲ **STEP 09** **HIGHLIGHTING** From here on in, we're just going to add a little more polish to our presentation. The navigational structure is already complete. One flaw, though, is that the appearance of the thumbnail doesn't change to show you've clicked it. To get round this, we've created a semi-transparent circle that's simply placed over the relevant thumbnail on each slide.

▲ **STEP 10** **ANIMATING OBJECTS** Next, we're going to animate the text and arrows used to explain the photographs on the slides. We want the text box to be invisible when the slide first opens, but to appear when we click the mouse. To do this, we need to open the Animation section in the Formatting palette and click Custom Animation.

▲ **STEP 11** **MAKING TEXT 'APPEAR'** In the Custom Animation dialog, we click the Add Effect button at the top and choose Appear from the Animation Effects list. As the name suggests, this means the text box will simply appear when the user clicks the mouse button. There are plenty of other effects, but they're easily overdone and can become tiresome.

▲ **STEP 12** **ADDING ARROWS** We can do the same with the arrows we've placed over some of the photographs to illustrate the compositional effects. When more than one object on a slide is animated, they appear as a list in the Custom Animation dialog so that it's possible to check the order in which objects appear. It's a very effective way to choreograph a number of objects.

MASTERCLASS
Using Hyperlinks in Keynote

Keynote isn't just for linear slideshows. With hyperlinks you can create interactive tutorials with non-linear navigation – quite apart from links to external websites.

Kit required iWork 08
Time 30 minutes
Goal Use hyperlinks for navigation in Keynote
Skill level Intermediate

Conventional Keynote presentations are all very well if you're standing at the front of the room and talking your audience through a set of arguments or points in a specific order. But there are times when you want to take a different approach. Maybe you want to use Keynote as an interactive learning aid for people to use on their own. Here, this conventional linear path isn't much use; your users will want to skip back and forth between topics to check things they didn't quite understand the first time around. Either that or jump past stuff that they know already to the things that really interest them. This is easy to do with hyperlinks. They disguise the linear nature of the slide show so that it behaves more like random-access multimedia.

Our workthrough's been kept simple just to demonstrate the basic principles but they'll also work with much more elaborate projects. In particular, Keynote's support for multiple Master slides means that you can create different sections within the presentation, each with its own navigational controls and layouts. For example, we could expand the presentation we've created here to include slides containing sample photos, together with a return button to get us back to the slide we were looking at. Hyperlinks are a very simple tool, with a great deal of potential. We used the instant alpha tool to produce the camera cutouts on our slides. For something so quick and simple, it's startlingly effective.

INTERFACE

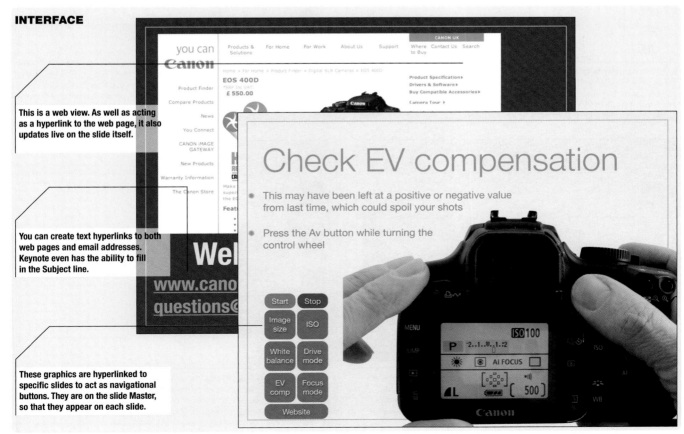

This is a web view. As well as acting as a hyperlink to the web page, it also updates live on the slide itself.

You can create text hyperlinks to both web pages and email addresses. Keynote even has the ability to fill in the Subject line.

These graphics are hyperlinked to specific slides to act as navigational buttons. They are on the slide Master, so that they appear on each slide.

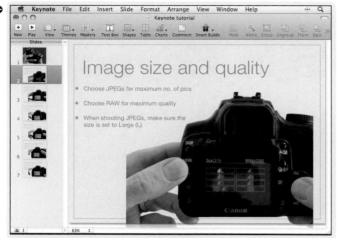

▲ **STEP 01 START WITH YOUR SLIDES** Our Keynote presentation is already complete as far as the content is concerned. It has an intro slide and six more that give specific information about camera settings. These are visible in the Navigator pane on the left of the screen. We need all the slides in place before we can start on the navigational hyperlinks.

▲ **STEP 02 EDITING MASTER SLIDES** There's no point in creating navigational buttons on every slide when we can simply create a single set on the slide Master. You can display Master slides using the View > Show Master Slides command. Our six main slides share the same Title & Bullets layout selected here for editing in the main window.

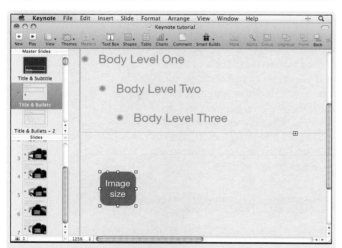

▲ **STEP 03 ADDING A BUTTON** We create our first button by choosing the round-cornered rectangle from the Shapes pop-up. These default to the current design theme's colours, though you can use the Inspector to change the colour if you want to. To add text to a graphic, just double-click and start typing, changing the text size if necessary.

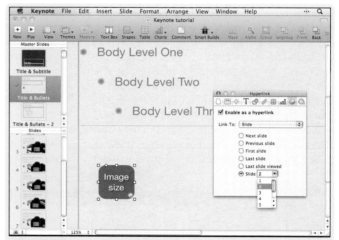

▲ **STEP 04 ASSIGNING A HYPERLINK** Any object you create in this way can be turned into a navigational button. Just select the object, open the Inspector (if it's not visible already) and select the Hyperlink tab second from the right. Check the Enable as a hyperlink box, select Slide from the pop-up Link To menu and choose the number of the slide you want to link to.

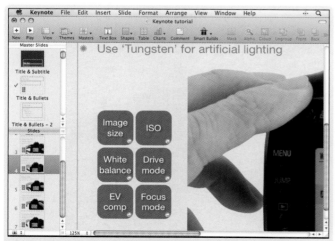

▲ **STEP 05 ADDING THE REMAINING BUTTONS** Here we've created buttons for all six slides, linking each one individually to the relevant slide. Remember that all this is being done on the slide Master, so the buttons will appear on every slide that uses it as long as you don't cover them up with anything (slide content will always overlay Master objects).

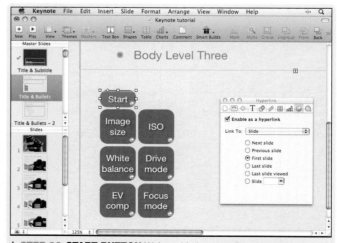

▲ **STEP 06 START BUTTON** We've added a green Start button at this point. This takes users right back to the first slide in the presentation in case they need to start again. We've linked to a Slide, using the pop-up menu in the Inspector but here we don't need its number – we just need to click the First slide radio button. You can also choose the Next, Previous and Last slides.

▲ STEP 07 **STOP BUTTON** This red Stop button exits the presentation. It's another one of the possible Hyperlink actions available in the Inspector. As you'll see from the list you can also link to other Keynote files, web pages and email addresses. We'll take a look at these last two options when we create a final links slide at the end of the presentation.

▲ STEP 08 **A FINAL SLIDE FOR LINKS** Here's our final slide. We've used a different slide Master for this because we don't want the navigational buttons appearing here. We've put the main heading low down on the page to make room for a graphic that we're adding shortly. Underneath, there's a URL that users should click on to visit a web page where they can find out more.

▲ STEP 09 **ADDING A TEXT HYPERLINK** Text hyperlinks are really straightforward. Just select the text and choose the Insert > Text Hyperlink > Webpage command. If the text itself is a URL, it will appear in the Inspector as the page that the hyperlink points to, so you don't need to do any more. If it isn't, you'll need to type the URL into the Inspector manually.

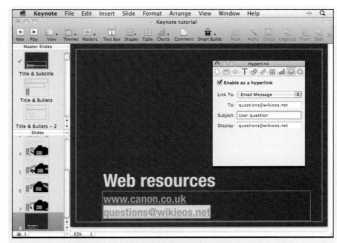

▲ STEP 10 **INSERTING AN EMAIL HYPERLINK** Email hyperlinks are just as easy. Here, you choose Insert > Text Hyperlink > Email message instead. Again if the text is already formatted as an email address, it will appear automatically in the Inspector. You'll notice here though that there's a Subject field – this automatically fills in the subject line in the email message.

▲ STEP 11 **ADDING A WEB VIEW** Now for one of Keynote's cleverer options. We would like to illustrate this final page with the web page that it links to and we can do this easily enough by opening it up in Safari, then dragging the page icon from the address bar on to the Keynote slide. This doesn't produce a static screen shot of the web page – it's a live web view.

▲ STEP 12 **WEB VIEW PROPERTIES** You can click on these web view objects to adjust their properties in the Hyperlink Inspector. By default the web view acts as a hyperlink – clicking it opens that page in Safari (or whatever web browser you use). But there's also an Update automatically option. With this enabled, the page is updated whenever the presentation is viewed.

MASTERCLASS
Sharing with iMovie HD 6

.Mac, YouTube, weblogs, iPods, iPhones, email, DVD – or back where it came from. You can send your iMovie projects to any or all of these places and more besides. Here's how.

Kit required iMovie HD 6
Time 15 minutes
Goal To export video with custom quality presets for various uses
Skill level Beginner

Sharing video with iMovie HD 6 couldn't be simpler. The Share menu is the route by which your completed projects can find their way onto your iPod, the Internet or be sent to individuals via email with a single click of the mouse.

The problem is that, as with most of the simple things in iLife, you don't have much control over the outcome. The one-click presets encode your video to a given size, usually pretty small, at a specific frame rate and with image quality determined by a fixed data rate defined in kilobits per second.

If you're in a rush or can't be doing with fiddling around with bitrates, this is all just great, but what if you'd like to make your video blog available to fast

broadband users at a larger size or better quality, or both? Then it's time you started experimenting with the QuickTime Expert settings. These allow you to export your video using the same codecs as the one-click presets, but you get to choose the image size and quality settings.

In this Masterclass, you'll discover that exporting video using your own encoding settings isn't all that difficult and can produce better results than iMovie's one-click presets. Another advantage of using iMovie's QuickTime export is that it provides export options for devices such as the iPhone and Apple TV, as well as any other codecs you may have installed, for example, Flip4Mac's WMV codec.

INTERFACE

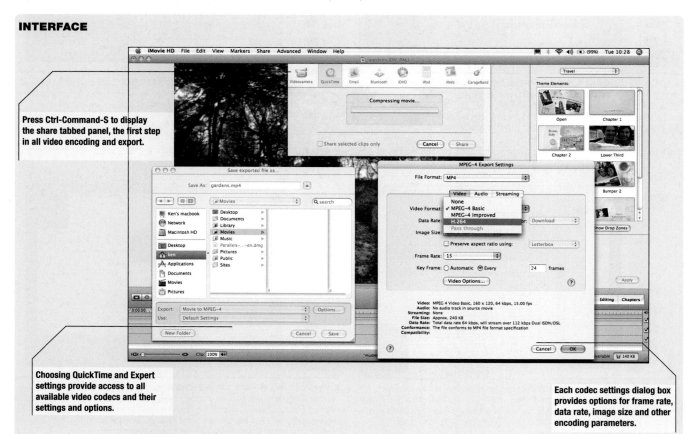

Press Ctrl-Command-S to display the share tabbed panel, the first step in all video encoding and export.

Choosing QuickTime and Expert settings provide access to all available video codecs and their settings and options.

Each codec settings dialog box provides options for frame rate, data rate, image size and other encoding parameters.

▲ **STEP 1 SHARE ALIKE** The share menu contains a number of options for exporting video but, whatever you select, the same tabbed panel, which you can open with the keyboard shortcut Ctrl-Command-S, opens providing access to all of the export presets via buttons at the top.

▲ **STEP 2 SHARE OPTIONS** With the exception of Video camera, iDVD and GarageBand, each of the preset buttons encodes the video using one of the available codecs and saves it to a file. The iPod button resizes the movie to 320 x 240, compresses it using the H.264 video codec (part of the Mpeg-4 standard) and places it in your iTunes library.

▲ **STEP 3 PROJECT SHARING** The iDVD preset button doesn't encode anything, but exports the project to iDVD where you can add chapter markers and create menu screens. iDVD does the (Mpeg-2) encoding as part of the burning process. Similarly, GarageBand allows you to add additional audio and music to the project.

▲ **STEP 4 WEB SHARING** The iWeb preset button provides two options – Share For Web and Share For Video Podcast. As well as different iWeb templates, the two options use different compression settings for the H.264 video codec. Share For Video Podcast produces better quality 320 x 240 video with correspondingly larger file sizes.

▲ **STEP 5 ACCESSING ENCODING OPTIONS** The preset buttons are convenient, but use a one-size fits all approach. For access to all the encoding options, click on the QuickTime button and choose Expert Settings from the Compress Movie For pull-down menu, then click on the Share button. This opens the Save Exported File As dialog box.

▲ **STEP 6 H.264 ENCODING** From the Export menu choose Movie to Mpeg-4 and press the Options button. Leave the Use menu on Default Settings and click on the Options button. In the Video tab of the Mpeg-4 Export Settings dialog box select MP4 from the File format pull-down menu, then select H.264 from the Video Format pull-down menu.

▲ **STEP 7 DECIDING THE DATA RATE** The data rate is the major determinant of video quality – higher data rates make for better quality video, but larger files with longer download times. There's no correct bitrate for a given delivery method, say for broadband. You have to choose based on the length of your movie, expected speed of the connection and other factors.

▲ **STEP 8 RESIZING** Image size obviously plays a large part in the quality of the viewing experience, but don't expect to be able to produce full-screen video at high bitrates for the web. If your clip is only a few seconds long, you can get away with 640 x 480, for anything longer choose 320 x 240.

▲ **STEP 9 FRAME RATE AND ASPECT RATIO** Setting the Frame Rate to Current will produce best results, but if your encoded files are coming out on the large side, try reducing this to 15fps. If your video is getting squeezed using one of the preset sizes, check the Preserve Aspect Ratio box and select a method from the pull-down menu.

▲ **STEP 10 USING PRESETS** If you are unsure about where to start with changing encoding parameters, use the presets as a starting point. Click on Cancel in the Mpeg-4 Export Settings dialog box and select Broadband – Medium from the Use pull-down menu, then click on the Options button to return to the Mpeg-4 Export Settings dialog box.

▲ **STEP 11 COMPARING PRESETS** The Broadband Medium preset encodes 320 x 240 video at 220Kbits/sec at 15fps. Click on Cancel, select the Broadband High preset and click on Options to return to the Mpeg-4 Export Settings dialog box. This preset encodes 480 x 360 video at the existing frame rate (25fps if the source is DV) at 672Kbits/sec.

▲ **STEP 12 OTHER CODECS** You don't have to encode using H.264, but bear in mind that, for web playback the viewer will need the right codec to play back your content in their browser or media player. For the iPhone, Apple TV, and other devices, using the presets is the best way to ensure compatibility and trouble-free playback.

MASTERCLASS
Recording a voiceover in iMovie

How to record a voiceover for a movie or slideshow using either a microphone plugged into your Mac or your DV camcorder.

Kit required iMovie and a Mac with a built in mic + a USB mic or iSight, or a DV camcorder
Time 10 minutes
Goal To record and add an iMovie voiceover
Skill level Beginner

▲ **STEP 01 TESTING, ONE, TWO** Position the playhead in the Timeline viewer where you want to begin recording and click on the audio button at the top of the Media pane. Speak into the mic to check it's working – you'll see green bars appear in the microphone level meter at the bottom of the Media pane.

▲ **STEP 02 CHECK THE MIC** If you can't see anything in the level meter the mic isn't working. If the meter goes into the red area the input recording level is set too high. In either case you'll need to select System Preferences from the Apple menu, click on the sound icon and select the correct input device from the list. Reduce the Input volume slider if necessary.

▲ **STEP 03 RECORDING** Close the sound control panel and click on the red record button on iMovie's Media pane to begin recording your voiceover. You can't playback the timeline while recording, so it might help to make a few dry runs while playing back your movie to get the timing right.

▲ **STEP 04 USING THE CAMCORDER** To record a voiceover with your camcorder, press record and speak into the camcorder's built-in mic. Capture the footage into iMovie in the usual way and place the clip on the timeline. Press Command-J, or select Extract audio from the advanced menu. This places the audio in the track below the unwanted video clip which you can delete.

MASTERCLASS
Making a DVD slideshow

Create a quick and easy slideshow in iMovie with dissolve transitions and backing music, then add a themed menu and burn it to DVD in iDVD.

Kit required iMovie + iDVD + some photos
Time 10 minutes
Goal To produced an iMovie slideshow and burn it to DVD
Skill level Beginner

▲ **STEP 01 IMPORT PHOTOS** Launch iMovie and create a new project. The simplest way to import photos is to drag a folder of pictures from the Finder onto the Clip viewer or into the Clips pane. To import photos from your iPhoto library click the media button then the Photos button at the top of the Media pane.

▲ **STEP 02 KEN BURNS** The default duration for imported photos is five seconds. If you playback the project you'll also discover that every image has a Ken Burns zoom applied and the default transition is a straight cut. Press Command-A to select all the photos and click on the Show Photo Settings button on the Photos tab of the Media pane.

▲ **STEP 03 NEW DURATION** To turn off the effect, uncheck the Ken Burns Effect checkbox. To change the length of time each photo is displayed for, drag the lower duration slider or enter a value in the form seconds:frames in the input box. Click on the update box to apply the new settings, which will become the defaults for images imported in future.

▲ **STEP 04 CHOOSE A TRANSITION** Click the Transitions button on the Editing pane and select the cross dissolve transition. Drag the speed slider to set an appropriate duration, don't make it too long or your slide will begin to dissolve into the next one before it's been on screen for more than a second or two. Position the playhead and click the transition in the Editing pane to see a preview.

When it comes to sharing photos one of the most popular options is to create a slideshow and put it on a DVD video. Using a video format for still photos might sound like an odd thing to do, but the widespread availability of DVD players coupled to domestic TVs means that wherever you go you can be sure the show will go on.

There are lots of ways you can get your photos onto a DVD. You can simply copy the Jpegs onto a data disc, which most DVD players will be able to read and display. You can start by creating a slideshow in iPhoto, or, as in this Masterclass, you can drag your pictures directly onto the iMovie Clip viewer and take it from there.

We've chosen this method because it's one of the quickest and easiest routes to a finished product so it's ideal if you're new to the iLife suite or if you're just more familiar with iMovie than either iPhoto or iDVD.

iMovie leaves you plenty of room to manoeuvre with titles, transitions and audio. It's easy to add the same transition throughout, or edit them individually. You can use the Title pane to add an introductory title to the show and to caption individual slides. Adding a music backing track from GarageBand or your iTunes library is easy and iMovie provides the audio tools to balance audio levels between a backing track and voiceover narration.

▲ **STEP 05 APPLY THE TRANSITION** With all of the images still selected, click the Add button to add the transition between every clip. Don't drag the dissolve onto clips in the Clip viewer or it will only be added between the two adjacent clips where it is dropped. You can still change the duration of all the transitions by adjusting the speed slider and clicking the Update button.

▲ **STEP 06 ADD A TITLE** Select a title style from the Titles pane, enter your title text in the boxes provided and format it. Uncheck the Over black box to superimpose the text on the opening photo and set the speed and pause sliders so that the title sequence finishes just before the transition. Adjust the duration of the opening slide to make it longer if necessary.

▲ **STEP 07 ADD MUSIC** You can add a music backing track by dragging it from the Finder and dropping it onto one of the two audio tacks in the Clip or Timeline viewer. You can also add music from GarageBand or your iTunes library – click on the audio button in the Media pane, navigate to the track you want and drag and drop it in the audio track underneath the slideshow in the Clip viewer.

▲ **STEP 08 BURN TO DVD** Select iDVD from the Share menu and select Render and Proceed from the alert box to render the images and open the project in iDVD. Choose a theme and select Autofill Drop Zones from the Project menu. Click on the playback button to preview the DVD, then exit and choose Burn DVD from the File menu. ✪

MASTERCLASS
Creating cool photo cubes

Photocubes are a fun and different way to display your photos, so work your way through this tutorial and you'll be well on your way to getting all squared up.

Kit required iWork
Time No more than 20 minutes
Goal To understand image placeholders, and create customisable photo cubes
Skill level Beginner

One of the very handy but often overlooked features of the two applications in the iWork suite is the ability to drop pictures from your media libraries into predefined drop zones. Professional designers have been doing this for years – indeed, QuarkXPress and InDesign ostensibly insist on a target frame being drawn on the page into which you drop your graphic – but it's something that's new to the consumer end of the market.

Perhaps unknowingly, you've used this feature already, as any time you open a template in Pages or Keynote, and replace a placeholder photo with one of your own, you're using these drop zones. They're easy to define yourself,

and by way of illustrating this, we'll show you how to create a template for a photo cube. Simply put, this is nothing more than a cube with a photo on each side, but they're very satisfying objects, and could be used for everything from a novel way to send pictures to friends and relatives, to a promotional unit, or even an oversized, personalised die if you feel like it.

You can expand on the principles outlined here to create complex layouts in Pages without having to resort to the pre-defined templates. You can also use the same techniques in high-end professional desktop publishing applications, making Pages the ideal first step for the budding designer.

INTERFACE

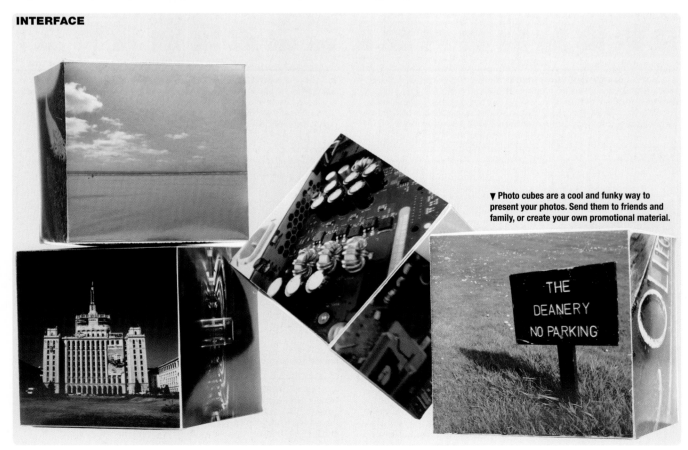

▼ Photo cubes are a cool and funky way to present your photos. Send them to friends and family, or create your own promotional material.

▲ **STEP 01 PLACE GRAPHIC** Launch Pages, and create a new, blank document. Click towards the edge of the page so that when you import a graphic, it will be placed as a floating graphic rather than inline as part of a block of text. The easiest way to insert images is from your iPhoto Library – just use the Media palette and drag a photo onto the page.

▲ **STEP 02 DRAW MASKING SHAPE** Now draw a square onto the page, accessible from the Objects menu in the toolbar. There's no need to alter the default fill and stroke colours or styles, as we'll simply be using this as a mask. Use the Metrics tab of the Inspector palette to alter the size – we're using a 6 x 6cm square in this example – and centre it on the page.

▲ **STEP 03 MASK GRAPHIC WITH SHAPE** With both the placed picture and the drawn shape selected, choose Format > Mask With Shape. You'll see that the image is now cropped within the boundaries of the drawn shape. This applies to any shape drawn within the iWork suite's applications, obviously, but it's the basic rectangle that matters to us for this Masterclass.

▲ **STEP 04 POSITION GRAPHIC WITHIN MASK** You may find that the image doesn't fit perfectly within the mask, but this is easily resolved. Simply double-click the image, and the original image that's being cropped will appear as a ghosted image. Resize, rotate, and move this image however you like; just click outside the graphic to confirm your changes.

▲ **STEP 05 DEFINE OBJECT PLACEHOLDER** We want to make this template easily reusable, so select your masked graphic, and pick Format > Advanced > Define as Image Placeholder. Also, any rotations or effects applied with the Adjust palette are tied to the masking square, not to the graphic in that mask; drop in a fresh graphic, and the same effects will be applied.

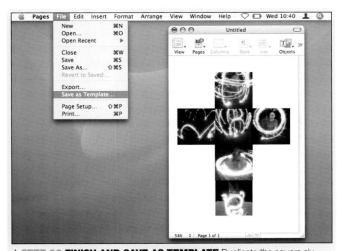

▲ **STEP 06 FINISH AND SAVE AS TEMPLATE** Duplicate the square six times into a crucifix shape – using the Metrics palette to position pictures exactly – and, if desired, add tabs to show people where to have the cubes fasten up. Once you're happy with the design, choose File > Save as Template, which you can then share with friends, colleagues and magazine readers.

MASTERCLASS
Automatically resize images

If you're uploading a lot of images to a website and you need to change their dimensions then it can be a boring and repetitive job. Using the power of Preview and Automator can simplify and speed up the task.

Kit required Mac OS X 10.4 Tiger or later
Time 10 minutes
Goal To set-up a simple batch process tool
Skill level Beginner

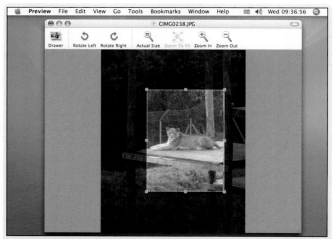

▲ **STEP 01 PREVIEW'S HIDDEN TOOLS** If you look at images in preview you'd be forgiven for thinking that it's nothing more than a fast tool for opening images and not much else. In fact, you can crop your images simply by clicking and dragging and saving a new image. If you want to resize your images, though, you have to be a bit tricky.

▲ **STEP 02 UNLOCK THE HIDDEN FEATURES OF PREVIEW** To get to some of the more interesting features of Preview you need to use Automator. Open the application and click on the Preview option in the Library pane. This reveals the options for Preview in the Action pane. Drag the Scale Images action to the workflow section.

▲ **STEP 03 SET THE SCALE** Once you've created your basic workflow, you can choose how to scale your images. You can select the exact pixel dimensions or just a percentage. If you want an exact percentage then click in the box and enter it. You can also use the arrows to give increments of 5% for each click.

▲ **STEP 04 SAVE THE ACTION** Choose Save As from the File menu, name your workflow and change the File Format drop-down menu to Application. Now all you have to do is drag and drop your images on to the application icon and they will be batch processed in seconds. And that's it – you've created a really fast tool that will save you lots of time resizing images.

15 steps to better photos

Are your photos not living up to your memories? Well, with a few subtle adjustments in either iPhoto or Photoshop, you can really liven up lacklustre snaps.

It's 180 years since Nicéphore Niépce made the first photographic image; it was exposed onto a pewter plate covered with bitumen of Judea, a petroleum derivative. Until the advent of digital photography, anyone who wanted to improve their photos had to be more chemist than creative, but with software such as Photoshop and iPhoto, it's easy to turn lacklustre snaps into miniature works of art.

That's what we're here to help you do. Over the next five pages, you'll learn how to restore colour to faded photographs, produce stunning black-and-white images that leave the bland results of a quick Desaturate in Photoshop in the dust, create blemish-free skin and much more.

And the best bit is that you don't have to splash out on Photoshop to follow along. This flagship application of Adobe's may give you the most control and best results – and we'll be showing you how to best harness its power – but we'll also show you how to do the same task in iPhoto, which offers surprisingly sophisticated editing abilities, too.

What's more, it comes free on new Macs, so many of us can use the techniques described in this feature effectively without spending a penny.

Much of what makes a good photograph, though, happens before you press the shutter, not once you've imported it into an editing suite, so we'll also be showcasing essential tips to help you take good, novel, interesting and relevant photographs.

Put it all together, and you have *MacUser's* essential guide to getting the very best photographs possible. No longer will you have to worry about boring your friends and family with holiday snaps, or taking precious memories that don't capture the moment as well as you could.

TASK

HOW TO IN iPHOTO

Convert to monochrome

Many pictures can look much better in black and white. This is partly because we perceive differences in light and dark more readily than differences in colour, and partly because most colour photos actually display a narrow gamut of tonal variation. Converting to monochrome can make pictures dramatic and gives portraits an elegance that's difficult to achieve in any other way.

The first step is to convert your picture to greyscale, so bring up the Effects palette and click B&W, or click B&W in the toolbar at the bottom. The result looks insipid, so, if you're using iPhoto 6, click Boost Color. In either iPhoto 5 or 6, next drag the sliders in the Adjust palette to roughly match those shown here. You will need to tinker to suit, and you could try making the picture even more dramatic by dragging the left-most slider towards the right on the Levels control; avoid moving to more than 25%. In iPhoto 4, you're limited to brightness and contrast controls; move the former slightly leftwards and the latter a little to the right to punch up converted-to-greyscale images.

Cropping

We'd always encourage you to frame a picture properly before pressing the shutter. Occasionally, though, you may need to change format or alter the focus of the shot, or you may decide that your original framing was off, in which case, you can re-frame digitally. Remember that detail will be lost, and, particularly with compact cameras, you may not have enough pixels to allow you to crop in very far while retaining enough resolution to print successfully.

HOW TO IN iPHOTO

If you want to keep your picture constrained to the dimensions of normal photographic paper, pick one from the Constrain list; snaps are usually 4 x 6in. iPhoto will automatically select the maximum area to fit onto the chosen paper size; the proportions of many digital shots are different from those of traditional photographic paper. Move your cursor inside the selected area to move it around, or drag in the corners to change the size. By default, iPhoto will assume you want to keep the orientation the same, but an option at the bottom of the Constrain menu enables you to change the orientation for cropping. When you're happy, click Crop.

Correcting red-eye

Red-eye is caused by the camera's flash reflecting off the retinas of the photo's subjects, and is at its worst when the flash is positioned close to the lens. Many cameras now have a red-eye reduction feature that fires a pre-flash to contract the subjects' pupils, but even so you might find that some of your evening and night shots seem to be populated by demons.

HOW TO IN iPHOTO

In theory, this is very simple: just load up the photograph, click the Red-Eye tool and click in the centre of the affected eyes; in many cases, your job will be done. It's not perfect, however, especially where the pupils are small, either because the shot is relatively low resolution, or because the faces only take up a small area of the photo. In this case, if you have iPhoto 5 or 6, you can use an undocumented hack to dot out the red-eye manually. Select the Red-Eye tool, hold down Control and Caps Lock, and then tap 9 then Tab. Adjust the size of the eye-shaped target with the square bracket keys on your keyboard, then click on the pupil to correct.

HOW TO IN PHOTOSHOP

This method is quite labour-intensive, so if you just want a quick-and-dirty mono conversion, convert your working colour space to Lab (Image > Mode > Lab Color) and choose Image > Adjustments > Desaturate. The results are much punchier than the insipid Desaturate command when in RGB. You can then convert back to RGB (or CMYK) for further work.

To do it right, convert your colour image to Lab and select the Lightness channel from the Channels palette. Now switch the Mode to Greyscale, which will use the information from the lightness channel to build the mono image. Command-click on the new Grey channel to select it, and then invert the selection. Create a new fill layer (Layer > New Fill Layer > Solid Color) filled with solid black, and adjust the opacity of the fill layer to tinker with the strength of this 'punching up'. You may also want to add

another adjustments layer to control curves or levels, perhaps to control greyscale performance in shadows or highlights.

You can also 'crisp up' contrast to give your images a gallery feel. Duplicate the background by dragging it to the new layer icon at the bottom of the palette, and run the High Pass filter with a radius of about 10 for a 7-megapixel image. Change this layer's blend mode to Hard Light, and, again, adjust the opacity of the layer to change the strength of the effect.

Adding warmth to a pure monochrome image can make it look a little more human. You could either convert the colour space to duo-, tri- or even quadtone to achieve this, or you could simply convert to RGB and add a Photo Filter adjustment layer with one of the warming filters set to around 15%.

HOW TO IN PHOTOSHOP

Open the image and choose the regular rectangular marquee tool. If you just want to crop to your own proportions, simply select the area you want to crop and choose Image > Crop. To keep pictures cropped to aspect ratios of standard photo paper, simply change the framing style from Normal to Fixed Aspect Ratio, and enter the basic size of the paper onto which you want to print. Units are irrelevant, so you could enter 4 and 6 or 10 and 15 (inches and centimetres respectively, as it happens) for normal photographic paper. Once that's done, select the area you want to keep and choose Image > Crop. Enter the relevant dimensions in Image > Image Size.

FRAMING TIPS

When framing your shots, you want to try to create the right balance of tension and harmony. Don't go too far either way – a portrait shot with the head in the exact centre of the frame is harmonious, but dull. Cropping off parts of the face introduces plenty of tension, but destroys the purpose of the piece.

Never position the horizon of a photograph exactly in the centre of the frame – you'll get a much more interesting image if you frame your shots so the horizon is around a third of the way up from the bottom of the picture. Many people rely on the idea of the golden ratio to help with framing; you can use the illustration at *http://en.wikipedia. org/wiki/golden_ratio* to get an idea of where you could focus a shot.

HOW TO IN PHOTOSHOP

If you have Photoshop CS2 or CS3, you do have a dedicated red-eye removal tool at your disposal. It's a bit hidden away – look in the fly-out tool menu for the Healing brush – but select it and you'll get a set of cross-hairs for clicking in the centre of the pupils. The default size usually works well for most photos, but the default 50% darken is a little strong and looks artificial in most snaps. Try reducing it to around 30%. If you want more control, though, or you don't have CS2 or CS3, you'll need the techniques described below.

Open your image and create a new layer. Switch the bend mode from Normal to Saturation, and select a brush that's a little smaller than the pupil you want to correct and just a little soft. Either use the eye-dropper tool to pick up a colour from the iris, or just stick with plain black, and begin to paint over the pupils. Remember that they're rarely perfectly circular, so avoid the temptation simply to dot a single spot of colour on top of the red-eye. Instead, gradually build up the shape of the correcting mask. Once you're done you can flatten the layers back down, and if you need to darken the pupils, a little subtle work with the Burn tool should see you right.

Refreshing old photos

Old, faded photographs do have a charm all of their own, but sometimes you want to restore them to something of their former glory. The techniques we'll discuss here are really only concerned with correcting the colours, not repairing damage – some of the techniques discussed in the Blemish-free skin section would apply here. The trick to this is to spot what colour shifts have taken place and compensate for them.

Most faded photos have a warm, orange cast. Correct this by dragging the Temperature slider towards the blue – not too much, but just enough to neutralise the colours. You may find you need to tint the picture with a little green. Most old photos benefit from quite drastic sharpening, so don't be afraid to really turn it up. Be very sparing with contrast increases – you may find that clipping in the dark slider for the Levels control does a better job.

With monochrome images, convert to greyscale, drag the Temperature and Tint sliders to the left, drag exposure to about -40, and bump up the contrast slightly.

Punch it up

It doesn't take much to spruce up humble holiday snaps, and these techniques simply add a little punch to your photos. Whether you've shot landscapes or people, a few seconds spent on each image can pay dividends. They can add drama to the most unassuming shot, but use them with care and print to check that the results aren't too extreme, especially if your system isn't colour calibrated.

The first step is normally to increase saturation – not too much unless you're deliberately going for a cartoonish finish. Next, try adjusting the Temperature slider: many landscapes benefit from a little warming up, so drag the slider to the right. A little sharpening doesn't usually go amiss here, either. Overexposing the picture a little often works wonders, and clipping the levels slightly at both ends can add contrast more effectively than the Contrast slider.

Blemish-free skin

One of the unpleasant side-effects of taking photos late at night is that people are often a bit sweaty or make-up has smudged, and the use of flash makes these problems worse. iPhoto's controls are a little coarse, but they do offer a way of removing the shine, and we'll show you a hack for iPhoto 5 and 6 to improve their Retouch controls. Photoshop offers finer controls, and we'll show you how to use a simple but effective technique.

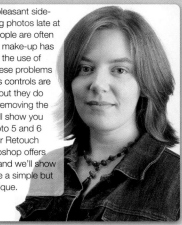

If you're using iPhoto 4, click the Retouch tool and dab away at the shiny highlights to 'matte them out'. If you have iPhoto 5 or later, select the Retouch tool, hold down Control and Caps Lock, and then tap 9. Press Tab and you'll get a dotted circle with a figure below. Use the square brackets keys to adjust the size of this circle, and the curly brackets (Shift-square brackets) to adjust the strength of the effect. A large-diameter circle with low strength (about 0.25) works well for de-shining; use multiple clicks, dotted around the affected area.

MASTERCLASS
Make your own RSS screen saver

The RSS screen saver built into Mac OS X is a great way to display the latest news. It's limited to RSS feeds from Safari, but it's possible to build your own and change the display to suit you using Quartz Composer.

Kit Required Quartz Composer (free on install disks)
Time 10 minutes
Goal To make your own RSS screen saver
Skill Level Intermediate

▲ **STEP 01 SCREEN SAVERS** You access the built-in RSS screen saver through the System Preferences control panel. It only gives you access to the RSS feeds you have in Safari, so you're stuck if you don't use the Apple browser to save your RSS feeds. To make matters worse, the design and colour scheme are static.

▲ **STEP 02 QUARTZ COMPOSER** Quartz Composer is a free application that can be found in the Developer Tools folder on your install disks. Open it and from the New Composition Assistant select Mac OS X RSS Screen Saver, which contains all you need to create your screen saver. First, you're taken to the setup screen and it's very simple to follow from there.

▲ **STEP 03 NAME YOUR SCREEN SAVER** The next step is to give your screen saver a name. This is how it will show up in the System Preferences control panel, so give it a memorable name. You can also choose to make the screen saver accessible to all the users of your Mac or just you.

▲ **STEP 04 ADD RSS FEED AND EDIT** In the Quartz Composer window, click on the RSS Feed so it's highlighted and then on the Inspector, where you then select Input Parameters and put the RSS feed address in to the URL field. If you want to change the screen saver, select the element on the Quartz Composer window and change its settings from the Inspector.

MacUser

FREE Portable iPod Speaker
Subscription Application Form

☐ **YES!** Please start my subscription to MacUser with 3 issues for £1 and send me my FREE Portable iPod Speaker. I understand that my subscription will continue at the low rate shown below, unless I write to cancel within my trial period.

☐ I am an existing subscriber, please extend my subscription to MacUser with this offer and send me my FREE gift.

① COMPLETE YOUR DETAILS

Mr/Mrs/Ms _____ Forename _____ Surname _____

Address _____

_____ Postcode _____

Job title _____ Company name _____

Daytime phone _____

Mobile phone _____

Email _____ Year of birth _____

② SELECT YOUR PAYMENT METHOD:

☐ Direct Debit Payment only £17.95 every 6 issues – UK Only (Save 24% on the shop price)

Dennis Instruction to your Bank or Building Society to pay by Direct Debit — **DIRECT Debit**

Please complete and send to: Freepost RLZS-ETGT-BCZR, Dennis Publishing Ltd, 800 Guillat Ave, Kent Science Park, Sittingbourne ME9 8GU

Name and full postal address of your Bank or Building Society

To the manager: Bank name _____

Address _____

Postcode _____

Account in the name(s) of _____

Originator's Identification Number

7	2	4	6	8	0

Ref no. to be completed by Dennis Publishing

Instructions to your Bank or Building Society
Please pay Dennis Publishing Ltd. Direct Debits from the account detailed in this instruction subject to the safeguards assured by the Direct Debit Guarantee. I understand that this instruction may remain with Dennis Publishing Ltd and, if so, details will be passed electronically to my Bank/Building Society.

Branch sort code ☐☐ ☐☐ ☐☐

Bank/Building Society account number ☐☐☐☐☐☐☐☐

Signature(s) _____

Date _____

Banks and building societies may not accept Direct Debit instructions for some types of account

---

Cheque or Credit/Debit Card Payment – 1 year (25 issues)

☐ UK £78.99 (SAVE 20%) ☐ Europe £89.00 ☐ World £132.00

☐ I enclose a cheque made payable to Dennis Publishing Ltd.

☐ Please charge my:

☐ Visa / ☐ MasterCard / ☐ AMEX / ☐ Switch (Issue No. ☐)

CARD NO. ☐☐☐☐☐☐☐☐☐☐☐☐☐☐☐☐ ☐☐☐

START DATE ☐☐☐☐ EXPIRY DATE ☐☐☐☐

SIGNED _____ DATE _____

③ Return this order form to

**Freepost RLZS-ETGT-BCZR,
MacUser Subscriptions Department,
800 Guillat Avenue, Kent Science Park,
Sittingbourne ME9 8GU**

(This address can be used on an envelope – no stamp required)

You will be able to view your subscription details online at www.subsinfo.co.uk

Offer Code: D0810BKZ

YOUR GREAT DEAL:

◼ **FREE** limited edition Portable iPod Speaker

◼ Start your subscription with **3 issues for £1**

◼ **Save 24%** a year on the shop price (when you pay by direct debit)

◼ Pay as little as **£17.95 every 6 issues**

◼ **FREE delivery** of your copies, before they hit the shelves

History of the Mac

'Apple ignited the personal computer revolution in the 1970s with the Apple II and reinvented the personal computer in the 1980s with the Macintosh. Today, Apple continues to lead the industry in innovation with its award-winning computers, OS X operating system and iLife and professional applications. Apple is also spearheading the digital media revolution with its iPod portable music and video players and iTunes online store, and has entered the mobile phone market with its revolutionary iPhone,' – positioning that appears at the end of all Apple marketing and press literature.

Apple, the company behind the Mac, was founded in California on 1 April 1976. Though it's never been confirmed, many believe it was named after Apple Corps, the Beatles' publisher; a poor choice of name that led to much legal wranglings over the years. Apple Corps dragged Apple Computer through the courts, made expensive financial settlements, and was assured by Apple Computer that it would keep out of the music business – a promise that was called into question with the arrival of the iPod, iTunes and online music store.

In retrospect, in a world where you can barely ride a train or bus without seeing a pair of distinctive white iPod headphones, it may have seemed a rash move to choose that name, but in 1976 the world was a very different place. Computers were primitive, the Internet was non-existent, and music came not on hard drives but flexible vinyl discs. That was the world into which Apple was born.

The two men we must thank for bringing us, over 30 years later, such masterpieces as the iMac, iPod and iPhone are Steve Jobs, the company's current CEO, and Steve Wozniak.

They met at the Homebrew Computer Club, a gathering of wannabe geeks in Silicon Valley. Despite the differences in their ages (Wozniak is almost five years older) the two men struck up a friendship, and started working on projects together. Jobs had spent some time as a programmer for Atari, then a leading light in video games production, while Wozniak had written a programming language and designed a circuit board for a brand new computer microprocessor. It was almost inevitable that the two men should found a computer company, along with friend Ronald Wayne, who we can thank for drawing

the original Apple logo, which depicted Newton sitting beneath his famed apple tree.

The story of how they funded their first product – the circuit board Wozniak had designed and which they christened the Apple I – is well-known. Jobs had sold his camper van; Wozniak his programmable calculator. Finally they had start-up funding, but neither of them could have known that those few dollars they raised would be the foundations of a multi-billion dollar corporation.

If you look at the Apple I today, it doesn't look much like what any of us would consider to be a computer. It was quite literally a bare bones system that you had to put together yourself. Many of the photos that you can find of it on the Internet show it in a wooden case with the word Apple crudely sawn into the top, but this was a mere stopgap, and as such every Apple I would be unique.

The Apple II arrived the following year, and proved to be a revolutionary machine. For starters, it boasted colour graphics, and after initially shipping with a tape recorder for storage that was soon swapped out for a floppy disk drive. Despite this, it wasn't until VisiCalc arrived on the platform, allowing businesses to do their spreadsheeting tasks on a computer rather than squared paper, that it became a must-have machine.

By now, Ronald Wayne had already bailed out of Apple Computer and had sold his 10% stake in the company to Steve Jobs for a paltry $800; a move he should now be regretting, with its stock having accelerated to sky-high prices. Jobs had brought in a third partner, Mark Markkula, a one-time employee of Intel, who helped the company to secure funding to the tune of $250,000.

Steves Wozniak and Jobs meet
1971

They start working at Hewlett-Packard
1975

Apple Computer founded
1975

Illustration Chris Robson *chrisrobson.com*

Perhaps inevitably, the Apple II was followed by the Apple III at the start of the 1980s, and then the III+.

By then, though, Jobs had paid a visit to Xerox' research facilities at Palo Alto, the so-called Parc, where he saw the Alto Computer. This was a radical departure from the accepted norms of computing, as it eschewed screens full of text for a graphical interface, in which the three-button mouse was king. Jobs, and colleague Jef Raskin, were impressed by what they saw, and when they returned to Apple they started working on integrating a similar interface into two computers in its labs at that time: the high-end Lisa business machine, and the low-end consumer Macintosh, named in honour of Jef Raskin's favourite variety of apple.

Although the Lisa came out first, and was the first commercial computer to support a graphical user interface (GUI), it was hugely expensive, and didn't have the staying power of the Macintosh, which is the direct predecessor of today's Mac computers.

The Macintosh was finally sent to the shops in January 1984, and promoted with a memorable advert that aired in a break of the televised Superbowl that year. The ad, which cost a reported $1.5 million, portrayed a world not unlike that in George Orwell's book *1984*, which was brought crashing down by the appearance of an athletic saviour with a hammer, which she hurled through one of the iconic telescreens that are a central focus of the novel.

'On January 24th, Apple Computer will introduce Macintosh. And you'll see why 1984 won't be like "1984",' said the voiceover and on-screen legend. How true it was.

The advert itself was almost as revolutionary as the computer it promoted. Directed by Ridley Scott, who

had just finished directing *Blade Runner*, it is held up as an icon of good advertising. Advertising Industry publication *Advertising Age* called it the best commercial of the 1980s and *TV Guide* names it the greatest commercial of all time, according to reports on CNN. It is much-quoted, reproduced in still photos and, at the time, received free replays by stations discussing its content, which would have gone a long way towards recouping the original cost of the slot in which it aired.

The advert was a dig at the growing influence of IBM – the largest computer company at the time – and the standards it had set with its PC, which still form the basis of all PCs sold to this day. Apple's advert portrayed IBM as Big Brother in Orwell's dystopian future, while it saw itself as the bright light that would free the world from IBM's domination.

Although Jobs loved the ad, and had even travelled to Shepperton Studios in the UK to oversee its week-long, $750,000 shoot in a studio filled with 200 British skinheads – not actors – the board was less keen and tried to offload the slots they had already bought in which to air it. Ad agency Chiat-Day, which had orchestrated the whole campaign claimed it was impossible at such a late stage, so the ad ran nonetheless.

Andy Herzfeld, a member of the original Macintosh team, recounts the board's reaction after the airing, and subsequent media interest on his site *folklore.org*: 'A week after the Macintosh launch, Apple held its January board meeting. The Macintosh executive staff was invited to attend, not knowing what to expect. When the Mac people entered the room, everyone on the board rose and gave them a standing ovation, acknowledging that they were wrong about ➊

Apple I goes
on sale
1976

Apple II hits
the shops
1977

Apple II gets
a floppy drive
1978

the commercial and congratulating the team for pulling off a fantastic launch.'

And so the 'affordable' Mac was born. It had a 9in monochrome screen, an 8MHz processor and 128KB of memory. Storage was limited to a 3.5in floppy drive. A hard drive would have been unimaginably expensive at the time. The machine came bundled with MacPaint and MacWrite.

Those specs may sound very conservative today – as indeed they are – but at the time they were enough to bring this machine to the interest of desktop publishing professionals. At $2495, it massively undercut comparative products, and the introduction of an affordable laser printer, and PageMaker layout software should perhaps be given credit for the Mac's continued success – to this day – in the field of design and print.

The Macintosh was revamped several times, but despite its success it was to be the ultimate author of Jobs' downfall at the company.

He had recruited John Sculley, one-time president of Pepsi, to act as Apple's CEO. He was a solid businessman, and found himself overseeing a company virtually split in two. The Macintosh team was proclaiming itself to be custodians of the company's future, while the Lisa team, selling its computers at $10,000 a pop, claimed it was the source of the company's income. Inevitably, the two didn't get on. Jobs' Macintosh team almost became a separate entity inside Apple, which was clearly something no CEO or board could condone.

Sculley and the board took the only course of action open to them; they stripped Jobs of his responsibilities. Jobs sold all but one of his shares in Apple and left to found NeXT Computer, a firm that developed extremely high-end machines, and a revolutionary operating system called NeXTstep.

Skip forward 10 years, and NeXT is doing well. Apple, though, less so. It had had a good few years, releasing a string of successful products, like the PowerBook and the Newton handheld computer. However, it had steadily lost market share to PCs running Microsoft Windows, and was valiantly trying to keep up the battle by licensing its own operating system to third-party hardware developers, while simultaneously running abortive projects to develop ever better versions, which never saw the light of day.

Nonetheless, it had the reserves to buy Jobs' new company, and in doing so bring him back into the fold, as a consultant. Now it was Jobs' turn to start bossing around the board. He ousted the current CEO at the time – Gil Amelio – and started to make immediate changes. He canned the failing operating system projects, terminated the Newton and cancelled the contracts with third-party developers to make Macintosh-compatible computers of their own. Apple was set to resume its role as the sole arbiter of both the hardware and software sides of its business.

Work started on porting the NeXTstep operating system from NeXT's own machines to the Mac, and it is that push that brought us to the Mac OS X environment that runs our Macs to this very day.

Almost straight away, Apple's fortunes were revived. Microsoft invested $150 million in the company and pledged to continue producing Microsoft Office for the platform, guaranteeing its continued viability in the business world. The following year, in May 1998, the most revolutionary product since the original Macintosh was unveiled by then interim CEO Jobs to an assembled crowd in San Francisco. It was the iMac.

Apple stock floated
1980

First Apple shareholders' meeting
1981

Apple releases the $10,000 Lisa
1983

This machine was both a nod to the past and a pointer to the future. It was an all-in-one device, where the guts of the computer were built into the back of the monitor, and it sported a design like nothing that had gone before it. Out went boring beige boxes, in came translucent plastics in funky colours. Jobs had teamed up with young British designer Jonathan Ive to breathe new life into the computer world, and it had worked.

Suddenly Apple was back in the spotlight. It was the new darling of the computer world, and countless peripheral manufacturers jumped onboard. Printers, scanners, mice, keyboards… seemingly everything now incorporated a flash of colourful plastic in an effort to make PCs look as trendy and desirable as the iMac, but none of them quite pulled it off.

That original iMac went through several iterations, which saw it evolve from a simple home business/web browsing/emailing machine into a fully-fledged multimedia device with video editing tools. It was eventually joined by the iBook, which took its cues from the iMac, being moulded from similar translucent plastics (in tangerine and blueberry colours), and integrating a carry handle by the hinge (the iMac had a carry handle in the top). It was a love-it or hate-it product, which bore a striking resemblance to a plastic toilet seat. Fortunately this wasn't sufficient a problem to put off the countless users who bought one and it was particularly popular in the education market.

2001 and 2002 saw radical redesigns of these two product lines. In 2001, the iBook was given a more sober white casing, and lost its bulging curves. In 2002, the iMac swapped its TV-style monitor for a flat screen, with the workings of the computer now housed in a dome below, rather than behind the

screen. Sales continued to rise. It seemed that the 'i' badged range of products was just what the world had been waiting for.

By now Jobs was officially back in control. He was no longer the interim CEO; he had the confidence of the board and he was breathing life back into a company that many, including Dell CEO Michael Dell, had pretty much written off.

New products followed, each one better than the last, and although not all seemed like logical additions to the range, such as the Mac mini, which looked good but was considered by some to be under-powered and over-priced in comparison to PC equivalents, it seemed that Jobs and Ive, between them, had an almost faultless understanding of their customers' wants and desires.

But then Apple hit something of a wall. It had put all of its eggs in one basket where processors were concerned. While most PC manufacturers split their ranges between chips from Intel and AMD, Apple was tied in to deals that saw it centre its designs on PowerPC processors from IBM and Motorola. They had served the company well for many years, but suddenly they seemed to top out. While customers clamoured for ever faster chips, the factories struggled to produce them. In a desperate attempt to sate public cries of frustration, it rigged up a Power Mac, one of its professional desktop computers, with a liquid-based cooling system that allowed the processor to be run at a faster speed than that for which it was designed. In true Apple style, it was an elegant implementation, but still it was something of a get around.

Next the notebook line-up started to suffer. PC competitors started to pull ahead with cooler, faster ●

Macintosh ships, and changes everything
1984

Steve Jobs leaves Apple; Apple's fortunes decline
1985

Steve Jobs returns; Apple's fortunes revived
1997

chips from Intel and Apple was starting to lag. A mobile edition of the G5 processor used in the latest desktop machines seemed as far away as ever and, taking the only course of action open to it, Apple announced in 2005 that it was to move away from the PowerPC processor, and standardise on the Intel platform, making its machines more like regular PCs than ever before.

This sent shock waves through the community. For customers it was great news; they'd finally have the speedy machines they were after, and perhaps at lower prices. For developers it was potentially terrible news. They had written their software to work with the PowerPC processor, and now they'd have to re-code it for an entirely new architecture.

Apple calmed their nerves somewhat by explaining that it would initially build in a compatibility routine to the operating systems on its new Intel machines. Called Rosetta, this would translate the instructions coming from the older software into the language understood by the new processors. It also demonstrated how easy it was to make the old PowerPC software natively compatible with the Intel chips.

However, the ease at which applications could be ported across depended entirely on their complexity. Simple tools like text editors could often be automatically re-encoded by the tools that translated the code from something humans would understand to the kind of low-level binary numbers understood by processors and memory. Other, more ambitious applications like Microsoft's Office Suite, or Adobe's Photoshop, required more serious surgery, and a lot of work and investment from their publishers.

Fortunately very few headline applications failed to make the move, so that by January 2008 order had

been restored with every major Mac application, including Word, Excel, PowerPoint, Photoshop, InDesign, Dreamweaver, QuarkXPress and a host of other staples now running more happily and more efficiently on Apple's new Intel processors.

But of course the story of the Mac isn't just about products starting with 'i'. Over the years Apple has worked on first consolidating and later diversifying its product line up to include servers, ultra-light notebooks, consumer and professional desktop machines and media boxes that sit underneath a television to stream movies and music direct to the living room.

FUTURE OF THE MAC

So where does it go from here? That question could be answered in any number of ways, but it's almost certain that the correct answer won't involve the company licensing its operating system for use by third-party developers again. It tried that for a while, and it wasn't a success. Now, with Microsoft Windows in an even more dominant position, it can't afford to try it again.

Apple's financial outlook has never looked better than it does right now, thanks to a close-to-perfect fusion of hardware and software that couldn't possibly be maintained if it allowed others a modicum of control over the products on which its operating system is used.

Almost all of those products are based on various editions of its operating system. That means, beside its closely-integrated music and movie download businesses, Mac OS X has become the key to the company's future existence. It is one of the world's most advanced operating systems, and finally

Apple drops the coloured stripes from its logo
1998

The iMac is introduced to the world
1998

Apple opens its first retail store
2001

increased sales are starting to do it justice. It has won plaudits from old hands and new arrivals alike, and it's getting rave reviews in the traditionally Windows-focused computer press. Meanwhile, the company is working hard to build it into an ever-increasing range of products, as it forms the basis of the iPhone and all recent iPods, apart from the shuffle. That's no mean feat, considering the system requirements of its competitors.

While brands like iTunes, iPhone and iPod remain the company's most visible icons, the word 'Mac' will live on for the foreseeable future for as long as Apple keeps on updating its operating system, and it's highly unlikely that it stop doing that. Microsoft is seeing its market share being slowly eroded and the best-placed company to benefit from this is Apple. That's not to say it will become the dominant player – it won't – but it offers great potential.

At the moment we are seeing more and more software applications move off computers' local hard drives and onto the web. Google is stealing a march with its highly competent online office suite, which gets better every day. Adobe is following its lead with Buzzword, an online word processor and, in early 2008, released a public test version of an online edition of Photoshop.

You might think that this is bad news for the Mac, but that couldn't be further from the truth. Once we're all running out software online, it won't matter what kind of computer we have or what operating system it runs, so nobody will be asking whether it will work with their computer – all they'll be interested in is how easy it is to get their Mac or PC online so they can use it. Here, the Mac has a trump card. It's supremely easy to get online, and it's just as happy running its

own browser, Safari, as it is with the cross-platform Firefox, which you'll find on as many PCs as Macs.

Apple, then, will continue to develop, improve and sell the Mac. That's a relief to many. With the arrival of the iPhone there was concern from some quarters that Apple had taken its eye off the ball where its computers were concerned. Developers were taken away from coding the latest release of Mac OS X and reassigned to the mobile phone project, much to the distress of faithful Apple computer users who saw the release date of their next software upgrade slipping back at a terrifying rate. When it arrived, though, Leopard was better than most had dared hope – a few grumbles aside – and it was clear that the delay was nothing more serious than a minor blip.

Apple is now making more money from selling computers than at any point in its history. It is gaining ground as one of the world's biggest manufacturers of notebook computers, trouncing the one-time big names of the industry. Investing in a Mac today gets you in at the ground floor.

However, there is one major sticking point for the Apple watcher, and that's what will happen to the company – and the Mac – once Steve Jobs moves on. He can't stay at the helm forever, and there is no obvious successor in place. Internal plans may be in place to handle this eventuality, but whatever happens and whenever it happens, Jobs' departure is sure to rock the company, its stock and its customers.

Right now Jobs seems as important to the company as its operating system and the Mac brand. After a brief brush with cancer a couple of years ago, Jobs has made the issue far more pertinent and pressing. Jobs is Apple, and Apple is Jobs as much as it is the Mac. ⊗

Mac OS X becomes the Mac's operating system
2001

Arrival of the iPod
2001

Apple drops 'Computer' to become Apple Inc
2007

Glossary

The Mac may be wonderfully easy to use, but the world of computing remains littered with technical terminology and acronyms, some of which is specific to the Mac, and some of which is in more general everyday use. A familiarity with these terms will greatly help in understanding and enjoying your Mac.

.Mac

Online service owned and run by Apple. .Mac offers remote storage of files, Hotmail-style webmail, photo galleries and web publishing. It is a paid-for extra, but as it is so well integrated into the Mac operating system and many of Apple's applications – in particular those in the iLife suite – it is a worthwhile investment for many users. More details can be found at *mac.com*.

Apple TV

Small box-like device used to download TV shows and movies from the iTunes Store and play back the media on a high-definition television. It can also share music and video libraries stored on a Mac. First introduced in January 2007, it received a significant free software upgrade in January 2008, indicating that Apple sees media downloads as an increasingly important part of its future.

Boot Camp

Application shipped as part of Mac OS X 10.5 Leopard that allows you to run Microsoft Windows on Apple computers with Intel processors. It gives Windows full access to all of the Mac's internal hardware so that it can work directly with the processor, memory and storage. This delivers excellent performance making the Mac – surprisingly – one of the best computers on which to run Windows.

Click Wheel

The circular controller on the front of an iPod, under which four buttons arranged at the points of a compass allow you to skip backwards and forwards through tracks and navigate the menus.

Cover Flow

Feature found in iTunes and the latest generation of iPods and the iPhone, which allows you to flick through the covers of the albums in your music collection. With the iPhone and iPod touch, you can also tap the albums to access their tracks. A similar feature in Mac OS X 10.5 Leopard allows you to flick through files in the Finder in the same way.

Creative Suite

Series of application bundles from Adobe, comprising a combination of its most popular programs, including Photoshop, InDesign, Dreamweaver, Flash and Premiere. At present, Creative Suite is at version 3 and is a cost-effective way to buy more than one Adobe application at a time, as most bundles cost little more than two of the programs that make them up.

Cursor

Vertical bar used in word processors to indicate the point at which your typing will appear.

Dashboard

A hidden layer of Mac OS X 10.4 Tiger and 10.5 Leopard on which you can run mini applications called Widgets. These run like sections of web pages to perform specific tasks, such as tracking stock prices, reporting the weather or translating words and phrases.

Desktop

This is the graphical main area of the screen on top of which windows open and applications run. Its background can be customised to show an image of your choice, and it can also be used as a temporary storage area for files on which you are working, although this is not to be recommended as it shows poor file management and can impact on your Mac's performance.

Dock

Translucent bar running along the bottom of the screen housing icons that are shortcuts to your most regularly-used applications. By right-clicking or Ctrl-clicking on the dividing bar in the right half of the Dock you can access its customisation menu, and from there move it to one side of the screen, change its size or have it automatically hide itself when not in use.

Double-click

To click twice in quick succession on the button of a mouse, the button in front of a trackpad, or the trackpad itself. This action when executed, rather than just selecting the item clicked on, will open a file in its associated application or launch a piece of software.

DTP

Acronym for desktop publishing that describes the process of designing pages on a screen rather than using molten metal, as was once the case with all printed matter. All magazines and newspapers, fliers and brochures are now designed using DTP software, which is a mainstay of the Mac platform. The two leading DTP applications are Adobe InDesign and QuarkXPress, although Apple Pages (part of iWork 08) and Microsoft Word offer similar tools tailored to home and small business users.

Exposé

Utility that reorganises your open windows to help you work more efficiently with your files. It is activated through the keyboard and can either display all active applications, split up active windows in the current application or clear the screen altogether to give you access to the Mac OS X Desktop.

Finder

The part of the Mac's operating system that handles navigation through files and folders. When you have no applications open, and are viewing the Desktop background you are in a pure Finder environment, as indicated by the word Finder at the left of the Menu bar.

Font

Term usually taken to describe the visual look of a set of characters (letters, numbers and symbols) and used interchangeably with the term typeface. However, it can also be taken to mean more than just the style of the characters but also their dimensions, weight and other attributes.

Front Row

Media playback software found on Apple TV and modern Macs, and included in Mac OS X 10.5 Leopard. It comprises large menus optimised for viewing on a regular TV screen, and is controlled by the standard Apple Remote, which if it didn't come with your Mac can be bought for £19.

GarageBand

Home-user music creation application found in iLife in which songs are constructed by dragging pre-recorded musical clips, called Loops, into the working area.

GB

Abbreviation for gigabyte, which is 1 million kilobytes of information. A single gigabyte is enough to store around 250 music tracks on an iPod.

iBook

Consumer notebook that appealed to students and less demanding home users. It was introduced shortly after the original iMac and after several iterations finally retired in 2006. Its closest current equivalent is the bottom-end MacBook.

iCal

Calendaring application bundled with Mac OS X that lets you set reminders for upcoming appointments and track tasks that need to be completed. It uses industry-standard formats, allowing you to share appointments with people through a range of applications and operating systems, as well as publish your diary online.

iDisk

Web storage space that is included in a .Mac subscription. It can be made to work in exactly the same way as a local hard drive in Mac OS X, and will even show up in the list of drives in a Finder window. Certain applications such as iPhoto and iWeb can also use it as a place to publish photo galleries and websites.

iDVD

This is an application that is used to burn movies to DVD, complete with chapters and menus for use on a consumer DVD player and TV, or another computer. iDVD is found in the iLife suite.

iLife

Lifestyle suite produced by Apple, which comprises iTunes, iPhoto, iMovie, iDVD, iWeb and GarageBand. It receives an update roughly every 12 to 18 months, and can be seen as a creative companion to a regular office suite. It is included free with every new Mac.

iMac

An all-in-one computer, in which its inner workings are hidden behind the screen. The keyboard and mouse are the only external components. The current metal and glass iMac is the fourth generation of the machine, which started out as a semi-transparent computer in a curvy round case in a choice of colours, and is credited by many as being the computer that revived the ailing Apple's fortunes following its debut in 1998.

Inspector

A panel that is used in many software applications to examine the current attributes of an element. It is also used as a way of altering them. Examples include controllers for fonts and text sizes in a word processor, or the colour of objects in a graphics application.

Interface

The interface of any application is the collection of menus, buttons, text, graphics and panels that make up its on-screen appearance. In Mac OS X, this includes the menubar at the top of the screen, the Dock at the bottom (or on the left or right of the screen if you have changed its position), the windows containing files and applications and the icons that you click.

iPhone

Part pocket computer, part media player, part communications device, this is Apple's play for the mobile phone market. It sells itself on its cool looks and excellent software. It is only ever sold through one network in any country – in the UK, that network is O2 – and it attracts a high contract cost. This is somewhat offset, however, in that the contract includes unlimited use of the Internet and a generous allocation of bundled calls.

iPod

The world's best-selling music player, which is also made by Apple. There are four distinct varieties of iPod: shuffle, nano, classic and touch. In the past there has also been the iPod mini, but this was phased out when the nano arrived. All but the shuffle can play video, and all work with iTunes, on either the Mac or PC.

iTunes

Free application for PCs and the Mac used for downloading and organising music and podcasts, as well as listening to Internet radio streams and uploading music to an iPod. It is also the home of the iTunes Store through which Apple sells music, movies and TV shows.

iWeb

Web design software included in the iLife suite of applications. It can publish to regular web hosting space, but is designed to work primarily with the webspace included as part of Apple's .Mac online service. As such, it takes advantage of server-specific features that are not available as a part of third-party hosting packages.

iWork

Apple's own office suite, comprising Pages (word processor), Numbers (spreadsheet) and Keynote (presentation package). Each application in the suite uses its own file format, but it can also import and export Microsoft Office files for compatibility. Each application prides itself on the quality of its output, boasting many low-level desktop publishing-style tools.

Keynote

Presentation application used for creating slides, comprising text, images, sound, movies and transitions. It is not directly compatible with PowerPoint, although it can read and write those files.

MacBook

The family name for Apple's range of notebook computers. It comprises three different lines; the consumer MacBook, the high-end MacBook Pro and the highly desirable, ultra-slim MacBook Air. Together their screens range in size from 13in to 17in, while their prices span from less than £700 to more than £2000 in their standard configurations. Each has a built-in web camera, called iSight, in the lid and ships with the latest version of the Mac operating system, although as they feature the same Intel processors as you'd find in a PC notebook, they are also capable of running Microsoft Windows.

Mac mini

Small, consumer computer, about the size of a box of biscuits. Seen by many as the ideal media computer because of its integrated DVD drive and media playback software, combined with a compact chassis

that makes it perfect for slipping under the TV, it seems likely that it is the Mac found in more living rooms more than any other.

Mac OS X

Apple's native operating system. The current edition is version 10.5, with each new release incrementing the number after the dot. Each one is given a wildcat-related codename in development, with the latest one being Leopard. This was preceded by Tiger, Panther, Jaguar and Cheetah. It was developed out of work done by NeXT, a company founded by Apple co-founder Steve Jobs, and later bought by Apple, hence bringing Jobs back into the company fold. It is based on a business operating environment called Unix, which makes it very secure and robust and less prone to infection from viruses and spyware than Microsoft Windows.

Mac Pro

Apple's professional-level computer. It ships without a monitor, in a drilled aluminium case. It is more powerful than an iMac or any portable computer Apple produces, but the primary reason for buying it is the expansion options it offers, with room for more memory and hard drives than Apple's consumer computers. It also ships as standard with two processors, rather than the usual one, to crunch through intensive tasks more quickly.

MB

Short for megabyte, which is 1000 kilobytes. Old-style 3.5in floppy disks used to hold about 1MB of data, but these days even a simple Microsoft Excel spreadsheet can be many times this size. As such, fewer and fewer measurements in computing are expressed in terms of megabytes, with gigabyte measurements becoming more common usage to describe file sizes.

Menubar
Strip of drop-down menus found at the top of the screen. It performs the same function as the bar of menus attached to the top of every individual application in Windows, but as it's not attached to the application window itself it instead tailors itself to feature only those options relevant to whichever application is foremost on the screen at any one time.

Multi-touch
Term used to describe hardware devices employed by Apple in the iPhone and MacBook Air that allow you to manipulate on-screen elements by sliding, twisting, flicking and pinching your fingers on a screen or trackpad.

Numbers
Apple's spreadsheet application, forming part of the iWork suite. It was introduced in 2008 and has its own file format, although it can import and export Microsoft Excel-compatible files. It has excellent design tools, which go a long way to making your spreadsheets look attractive and engaging, but its unique ability is to include more than one table on a single page. Excel can include only one.

Office
Generic term used to describe Microsoft's business applications suite comprising Word (word processor), Excel (spreadsheet), PowerPoint (presentation, and various email

and database applications, depending on the year of release and whether it is a PC or Mac edition. Its native file formats have become something of a business standard adhered to by many rival applications.

Operating System
Software that controls the most fundamental hardware of a computer and passes instructions to it from the applications that they run. Mac OS X and Windows are both operating systems, but other popular alternatives include Linux and Unix.

Pages
Apple's own word processing application, found in the iWork suite. It boasts good home-user desktop publishing features, which were once to the detriment of its tools for regular plain text writing, although in later editions this imbalance has been redressed, making Pages a first-class text creation and editing tool.

Pointer
The on-screen arrow moved using the mouse or trackpad. In a spreadsheet such as Excel or Numbers, it is usually replaced by a cross when moving over the grid of cells in a table.

PowerBook
Now outdated notebook computer produced by Apple using its older generation of PowerPC processors. Physically it looked almost identical to the current MacBook Pro and, because of its build quality and the conservative demands on recent releases of Mac OS X, many are still in use.

Power Mac
The predecessor of the Mac Pro, once forming the upper echelons of Apple's desktop computer line and favoured by professional users, particularly in creative and design environments.

Preferences
Each application has a section dedicated to adjustable settings, called Preferences. You'll find it by clicking on the application's name in the menubar at the top of the screen, and then clicking on Preferences in the menu that drops down. More extensive settings used to control how the Mac works in general are found in System Preferences. Find this by clicking on the Apple icon in the top left-hand corner of the screen.

Processor
The brain of your computer, the processor is the chip that does all of the calculations that make it work. There are several processors in every machine, covering general system tasks and graphics. All recent Macs use the same kind of main processor as a PC, made by Intel, but older Macs use the so-called PowerPC processor line, and may be unable to run some of the latest software releases, including Adobe Premiere (professional video editing application) and FileMaker Bento (database for home-users).

RAM
Acronym for Random Access Memory; a series of fast chips used by the processor to temporarily store information while it is being worked on. All data stored in the Ram is lost when the Mac is turned off or rebooted. As such, files should be saved at regular intervals.

Right-click

Clicking with the right-hand button of a mouse to bring up a menu of options relevant to the item on which you have clicked. The mice that Apple used to ship came with only one button, so right-clicking was could be performed by holding down the Ctrl key while clicking to call up the same menu. Apple's current mouse offering, the Apple Mighty Mouse, can be configured for two-button use in System Preferences, while plugging in any two-button mouse works without any trouble.

Software Update

Small application found by clicking on the Apple icon in the top-left corner of the screen, which checks with Apple's servers for new and updated versions of the software on your Mac. It will automatically run every so often on its own, but if you notice it has not run in the last couple of weeks, it's worth invoking manually. This is the Mac equivalent of Windows Update and Office Update on the PC.

Spaces

Feature of Mac OS X 10.5 Leopard that allows you to have up to 16 virtual screens running on your Mac at the same time. This allows you to organise your active applications according to function, or run 16 of them in full-screen mode, rather than smaller windows.

Time Capsule

Hard drive with wireless features, allowing Macs and PCs to connect and use it for storage. It was designed specifically to work hand-in-hand with Time Machine. Time Capsule replaced a feature that was included

in pre-release versions of Mac OS X 10.5 Leopard that allowed Time Machine back ups to be made over a wireless network.

Time Machine

Automatic backup system built in to Mac OS X 10.5 Leopard. Once you have plugged in an external hard drive and given Time Machine permission to use it, the application will copy changes made to your system every hour. Should you lose an important file or make changes that you should not have done you can then roll back through each hour of changes to find the file and return the data to its previous state.

Trackpad

Touch-sensitive area on a notebook computer, between the user and the keyboard. Sliding your finger across its surface will move an on-screen cursor, while tapping it will cause the pointer to select the item over which it sits. Usually accompanied by one or two selection buttons just beneath it to perform a similar task. Using two fingers on the trackpad of any MacBook-based notebook scrolls the contents of the current open window.

Trash

Found on the Dock, the Trash is where you drag files and applications when you want to delete them from your system. Other applications, such as iTunes, may also send files here when you delete them from within their own environment. Items sent to the Trash are not immediately deleted, allowing them to be recovered at a later date if deleted in error. Once emptied, however, the files are lost forever. The direct equivalent in Windows is the Recycle Bin.

USB

Universal Serial Bus; a port and cable combination that lets you transfer data to and from your Mac. It is used to connect almost every kind of device (hence the Universal part of its name) including printers, scanners, iPods and cameras.

Widget

See Dashboard.

Wifi

Colloquial term used to describe a wide range of wireless networking technologies. It can usually be taken to mean any kind of wireless connection over which you might browse the web or send and receive email.

Window

The container holding an application or an open file on the screen in any graphical operating system, such as Mac OS X.

Windows

Microsoft's operating system. The current edition is Windows Vista, but its predecessor, Windows XP, remains popular as some users have shown a reluctance to upgrade. It will only run on the Mac with the help of software built into Mac OS X 10.5 Leopard, or Parallels and Fusion from third-party developers (see page 98).

WWDC

Worldwide Developers' Conference held every summer at which Apple outlines its future strategy for Mac OS X and other key technologies, and makes an announcement for a high-end product or two.